THE INNOVATOR'S DNA

THE INNOVATOR'S DNA

MASTERING THE FIVE SKILLS OF DISRUPTIVE INNOVATORS

Jeff Dyer
Hal Gregersen
Clayton M. Christensen

HARVARD BUSINESS REVIEW PRESS
BOSTON, MASSACHUSETTS

Printed in the United States of America
20 19 18 17 16 15

Library of Congress Cataloging-in-Publication Data

Dyer, Jeff.
The innovator's DNA : mastering the five skills of disruptive innovators/ Jeff Dyer, Hal Gregersen, Clayton M. Christensen.
p. cm.
ISBN 978-1-4221-3481-8 (hardback)
1. Creative ability in business. 2. Technological innovations. 3. Entrepreneurship. I. Gregersen, Hal B., 1958– II. Christensen, Clayton M. III. Title.
HD53.D94 2011
658.4'063—dc22

2011008440

The paper used in this publication meets the requirements of the American National Standard for Permanence of Paper for Publications and Documents in Libraries and Archives Z39.48-1992.

Contents

Introduction

INNOVATION. It's the lifeblood of our global economy and a strategic priority for virtually every CEO around the world. In fact, a recent IBM poll of fifteen hundred CEOs identified creativity as the number-one "leadership competency" of the future.[1] The power of innovative ideas to revolutionize industries and generate wealth is evident from history: Apple iPod outplays Sony Walkman, Starbucks's beans and atmosphere drown traditional coffee shops, Skype uses a strategy of "free" to beat AT&T and British Telecom, eBay crushes classified ads, and Southwest Airlines flies under the radar of American and Delta. In every case, the creative ideas of innovative entrepreneurs produced powerful competitive advantages and tremendous wealth for the pioneering company. Of course, the retrospective $1 million question is, how did they do it? And perhaps the prospective $10 million question is, how could I do it?

The Innovator's DNA tackles these fundamental questions—and more. The genesis of this book centered on the question that we posed years ago to "disruptive technologies" guru and coauthor Clayton Christensen: where do disruptive business models come from? Christensen's best-selling books, *The Innovator's*

Dilemma and *The Innovator's Solution,* conveyed important insight into the characteristics of disruptive technologies, business models, and companies. *The Innovator's DNA* emerged from an eight-year collaborative study in which we sought a richer understanding of disruptive innovators—who they are and the innovative companies they create. Our project's primary purpose was to uncover the origins of innovative—and often disruptive—business ideas. So we interviewed nearly a hundred inventors of revolutionary products and services, as well as founders and CEOs of game-changing companies built on innovative business ideas. These were people such as eBay's Pierre Omidyar, Amazon's Jeff Bezos, Research In Motion's Mike Lazaridis, and Salesforce.com's Marc Benioff. For a full list of innovators we interviewed whom we quote in this book, see appendix A; virtually all of the innovators we quote, with the exception of Steve Jobs (Apple), Richard Branson (Virgin), and Howard Schultz (Starbucks)—who have written autobiographies or have given numerous interviews about innovation—are from our interviews.

We also studied CEOs who ignited innovation in existing companies, such as Procter & Gamble's A. G. Lafley, eBay's Meg Whitman, and Bain & Company's Orit Gadiesh. Some entrepreneurs' companies that we studied were successful and well known; some were not (for example, Movie Mouth, Cow-Pie Clocks, Terra Nova BioSystems). But all offered a surprising and unique value proposition relative to incumbents. For example, each offered new or different features, pricing, convenience, or customizability compared to their competition. Our goal was less to investigate the companies' strategies than it was to dig into the thinking of the innovators themselves. We wanted to understand as much about these people as possible, including the moment (when and how) they came up with the creative ideas that launched new products or businesses. We asked them to tell us about the most valuable and novel business idea that they had generated during their business careers, and to tell us where those ideas came from. Their stories were provocative and insightful, and surprisingly similar.

As we reflected on the interviews, consistent patterns of action emerged. Innovative entrepreneurs and executives behaved similarly when discovering breakthrough ideas. Five primary discovery skills—skills that compose what we call *the innovator's DNA*—surfaced from our conversations. We found that innovators "Think Different," to use a well-known Apple slogan. Their minds excel at linking together ideas that aren't obviously related to produce original ideas (we call this cognitive skill "associational thinking" or "associating"). But to think different, innovators had to "act different." All were questioners, frequently asking questions that punctured the status quo. Some observed the world with intensity beyond the ordinary. Others networked with the most diverse people on the face of the earth. Still others placed experimentation at the center of their innovative activity. When engaged in consistently, these actions—questioning, observing, networking, and experimenting—triggered associational thinking to deliver new businesses, products, services, and/or processes. Most of us think creativity is an entirely cognitive skill; it all happens in the brain. A critical insight from our research is that *one's ability to generate innovative ideas is not merely a function of the mind, but also a function of behaviors.* This is good news for us all because it means that *if we change our behaviors, we can improve our creative impact.*

After surfacing these patterns of action for famous innovative entrepreneurs and executives, we turned our research lens to the less famous but equally capable innovators around the world. We built a survey based on our interviews that taps into the discovery skills of innovative leaders: associating, questioning, observing, networking, and experimenting. To date, we have collected self-reported and 360-degree data on these discovery skills from over five hundred innovators and over five thousand executives in more than seventy-five countries (for information about our assessments for individuals and companies, go to our Web site: http://www.InnovatorsDNA.com). We found the same pattern for famous as well as less famous leaders. Innovators were simply much more likely to question, observe, network, and experiment compared to typical executives. We published the results of our research in *Strategic Entrepreneurship Journal*, the top academic journal focused on entrepreneurs (details of our study are reported in appendix B).[2] We also published our findings in an article titled "The Innovator's DNA," which was the runner-up for the 2009 *Harvard Business Review* McKinsey Award.

We then turned to see what we could learn about the DNA of innovative organizations and teams. We started by looking at *BusinessWeek*'s annual ranking of innovative companies. This ranking, based on votes from executives, identified companies with a reputation for being innovative. A quick look at the *BusinessWeek* lists from 2005 to 2009 shows Apple as number one and Google, number two. OK, intuitively that sounds right. But we felt that the *BusinessWeek* methodology (executives voting on which companies are innovative) produces a list that is largely a popularity contest based on *past* performance. Indeed, do General Electric, Sony, Toyota, and BMW deserve to be on the list of most innovative companies today? Or are they simply there because they have been successful in the past?

To answer these questions, we developed our own list of innovative companies based on current innovation prowess (and expectations of future innovations). How did we do this? We thought the best way was to see whether investors—voting with their wallets—could give us insight into which companies they thought most likely to produce future innovations: new products, services, or markets. We teamed up with HOLT (a division of Credit Suisse Boston that had done a similar analysis for *The Innovator's*

Who Is Classified as an Innovator?

Perhaps one of the most surprising findings from the past thirty years of entrepreneurship research is that *entrepreneurs do not differ significantly (on personality traits or psychometric measures) from typical business executives.*[a] We usually meet this finding with skepticism, since most of us intuitively believe that entrepreneurs are somehow different from other executives. Note that our research focused on *innovators* and, in particular, *innovative* entrepreneurs rather than entrepreneurs. Here's why. Innovative entrepreneurs start companies that offer unique value to the market. When someone opens a dry cleaner or a mortgage business, or even a set of Volkswagen dealerships or McDonald's franchises, researchers put them all in the same category of entrepreneur as the founders of eBay (Pierre Omidyar) and Amazon (Jeff Bezos). This creates a categorization problem when trying to find out whether *innovative* entrepreneurs differ from typical executives. The fact is that most entrepreneurs launch ventures based on strategies that are not unique and certainly not disruptive. Among entrepreneurs as a whole, only 10 percent to 15 percent qualify as "innovative entrepreneurs" of the kind we're discussing.

Our study includes four types of innovators: (1) start-up entrepreneurs (as we described earlier), (2) corporate entrepreneurs (those who launch an innovative venture from within the corporation), (3) product innovators (those who invent a new product), and (4) process innovators (those who launch a breakthrough process). Our process inventor category includes folks like A. G. Lafley, who initiated a set of innovative processes at Procter & Gamble that sparked numerous new product innovations. In all cases, the original idea for the new

(continued)

business, product, or process must be the innovator's idea. While these different types of innovators have numerous similarities, they also have some differences, as we will show in the chapters that follow.

a. This is evident in the conclusions of numerous studies on entrepreneurs, including the following:

> "After a great deal of research, it is now often concluded that most of the psychological differences between entrepreneurs and managers in large organizations are small or non-existent" (L. W. Busenitz and J. B. Barney, "Differences Between Entrepreneurs and Managers in Large Organizations," *Journal of Business Venturing* 12, 1997).

> "There appears to be no discoverable pattern of personality characteristics that distinguish between successful entrepreneurs and non-entrepreneurs" (W. Guth, "Director's Corner: Research in Entrepreneurship," *The Entrepreneurship* Forum, winter 1991).

> "Most of the attempts to distinguish between entrepreneurs and small business owners or managers have discovered no differentiating features" (R. H. Brockhaus and P. S. Horwitz, "The Psychology of the Entrepreneur" in *The Art and Science of* Entrepreneurship, 1986).

Solution) to develop a methodology for determining what percentage of a firm's market value could be attributed to its existing businesses (products, services, markets). If the firm's market value was higher than the cash flows that could be attributed to its existing businesses, then the company would have a *growth and innovation premium* (for our purposes, we'll just call it an *innovation premium*). An innovation premium is the proportion of a company's market value that cannot be accounted for from cash flows of its current products or businesses in its current markets. It is the premium the market gives these companies because investors expect them to come up with new products or markets—*and* they expect the companies to be able to generate high profits from them (see chapter 7 for details on how the premium is calculated).

It is a premium that every executive, and every company, would like to have.

We unveil our list of the most innovative companies—ranked by innovation premium—in chapter 7. Not surprisingly, we found that our top twenty-five companies include some on the *BusinessWeek* list—such as Apple, Google, Amazon, and Procter & Gamble. These companies averaged at least a 35 percent innovation premium over the past five years. But we also learned that companies such as Salesforce.com (software), Intuitive Surgical (health care equipment), Hindustan Lever (household products), Alstom (electrical equipment), and Monsanto (chemicals) have similar premiums. And as we studied these firms in greater detail, we learned that they are also very innovative. As we examined both our list and the *BusinessWeek* list of innovative companies, we saw several patterns.

First, we noticed that compared to typical companies they were far more likely to be led by an innovative founder or a leader who scored extremely high on the five discovery skills that compose the innovator's DNA (their average discovery quotient was in the eighty-eighth percentile, which meant they scored higher than 88 percent of people taking our discovery skills assessment). Innovative companies are almost always led by innovative leaders. Let us say this again: *Innovative companies are almost always led by innovative leaders.* The bottom line: if you want innovation, you need creativity skills within the top management team of your company. We saw how innovative founders often imprinted their organizations with their behaviors. For example, Jeff Bezos personally excels at experimenting, so he helped create institutionalized processes within Amazon to push others to experiment. Similarly, Intuit's Scott Cook shines at observing, so he pushes observation at Intuit. Perhaps not surprisingly, we discovered that the DNA of innovative organizations mirrored the DNA of innovative individuals. In other words, innovative *people* systematically engage in questioning, observing, networking, and experimenting behaviors to spark new ideas. Similarly, innovative *organizations* systematically develop *processes* that encourage questioning, observing, networking, and experimenting by employees. Our chapters on building the innovator's DNA in your organization and team describe how you too can actively encourage and support others' innovation efforts.

Why the Ideas in This Book Should Matter to You

Over the last decade, many books on the topic of innovation and creativity have been written. Some books focus on disruptive innovation, such as Clayton Christensen's *The Innovator's Dilemma* and *The Innovator's Solution*. Others, such as *Ten Rules for Strategic Innovators* (Govindarajan and Trimble), *Game Changer* (A. G. Lafley and Ram Charan), and *The Entrepreneurial Mindset* (Rita McGrath and Ian MacMillan), examine how organizations, and organizational leaders, encourage and support innovation. Others look more specifically at product development and innovation processes within and across firms, such as *How Breakthroughs Happen* (Andrew Hargadon) and *The Sources of Innovation* (Eric von Hippel). Other books on innovation look at the roles individuals play in the innovation process within companies, such as *The Ten Faces of Innovation* and *The Art of Innovation* (both by Tom Kelley of IDEO), or *A Whole New Mind* (Daniel Pink). Finally, other books like *Creativity in Context* (Teresa Amabile) and *Creativity* (Mihaly Csikszentmihalyi) examine individual creativity and, more specifically, theories and research about creativity. Our book differs from the others in that it is focused squarely on individual creativity in the business context and is based on our study of a large sample of business innovators, including some big-name innovators such as Jeff Bezos (Amazon.com), Pierre Omidyar (eBay), Michael Lazaridis

A Disclaimer . . . Sort of

We think it is important to remember three significant points as you read *The Innovator's DNA*. First, engaging in the discovery skills doesn't ensure financial success. Throughout the book, we tell stories of people who were manifestly successful at innovating. We focus on the success stories because we are all more naturally drawn to success than failure. However, in our sample of five hundred innovators, only two-thirds launched ventures or products that met our criteria of success. Many were not successful. The innovators developed the right skills—questioning, observing, networking, and experimenting—that produced an innovative venture or product, but the result was not always a financial success. The point is that the discovery skills we describe are necessary, indeed critical, for generating innovative business ideas, but they don't guarantee success.

Second, failure (in a financial sense) often results from not being vigilant in engaging all discovery skills. The more financially successful innovators in our sample demonstrated a higher discovery quotient (scored higher on the discovery skills) than less successful ones. If you fail with an innovation, it may be that you didn't ask all the right questions, make all of the necessary observations, talk to a large enough group of diverse people, or run the right experiments. Of course, it is also possible that you did all these things but an even newer technology emerged or some other bright innovator came up with an even better idea. Or maybe you just didn't excel at executing on the idea or have the resources to compete with an established firm that imitated your invention. Many factors can prevent a new product or business idea from gaining traction in the market. But the better you are at asking the

(continued)

right questions, engaging in the right observations, eliciting ideas and feedback through networking with the right people, and running experiments, the less likely you are to fail.

Third, we spotlight different innovators and innovative companies to illustrate key ideas or principles, but not to set them up as perfect examples of how to be innovative. Some innovators we studied were "serial innovators," as they had developed quite a number of innovations over time and appeared motivated to continue doing so. Others benefitted by being in the right place at the right time to make a critical observation, talk to a key person with particularly useful knowledge, or serendipitously learn from an experiment. They made an important discovery once, but they might not necessarily be capable or motivated (perhaps due to financial success) to continue generating innovative ideas. In similar fashion, we have found that innovative companies can quickly lose their innovative prowess, while others can quickly improve it. In chapter 8, we show that Apple's innovation prowess (as measured by its innovation premium) dropped dramatically after Jobs left in 1984, but then jumped up dramatically a few years after he returned to lead the company. Procter & Gamble was a solid innovation performer before Lafley took the helm, but increased its innovation premium by 30 percent under his leadership. The point is that people and companies can change and may not always live up to our lofty expectations.

(Research In Motion/BlackBerry), Michael Dell (Dell), Marc Benioff (Salesforce.com), Niklas Zennström (Skype), Scott Cook (Intuit), Peter Thiel (PayPal), David Neeleman (JetBlue and Azul airlines), and so on. The premise of our book is that we explain how these big names got their "big ideas" and describe a process that readers can emulate. We describe in detail five skills that anyone can master to improve his or her own ability to be an innovative thinker.

Ask yourself: Am I good at generating innovative business ideas? Do I know how to find innovative people for my organization? Do I know how to train people to be more creative and innovative? Some executives respond to the last question by encouraging employees to think outside the box. But thinking outside the box is precisely what employees (and executives) are trying to figure out. We've even watched some executives answer the "How do I think outside the box?" question with another equally generic (and unhelpful) answer, "Be creative."

If you find yourself struggling with actionable answers to these questions, read on to gain a solid grasp of five skills that can make all the difference when facing your next innovation challenge. All leaders have problems and opportunities sitting in front of them for which they have no solution. It might be a new process. It might be a new product or service. It might be a new business model for an old business. In every case, the skills you build by putting into practice the innovator's DNA may literally save your job, your organization, and perhaps your community. Indeed, we've found that if you want to rise to the highest levels of your organization—to a business unit manager, president, or CEO position—you need strong discovery skills. And if you want to lead a truly innovative organization, you likely will need to excel at those skills.

We hope that *The Innovator's DNA* will encourage you to reclaim some of your youthful curiosity. Staying curious keeps us engaged and our organizations alive.[3] Imagine how competitive your company will be ten years from now without innovators if its people didn't find any new ways to improve its processes, products, or services. Clearly, your company would not survive. Innovators constitute the core of any company's, or even country's, ability to compete.

How *The Innovator's DNA* Unfolds

Like a pocket-sized map in a foreign place, our book serves as a guide to your innovation journey. The first part (chapters 1 through 6) explains why the innovator's DNA matters and how the pieces can combine into a personalized approach to innovation. We put flesh onto the "think different" slogan by explaining in detail the habits and techniques that allow innovators to think differently. The chapters in part one give rich detail about how to master the specific skills that are key to generating novel ideas—associating, questioning, observing, networking, and experimenting.

The second part (chapters 7 through 10) amplifies the building blocks of innovation by showing how the discovery skills of innovators described in part one operate in organizations and teams. Chapter 7 introduces our ranking of the world's most innovative companies based on each company's innovation premium, a market value premium based on investors' expectations of future innovations. We also provide a framework for seeing how the innovator's DNA works in the world's most innovative teams and organizations. We call this the "3P" framework because it contains the discovery-driven building blocks of highly innovative organizations or teams—*people, processes,* and *philosophies.* Chapter 8 focuses on building-block number one, *people,* and describes how innovative organizations achieve maximum impact by actively recruiting, encouraging, and rewarding people who display strong discovery skills—and blending innovators effectively with folks who have strong execution skills. Chapter 9 shows innovative team and company *processes* that mirror the five discovery skills of disruptive innovators. In other words, innovative companies rely on processes to encourage—even require—their people to engage in questioning, observing, networking, experimenting, and associating. Chapter 10 focuses on the fundamental *philosophies* that guide behavior within innovative teams and organizations. These philosophies not only guide disruptive innovators but also get imprinted in the organization, giving people the courage to innovate. Finally, for those interested in building discovery skills in yourself, your team, and even the next generation (young people you know), in appendix C we guide you through a process of taking your innovator's DNA to the next level.

We're delighted that you're starting or continuing your own innovation journey. We have watched scores of individuals take the ideas in this book to heart and who describe how they have dramatically improved their innovation skills as a result. They continually confirm that the journey is worth taking. We think you'll feel the same way once you've finished reading about and mastering the skills of a disruptive innovator.

PART ONE

Disruptive Innovation Starts with You

1

The DNA of Disruptive Innovators

"I want to put a ding in the universe."

—Steve Jobs, founder and CEO,
Apple Inc.

DO I KNOW HOW to generate innovative, even disruptive, business ideas? Do I know how to find creative people or how to train people to think outside the box? These questions stump most senior executives, who know that the ability to innovate is the "secret sauce" of business success. Unfortunately, most of us know very little about what makes one person more creative than another. Perhaps for this reason, we stand in awe of visionary entrepreneurs such as Apple's Steve Jobs, Amazon's Jeff Bezos, and eBay's Pierre Omidyar, and innovative executives like P&G's A. G. Lafley, Bain & Company's Orit Gadiesh, and eBay's Meg Whitman. How do these people come up with groundbreaking new ideas? If it were possible to discover the inner workings of the masters' minds, what could the rest of us learn about how innovation really happens?

Ideas for Innovation

Consider the case of Jobs, who was recently ranked the world's number-one best-performing CEO in a study published by *Harvard Business Review*.[1] You may recall Apple's famous "Think Different" ad campaign, whose slogan says it all. The campaign featured innovators from different fields, including Albert Einstein, Picasso, Richard Branson, and John Lennon, but Jobs's face might easily have been featured among the others. After all, everyone knows that Jobs is an innovative guy, that he knows how to think different. But the question is, just how does he do it? Indeed, how does any innovator think different?

The common answer is that the ability to think creatively is genetic. Most of us believe that some people, like Jobs, are simply born with creative genes, while others are not. Innovators are supposedly right brained, meaning that they are genetically endowed with creative abilities. The rest of us are left brained—logical, linear thinkers, with little or no ability to think creatively.

If you believe this, we're going to tell you that you are largely wrong. At least within the realm of business innovation, virtually everyone has some capacity for creativity and innovative thinking. Even you. So using the example of Jobs, let's explore this ability to think different. How did Jobs come up with some of his innovative ideas in the past? And what does his journey tell us?

Innovative Idea #1: Personal Computers Should Be Quiet and Small

One of the key innovations in the Apple II, the computer that launched Apple, came from Jobs's decision that it should be quiet. His conviction resulted, in part, from all the time he'd spent studying Zen and meditating.[2] He found the noise of a computer fan distracting. So Jobs was determined that the Apple II would have no fan, which was a fairly radical notion at the time. Nobody else had questioned the need for a fan because *all* computers required a fan to prevent overheating. Getting rid of the fan wouldn't be possible without a different type of power supply that generated less heat.

So Jobs went on the hunt for someone who could design a new power supply. Through his network of contacts, he found Rod Holt, a forty-something, chain-smoking socialist from the Atari crowd.[3] Pushed by Jobs, Holt abandoned the fifty-year-old conventional linear unit technology and created a switching power supply that revolutionized the way power was delivered to electronics products. Jobs's pursuit of quiet and Holt's ability to deliver an innovative power supply that didn't need a fan made the Apple II the quietest and smallest personal computer ever made (a smaller computer was possible because it didn't need extra space for the fan).

Had Jobs never asked, "Why does a computer need a fan?" and "How do we keep a computer cool without a fan?" the Apple computer as we know it would not exist.

Innovative Idea #2: The Macintosh User Interface, Operating System, and Mouse

The seed for the Macintosh, with its revolutionary operating system, was planted when Jobs visited Xerox PARC in 1979. Xerox, the copier company, created the Palo Alto Research Center (PARC), a research lab charged with designing the office of the future. Jobs wrangled a visit to PARC in exchange for offering Xerox an opportunity to invest in Apple. Xerox didn't know how to capitalize on the exciting things going on at PARC, but Jobs did.

Jobs carefully observed the PARC computer screen filled with icons, pull-down menus, and overlapping windows—all controlled by the click of a mouse. "What we saw was incomplete and flawed," Jobs said, "but the germ of the idea was there . . . within ten minutes it was obvious to me that all computers would work like this."[4] He spent the next five years at Apple leading the design team that would produce the Macintosh computer, the first personal computer with a graphical user interface (GUI) and mouse. Oh, and he saw something else during the PARC visit. He got his first taste of object-oriented programming, which became the key to the OSX operating system that Apple acquired from Jobs's other start-up, NeXT Computers. What if Jobs had never visited Xerox PARC to observe what was going on there?

Innovative Idea #3: Desktop Publishing on the Mac

The Macintosh, with its LaserWriter printer, was the first computer to bring desktop publishing to the masses. Jobs claims that the "beautiful typography" available on the Macintosh would never have been introduced if he hadn't dropped in on a calligraphy class at Reed College in Oregon. Says Jobs:

> Reed College offered perhaps the best calligraphy instruction in the country. Throughout the campus every poster, every label on every drawer, was beautifully hand-calligraphed. Because I had dropped out and didn't have to take the normal classes, I decided to take a calligraphy class to learn how to do this. I learned about serif and san serif typefaces, about varying the amount of space between different letter combinations, about what makes great typography great. It was beautiful, historical, artistically subtle in a way that science can't capture, and I found it fascinating. None of this had even a hope of any practical application in my life. But ten years later, when we were designing the first Macintosh computer, it all came back to me. And we designed it all into the Mac. It

> was the first computer with beautiful typography. If I had never dropped in on that single course in college, the Mac would have never had multiple typefaces or proportionally spaced fonts. And since Windows just copied the Mac, it's likely that no personal computer would have them.[5]

What if Jobs hadn't decided to drop in on the calligraphy classes when he had dropped out of college?

So what do we learn from Jobs's ability to think different? Well, first we see that his innovative ideas didn't spring fully formed from his head, as if they were a gift from the Idea Fairy. When we examine the origins of these ideas, we typically find that the catalyst was: (1) a question that challenged the status quo, (2) an observation of a technology, company, or customer, (3) an experience or experiment where he was trying out something new, or (4) a conversation with someone who alerted him to an important piece of knowledge or opportunity. In fact, by carefully examining Jobs's *behaviors* and, specifically, how those behaviors brought in new diverse knowledge that triggered an innovative idea, we can trace his innovative ideas to their source.

What is the moral of this story? We want to convince you that creativity is not just a genetic endowment and not just a cognitive skill. Rather, we've learned that creative ideas spring from behavioral skills that you, too, can acquire to catalyze innovative ideas in yourself and in others.

What Makes Innovators Different?

So what makes innovators different from the rest of us? Most of us believe this question has been answered. It's a genetic endowment. Some people are right brained, which allows them to be more intuitive and divergent thinkers. Either you have it or you don't. But does research really support this idea? Our research confirms others' work that creativity skills are not simply genetic traits endowed at birth, but that they can be developed. In fact, the most comprehensive study confirming this was done by a group of researchers, Merton Reznikoff, George Domino, Carolyn Bridges, and Merton Honeymon, who studied creative abilities in 117 pairs of identical and fraternal twins. Testing twins aged fifteen to twenty-two, they found that only about 30 percent of the performance of identical twins on a battery of ten creativity tests could be attributed to genetics.[6] In contrast, roughly 80 percent to 85 percent of the twins' performance on general intelligence (IQ) tests could be attributed to genetics.[7] So general intelligence (at least the way scientists measure it) is basically a genetic endowment, but creativity is not. *Nurture trumps nature as far as creativity goes.* Six other creativity studies of identical twins confirm the Reznikoff et al. result: roughly 25 percent to 40 percent of what we do innovatively stems from genetics.[8] That means that roughly two-thirds of our innovation skills *still* come through learning—from first understanding the skill, then practicing it, and ultimately gaining confidence in our capacity to create.

This is one reason that individuals who grow up in societies that promote community versus individualism and hierarchy over merit—such as Japan, China, Korea, and many Arab nations—are less likely to creatively challenge the status quo and turn out innovations (or win Nobel prizes). To be sure, many innovators in our study seemed genetically gifted. But more importantly, they often described how they acquired innovation skills from role models who made it "safe" as well as exciting to discover new ways of doing things.

If innovators can be made and not just born, how then do they come up with great new ideas? Our research on roughly five hundred innovators compared to roughly five thousand executives led us to identify five discovery skills that distinguish innovators from typical executives (for detail on the research methods, see appendix B). First and foremost, innovators count on a cognitive skill that we call "associational thinking" or simply "associating." Associating happens as the brain tries to synthesize and make sense of novel inputs. It helps innovators discover new directions by making connections across seemingly unrelated questions, problems, or ideas. Innovative breakthroughs often happen at the intersection of diverse disciplines and fields. Author Frans Johanssen described this phenomenon as "the Medici effect," referring to the creative explosion in Florence when the Medici family brought together creators from a wide range of disciplines—sculptors, scientist, poets, philosophers, painters, and architects. As these individuals connected, they created new ideas at the intersection of their respective fields, thereby spawning the Renaissance, one of the most innovative eras in history. Put simply, innovative thinkers connect fields, problems, or ideas that others find unrelated.

The other four discovery skills trigger associational thinking by helping innovators increase their stock of building-block ideas from which innovative ideas spring. Specifically, innovators engage the following behavioral skills more frequently:

Questioning. Innovators are consummate questioners who show a passion for inquiry. Their queries frequently challenge the status quo, just as Jobs did when he asked, "Why does a computer need a fan?" They love to ask, "If we tried this, what would happen?" Innovators, like Jobs, ask questions to understand how things really are today, why they are that way, and how they might be changed or disrupted. Collectively, their questions provoke new insights, connections, possibilities, and directions. We found that innovators consistently demonstrate a high Q/A ratio, where questions (Q) not only outnumber answers (A) in a typical conversation, but are valued at least as highly as good answers.

Observing. Innovators are also intense observers. They carefully watch the world around them—including customers, products, services, technologies, and companies—and the observations help them gain insights into and ideas for new ways of doing things. Jobs's observation trip to Xerox PARC provided the germ of insight that was the catalyst for both the Macintosh's innovative operating system and mouse, and Apple's current OSX operating system.

Networking. Innovators spend a lot of time and energy finding and testing ideas through a diverse network of individuals who vary wildly in their backgrounds and perspectives. Rather than simply doing social networking or networking for resources, they actively search for new ideas by talking to people who may offer a radically different view of things. For example, Jobs talked with an Apple Fellow named Alan Kay, who told him to "go visit these crazy guys up in San Rafael, California." The crazy guys were Ed Catmull and Alvy Ray, who headed up a small computer graphics operation called Industrial Light & Magic (the group created special effects for George Lucas's movies). Fascinated by their operation, Jobs bought Industrial Light & Magic for $10 million, renamed it Pixar, and eventually took it public for $1 billion. Had he never chatted with Kay, he would never have wound up purchasing Pixar, and the world might never have thrilled to wonderful animated films like *Toy Story, WALL-E,* and *Up*.

Experimenting. Finally, innovators are constantly trying out new experiences and piloting new ideas. Experimenters unceasingly explore the world intellectually and experientially, holding convictions at bay and testing hypotheses along the way. They visit new places, try new things, seek new information, and experiment to learn new things. Jobs, for example, has tried new experiences all his life—from meditation and living in an ashram in India to dropping in on a calligraphy class at Reed College. All these varied experiences would later trigger ideas for innovations at Apple Computer.

Collectively, these discovery skills—the cognitive skill of associating and the behavioral skills of questioning, observing, networking, and experimenting—constitute what we call the innovator's DNA, or the code for generating innovative business ideas.

The Courage to Innovate

Why do innovators question, observe, network, and experiment more than typical executives? As we examined what motivates them, we discovered two common themes. First, they actively desire to change the status quo. Second, they regularly take smart risks to make that change happen. Consider the consistency of language that innovators use to describe their motives. Jobs wants to "put a ding in the universe." Google cofounder Larry Page has said he's out to "change the world." These innovators steer entirely clear of a common cognitive trap called *the status quo bias*—the tendency to prefer an existing state of affairs to alternative ones. Most of us simply accept the status quo. We may even like routine and prefer not to rock the boat. We adhere to the saying, "if it ain't broke, don't fix it," while not really questioning whether "it" is "broke." In contrast, innovators see many things as "broke." And they want to fix them.

How do innovators break the status quo? One way is to refuse to be dictated by other people's schedules. Just glance at an innovative executive's typical calendar and you will find a radically different schedule compared to less inventive executives. *We found that innovative entrepreneurs (who are also CEOs) spend 50 percent more time on discovery activities (questioning, observing, experimenting, and networking) than CEOs with no innovation track record.* That translated into spending almost one more day each week on discovery activities. They understand that fulfilling their dreams to change the world means they've got to spend a significant amount of time trying to discover *how* to change the world. And having the courage to innovate means that they are actively looking for opportunities to change the world.

Embracing a mission for change makes it much easier to take smart risks, make mistakes, and most of all, learn quickly from them. Most innovative entrepreneurs we studied felt that mistakes are nothing to be ashamed of. In fact, they are an expected cost of doing business. "If the people running Amazon.com don't make some significant mistakes," Jeff Bezos told us, "then we won't be doing a good job for our shareholders because we won't be swinging for the fences." In short, innovators rely on their "courage to innovate"—an active bias against the status quo and an unflinching willingness to take smart risks—to transform ideas into powerful impact.

In summary, the DNA of innovators—or the code for generating innovative ideas—is expressed in the model shown in figure 1-1. The key skill for generating innovative ideas is the cognitive skill of associational thinking. The reason that some people generate more associations than others is partly because their brains are just wired that way. But a more critical reason is that they more frequently engage in the behavioral skills of questioning, observing, networking, and experimenting. These are the catalysts for associational thinking. Of course, the next question is, why do some people engage these four skills more than others? The answer is that they have the courage to innovate. They are willing to embrace a mission for change and take risks to make change happen. The bottom line is that to improve your ability to generate innovative ideas, you need to practice associational thinking and more frequently engage in questioning, observing,

FIGURE 1-1

The innovator's DNA model for generating innovative ideas

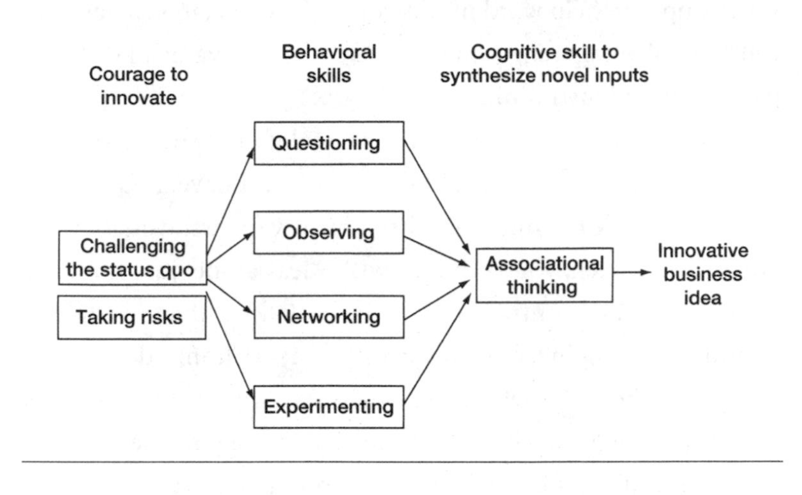

networking, and experimenting. That will likely only happen if you can somehow cultivate the courage to innovate.

As innovators actively engage in their discovery skills over a lifetime, they build discovery habits, and they become defined by them. They grow increasingly confident in their ability to discover what's next, and they believe deeply that generating creative insights is *their* job. It is not something to delegate to someone else. As A. G. Lafley declared, "innovation is the central job of every leader—business unit managers, functional leaders, and the CEO."[9]

The Innovator's DNA

We've just told you that the ability to be innovative is *not* based primarily on genetics. At the same time, we're using the DNA metaphor to describe the inner workings of innovators, which suggests that it is. Bear with us for a moment. (And welcome to the world of innovation, where the ability to synthesize two seemingly opposing ideas is the type of associating that produces novel insights.) Recent developments in the field of gene therapy show that it is possible to modify and strengthen your physical DNA, for example, to help ward off diseases.[10] Likewise, it is metaphorically possible to strengthen your personal innovator's DNA. Let us provide an illustration.

Imagine that you have an identical twin, endowed with the same brains and natural talents that you have. You're both given one week to come up with a creative new business idea. During that week, you come up with ideas alone, just thinking in your room. By contrast, your twin (1) talks with ten people—including an engineer, a musician, a stay-at-home dad, and a designer—about the venture; (2) visits three innovative start-ups to observe what they do; (3) samples five "new to the market" products and takes them apart; (4) shows a prototype he's built to five people, and (5) asks "What if I tried this?" and "What would make this not work?" at least ten times each day during these networking, observing, and experimenting activities. Who do you bet will come up with the more innovative (and usable) idea? My guess is that you'd bet on your twin, and not because he has better natural (genetic) creative abilities. Of course, the anchor weight of genetics is still there, but it is not the dominant predictor. People can learn to more capably come up with innovative solutions to problems by acting in the way that your twin did.

As figure 1-2 shows, innovative entrepreneurs rarely display across-the-board strength in observing, experimenting, and networking, and actually don't need to. All of the high-profile innovative entrepreneurs in our study scored above the seventieth percentile in associating and questioning. The innovators seemed to hold these two discovery skills more universally. But the innovators we studied didn't need world-class strength in the other behaviors. It certainly helped if they excelled at one of the four skills and were strong in at least two. If you hope to be a better

Discovery Skill Strengths Differ for Disruptive Innovators

To understand that innovative entrepreneurs develop and use different skills, look at figure 1-2. It shows the percentile rank scores on each of the five discovery skills for four well-known founders and innovators: Pierre Omidyar (eBay), Michael Dell (Dell), Michael Lazaridis (Research In Motion), and Scott Cook (Intuit). The percentile rank indicates the percentage of over five thousand executives and innovators in our database who scored lower on that particular skill. A particular skill is measured by the frequency and intensity with which these individuals engage in activities that compose the skill.

FIGURE 1-2

High-profile innovators' discovery skills profile

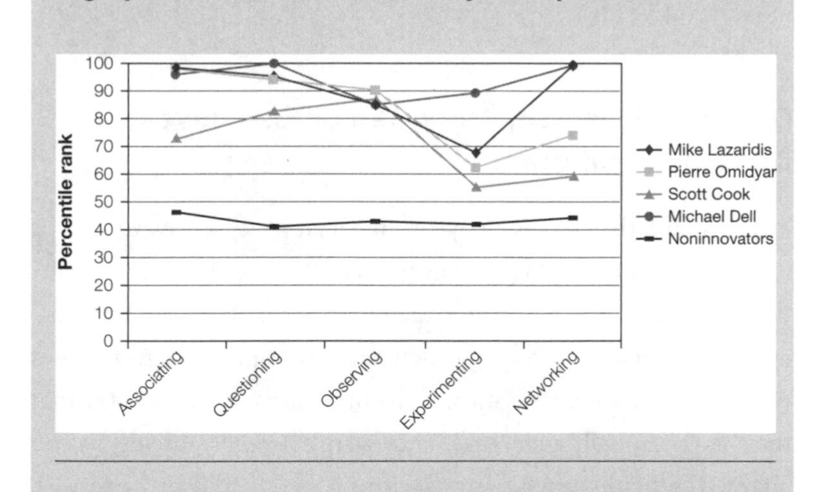

As you can see, the pattern for each innovative entrepreneur is different. For example, Omidyar is much more likely to acquire his ideas through questioning (ninety-fifty percentile) and

(continued)

observing (eighty-seventh percentile), Dell through experimenting (ninetieth percentile) and networking (ninety-eighth percentile), Cook through observing (eighty-eighth percentile) and questioning (eighty-third percentile), and Lazaridis through questioning (ninety-sixth percentile) and networking (ninety-eighth percentile). The point is that each of these innovative entrepreneurs did not score high on *all* five of the discovery skills. They each combined the discovery skills *uniquely* to forge new insights. Just as each person's physical DNA is unique, an innovator's DNA comprises a unique combination of skills and behaviors.

innovator, you will need to figure out which of these skills you can improve and which can be distinguishing skills to help you generate innovative ideas.

Delivery Skills: Why Most Senior Executives Don't Think Different

We've spent the past eight years interviewing scores of senior executives—mostly at large companies—asking them to describe the most novel and valuable strategic insights that they had generated during their careers. Somewhat surprisingly, we found that top executives rarely mentioned an innovative business idea that they had personally generated. They were extremely intelligent and talented individuals who were accomplished at delivering results, but they didn't have much direct, personal experience with generating innovative business ideas.

In contrast to innovators who seek to fundamentally change existing business models, products, or processes, most senior executives work hard to efficiently deliver the next thing that should be done *given* the existing business model. That is, they

I'm Not Steve Jobs . . . Is This Relevant?

OK, so you're not Steve Jobs. Or Jeff Bezos. Or any other famous business innovator. But that doesn't mean you can't learn from these innovators. You *can* get better at innovating, even if most of your innovations are somewhat incremental in nature. We've seen it happen, and we've seen that it can make a difference. We've seen a pharmaceutical executive practice a questioning technique (see chapter 3) each day to identify key strategic issues facing his division. After three months, his boss told him that he'd become the most effective strategic thinker on his team. Within six months, he was promoted to a corporate strategic planning job. "I just improved my ability to ask questions," he told us. We've seen MBA students in our classes use the observing, networking, and experimenting techniques to generate entrepreneurial business ideas. One got the idea for launching a company that uses bacteria to eat pollution from networking with someone he met at a neighborhood barbeque. Another observed that the best English speakers in Brazil were people who watched American movies and television. So he launched a company that sells software that helps people learn English by watching movies. Many innovative ideas may seem small, such as a new process for effectively screening job recruits or a better way to build customer loyalty, but they are valuable new ideas nonetheless. And if you come up with enough of them, they will definitely help you advance in your career. The point is this: you don't have to be Steve Jobs to generate innovative ideas for your business.

work inside the box. They shine at converting a vision or goal into the specific tasks to achieve the defined goal. They organize work and conscientiously execute logical, detailed, data-driven plans of action. In short, most executives excel at execution, including the following four delivery skills: *analyzing, planning, detail-oriented implementing,* and *disciplined executing.* (We'll say more about these skills later in the chapter and in chapter 8, but for now we need only note that they are critical for delivering results and translating an innovative idea into reality.)

Many innovators realize that they are deficient in these critical skills and, consequently, try to team up with others who possess them. For example, eBay founder Omidyar quickly recognized the need for execution skills, so he invited Jeff Skoll, a Stanford MBA, and Meg Whitman, a Harvard MBA, to join him. "Jeff Skoll and I had very complementary skills," Omidyar told us. "I'd say I did more of the creative work developing the product and solving problems around the product, while Jeff was involved in the more analytical and practical side of things. He was the one who would listen to an idea of mine and then say, 'Ok, let's figure out how to get this done.'" Skoll and Whitman professionalized the eBay Web site, added fixed-price auctions, drove international expansion, developed new categories such as autos, and integrated important capabilities such as PayPal.

Why do most senior executives excel in the delivery skills, but are only above average in discovery skills? It is vital to understand that the skills critical to an organization's success vary systematically throughout the business life cycle. (See figure 1-4). For example, in the start-up phase of an innovative venture, the founders are obviously more discovery-driven and entrepreneurial. Discovery skills are crucial early in the business life cycle because the company's key task is to generate new business ideas worth pursuing. Thus, discovery (exploration) skills are highly valued at this stage and delivery (execution) skills are secondary. However, once innovative entrepreneurs come up with a promising new business idea and then shape that idea into a bona fide business opportunity, the company begins to grow and then must pay attention to building the processes necessary to scale the idea.

The Discovery and Delivery Skills Matrix: How Innovators Stack Up

To test the assertion that innovative executives have a different set of skills than typical executives, we used our innovator's DNA assessment to measure the percentile rank of a sample of high-profile innovative entrepreneurs (founder CEOs of companies on *BusinessWeek*'s list of the top one hundred most innovative companies) on both the five discovery skills (associating, questioning, observing, networking, experimenting) and the four delivery or execution skills: analyzing, planning, detail-oriented implementing, and self-disciplined executing. We averaged their percentile rank scores across the five discovery skills to get an overall percentile rank, and then did the same thing across the four delivery skills to get an overall percentile rank. We refer to the overall percentile rank across the five discovery skills as the "discovery quotient" or DQ. While intellectual quotient (or IQ) tests are designed to measure general intelligence and emotional quotient (or EQ) assessments measure emotional intelligence (ability to identify, assess, and control the emotions of ourselves and others), discovery quotient (DQ) is designed to measure our ability to discover ideas for new ventures, products, and processes.

Figure 1-3 shows that the high-profile innovative entrepreneurs scored in the eighty-eighth percentile on discovery skills, but only scored in the fifty-sixth percentile on delivery skills. In short, they were just average at execution. We then conducted the same analysis for a sample of nonfounder CEOs (executives who had never started a new business). We found that most senior executives in large organizations were the mirror image of innovative entrepreneurs: they scored around the eightieth percentile on delivery skills, while scoring only above average on

(continued)

FIGURE 1-3

Discovery-delivery skills matrix

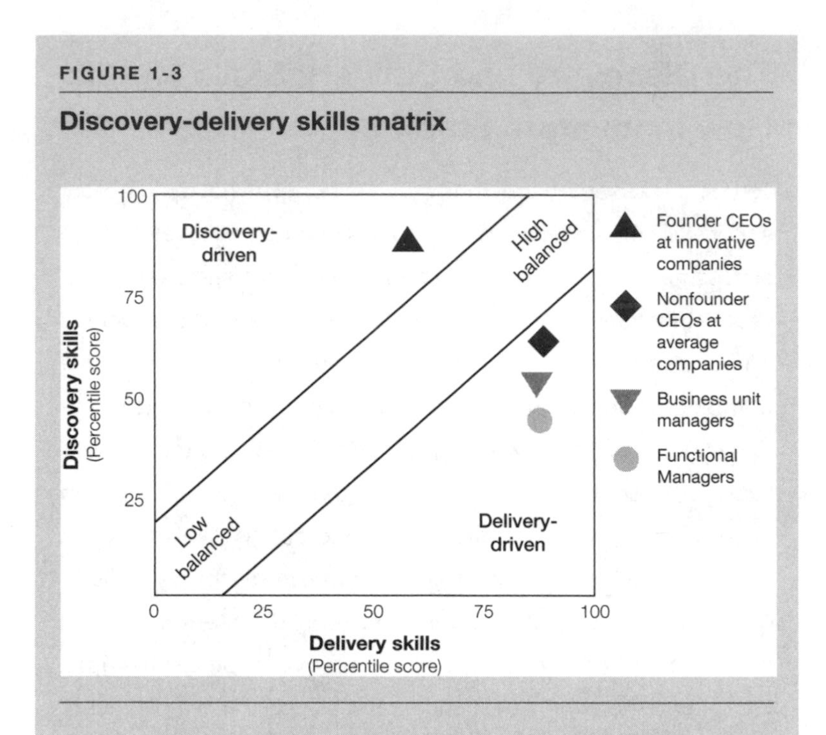

discovery skills (sixty-second percentile). In short, they are selected primarily for their execution skills. This focus on execution is even more pronounced in business unit managers and functional managers, who are worse at discovery than typical CEOs. This data shows that innovative organizations are led by individuals with a very high DQ. It also shows that even within an average organization, discovery skills tend to distinguish those who make it to the highest levels of the organization. So if you want to move up, you'd better learn how to innovate.

During the growth stage, the innovative entrepreneur may well leave the company, either because she has no interest in scaling the idea (which involves boring and routine work, at least to her) or because she does not have the skills to manage effectively in a large organization. Innovative entrepreneurs are often

FIGURE 1-4

The business and executive skill life cycles

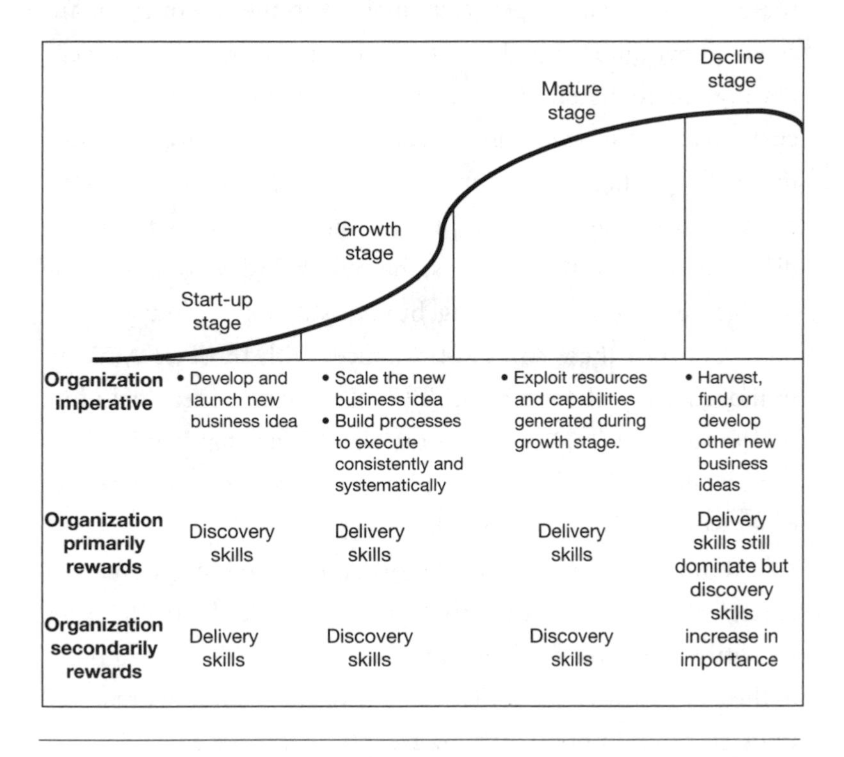

described as poor managers because they lack the ability to follow through on their new business ideas and are often irrationally overconfident in them. Moreover, they are more likely to make decisions based on hunches and personal biases rather than data-driven analysis.[11] Not surprisingly, the conventional prescription for these problems is to replace the entrepreneurs with professional managers—individuals with proven skills at delivering results. At this point in the business life cycle, professional managers who are better equipped to scale the business often replace the entrepreneur founders. When such replacement occurs, however, *key discovery skills walk away from the top management team.*

With the founder entrepreneur out of the picture, the ensuing growth and maturation stage of the business life cycle begins. In these stages, managers generally make it to the top of the management pyramid through great execution. This may involve generating incremental (sustaining) innovations for existing customers, but the focus is on execution, not building new businesses. Surprisingly few companies in this stage pay systematic attention to the selection or promotion of people with strong discovery skills. As this happens, the lack of discovery skills at the top becomes even more glaring, but it is still not necessarily obvious. (Contrast these common practices with those of Amazon founder Bezos, who systematically asks any new hire, including senior executives, to "tell me about something that you have invented." Bezos wants to hire people with an inventive attitude—in other words, people like himself.)

Eventually, for most organizations, the initial innovations that created the business in the first place complete their life cycle. Growth stalls as the business hits the downward inflection point in the well-known S curve. These mature and declining organizations are typically dominated by executives with excellent delivery skills. Meanwhile, investors demand new growth businesses, but senior executive teams can't seem to find them because the management ranks are dominated by folks with strong delivery skills. With discovery skills largely absent from the top management team, it becomes increasingly difficult to find new business opportunities to fuel new company growth. The company once again starts to see the imperative for discovery skills.

In sharp contrast, when entrepreneur founders stay through the growth stage, the company significantly outperforms its peers in growth and profitability.[12] An entrepreneurial founder is far more likely to surround herself with executives who are good at discovery, or who at least understand discovery. Could Apple have built new businesses in music (iTunes and iPod) and phones (iPhone) on top of an older computer business without the return of Jobs? We doubt it.

The key point here is that large companies typically fail at disruptive innovation because the top management team is dominated by individuals who have been selected for delivery skills, not discovery skills. As a result, most executives at large organizations don't know how to think different. It isn't something that they learn within their company, and it certainly isn't something they are taught in business school. Business schools teach people how to be deliverers, not discoverers.

For a moment, consider your company's track record of rewarding and promoting discovery skills. Does your company actively screen for people who have strong discovery skills? Does your company regularly reward discovery skills through annual performance assessments? If the answers are no, then it is likely that a severe discovery skill deficit exists at the top ranks of management in your company.

You Can Learn to Think Different

In this chapter, we've tried to convince you that creativity is not a just a genetic predisposition; it is an active endeavor. Apple's slogan "Think Different" is inspiring but incomplete. Innovators must consistently act different to think different. We acknowledge that genetics are at work within innovators, and that some have superior natural ability at associational thinking. However, *even if two individuals have the same genetic creative ability, one will be more successful at creative problem solving if he or she more frequently engages in the discovery skills we have identified.* By understanding—and engaging in—the five discovery skills, we believe that you can find ways to more successfully develop the creative spark within yourself and others. Read on as we describe how to master the five discovery skills in order to become a more innovative thinker.

Discovery and Delivery Skills Quiz: What's Your Profile?

To get a quick snapshot of your discovery-delivery skills profile, take the following self-assessment survey (1 = strongly disagree; 2 = somewhat disagree; 3 = neither agree nor disagree; 4 = somewhat agree; 5 = strongly agree). Remember to answer based on your actual behaviors, not what you would like to do.

1. Frequently, my ideas or perspectives diverge radically from others' perspectives.
2. I am very careful to avoid making any mistakes in my work.
3. I regularly ask questions that challenge the status quo.
4. I am extremely well organized at work.
5. New ideas often come to me when I am directly observing how people interact with products and services.
6. I must have everything finished "just right" when completing a work assignment.
7. I often find solutions to problems by drawing on solutions or ideas developed in other industries, fields, or disciplines.
8. I never jump into new projects and ventures and act quickly without carefully thinking through all of the issues.
9. I frequently experiment to create new ways of doing things.
10. I always follow through to complete a task, no matter what the obstacles.
11. I regularly talk with a diverse set of people (e.g., from different business functions, organizations, industries, geographies, etc.) to find and refine new ideas.

12. I excel at breaking down a goal or plan into the micro tasks required to achieve it.
13. I attend conferences (on my areas of expertise as well as unrelated areas) to meet new people and understand what issues are facing them.
14. I pay careful attention to details at work to ensure that nothing is overlooked.
15. I actively seek to identify emerging trends by reading books, articles, magazines, blogs, and so on.
16. I hold myself and others strictly accountable for getting results.
17. I frequently ask "what if" questions that provoke exploration of new possibilities and frontiers.
18. I consistently follow through on all commitments and finish what I've started.
19. I regularly observe the activities of customers, suppliers, or other organizations to get new ideas.
20. I consistently create detailed plans to get work done.

To score your survey:

Add your score on the odd-numbered items. You score very high on discovery skills if your total score is 45 or above, high on discovery if your score is 40–45, moderate to high on discovery if your score is between 35 and 40, moderate to low if you score 29–34; you score low on discovery if your score is 28 or less.

Add your score on the even-numbered items. You score very high on delivery skills if your total score is 45 or above, high on delivery if your score is 40–45, moderate to high on delivery if your score is between 35 and 40, moderate to low

(continued)

if you score 29–34; you score low on delivery if your score is 28 or less.

We have drawn this short survey from a more systematic seventy-item assessment (either a self-assessment or a 360-degree assessment) that we have developed to assess an individual's discovery skills and delivery skills. You can do this assessment through our Web site at http://www.InnovatorsDNA.com. Should you decide to complete an assessment, you will receive a *development guide* to walk you through your results and help you design a skill development plan. Your assessment will provide you with your DQ and percentile data for each discovery and delivery skill to compare your scores with the over five thousand executives and innovators in our dataset.

2

Discovery Skill #1

Associating

"Creativity is connecting things."

—Steve Jobs, founder and CEO,
Apple Inc.

INNOVATORS THINK DIFFERENTLY (to be grammatically correct), but as Steve Jobs put it, they really just think different by connecting the unconnected. Einstein once called creative thinking "combinatorial play" and saw it as "the essential feature in productive thought." Associating—or the ability to make surprising connections across areas of knowledge, industries, even geographies—is an often-taken-for-granted skill among the innovators we studied. Innovators actively pursue diverse new information and ideas through questioning, observing, networking, and experimenting—the key catalysts for creative associations.

To illustrate how associations produce innovative business ideas, consider how Marc Benioff came up with the idea for Salesforce.com, now a $13 billion software company. Benioff's experience with technology and software began when, as a fifteen-year-old, he built a small software company, Liberty Software, writing computer games (like "How to Juggle") on his Commodore 64. As a computer science and entrepreneurship undergraduate, Benioff worked summers at Apple during the build-up and launch of the first Mac, learning firsthand what it meant to work in a think-different world.

After graduation, Benioff joined Oracle, then a small start-up. By the time Benioff was twenty-five, he was leading Oracle's entire direct-marketing division and was beginning to see several streams of opportunity emerging on the Internet. "The nature of being successful with software is you always have to be looking for the next thing, so you have to condition your mind to think that way," Benioff told us. "I've seen a lot of different technological shifts over the last twenty-five years, so as I was sitting at my desk at Oracle in the late nineties and watching the emergence of Amazon.com and eBay . . . it felt like something significant was on the horizon."

Benioff decided it was time to think more deeply about the changing technological landscape—and his own career. So he took a sabbatical that started with a trip to India where he met a variety of diverse people, including spiritual leader and humanitarian, Mata Amritanandamayi (who helped strengthen his commitment to doing well and doing good in business). Benioff's next stop on this global journey was Hawaii, where he discussed various ideas for new businesses with an assortment of entrepreneurs and friends. While swimming with dolphins in the Pacific Ocean, the fundamental epiphany for Salesforce.com surfaced. He reflected: "I asked myself 'Why aren't all enterprise software applications built like Amazon and eBay? Why are we still loading and upgrading software the way that we have been doing all this time when we now have the Internet?' And that was a fundamental breakthrough for me, asking those questions. And that's the genesis of Salesforce. *It's basically enterprise software meets Amazon.*"

Benioff's synthesis of novel inputs or association—"enterprise software meets Amazon"—challenged the industry tradition of selling software on CD-ROMs and engaging companies in lengthy, customized (and expensive) installation processes, and instead focused on delivering software as a service over the Internet. That way, the software would be available 24/7, and companies would avoid all the costs and shutdowns associated with ongoing, large-scale IT system installations and upgrades. Given his substantial experience in sales and marketing at Oracle, Benioff felt that providing software services for managing a sales force and customer relations carried huge potential for small and medium-sized businesses that couldn't afford customized enterprise software. Thus, Salesforce.com was born.

Benioff's vision emerged from years of significant software industry experience combined with countless questions, observations, explorations, and conversations that ultimately helped him bring together things that had never been connected before. He borrowed elements of the Amazon business model and built a different one based on a software system that companies would pay for *as* they used it, instead of paying for all of the software systems *before* they used them (as most software providers did). It was truly revolutionary as it launched an era of "cloud computing" that seems obvious now, but was far from obvious then.

Ever the juggler with a mind hooked on "combinatorial play" (or playing around with new associations), Benioff and his Salesforce.com team have continued the innovation journey. He explained that pre-Salesforce.com, his critical question was "Why isn't all enterprise software like Amazon?" but post-Salesforce.com, a different question slowly took its place, "Why isn't all enterprise software (including Salesforce.com) like Facebook?" Benioff and his team hotly pursued the answer and invented Chatter, a new social software application that has been referred to as "Facebook for businesses." Chatter takes the best of Facebook and Twitter and applies it to enterprise collaboration (think of it as "Facebook and Twitter meet enterprise software," just as "enterprise software met Amazon" at Salesforce.com's genesis).

Chatter uses new ways of sharing information such as feeds and groups, so that without any effort, people can see what individuals and teams are focusing on, how projects are progressing, and what deals are closing. It changes the way companies collaborate on product development, customer acquisition, and content creation by making it easy for everyone to see what everyone else is doing. At companies using Chatter, e-mail in-boxes have shrunk dramatically (by 43 percent at Salesforce.com) because the majority of communications are now status updates and feeds in Chatter. "Employees now follow accounts, and updates are automatically broadcast to them in real-time via Chatter," Benioff told us. "This is the true power of Chatter—bringing to light the most important people and ideas that move our companies forward. I call this social intelligence, and it's giving everyone access to the people, the knowledge, and the insight they need to make a difference."

Associating: What It Is

The great innovative entrepreneur Walt Disney once described his role in the company he founded as creative catalyst. By that he meant that while he himself didn't actually do the drawings for the wonderful animated films or build the giant Matterhorn replica for Disneyland, he did put ideas together in ways that sparked creative insights throughout the company. One day, a little boy was curious about Disney's job, and Disney vividly recalled the conversation: "I was stumped one day when a little boy asked, 'Do you draw Mickey Mouse?' I had to admit I do not draw any more. 'Then you think up all the jokes and ideas?' 'No,' I said, 'I don't do that.' Finally, he looked at me and said, 'Mr. Disney, just what do you do?' 'Well,' I said, 'I think of myself as a little bee. I go from one area of the studio to another and gather pollen and sort of stimulate everybody.' I guess that's the job I do."[1] Not only did Disney spark others' ideas, he sparked his own as well by putting himself at the intersection of others' experiences. Over time, Disney's associational insights—including a string of industry firsts such as joining animation with full-length movies and putting themes into amusement parks—changed the face of entertainment.

Innovative leaders at well-known companies such as Apple, Amazon, and Virgin do exactly the same thing. They cross-pollinate ideas in their own heads and in others. They connect wildly different ideas, objects, services, technologies, and disciplines to dish up new and unusual innovations. "Creativity is connecting things," as Steve Jobs once put it. He continued, "When you ask creative people how they did something, they feel a little guilty because they didn't really do it, they just saw something . . . they were able to connect experiences they've had and synthesize new things."[2] This is how innovators think different, or what we call associating,[3] a cognitive skill at the core of the innovator's DNA. In this chapter, we look more deeply into the workings of associational thinking and offer some techniques for developing this cognitive ability.

Associating: Where It Happens

Innovative ideas flourish at the intersection of diverse experience, whether it be others' or our own. Throughout history, great ideas have emerged from these crossroads of culture and experience. Much like the twelve major streets of traffic converging on the accident-prone circular road surrounding the Arc de Triomphe in Paris, the more diverse our crossroads of experience, the more likely a serendipitous synthesis of the surprising will occur. Put simply, innovators intentionally maneuver themselves into the intersection, where diverse experiences flourish and foster the discovery of new insights. As we mentioned in chapter 1, Frans Johansson coined the term "Medici effect"[4] to describe the spark that occurs in a geographic space or market space where a combination of novel ideas coalesce into something quite surprising. Such Medici effects have occurred throughout history, ancient and contemporary.

For example, historians often refer to the eighth to thirteenth centuries of the Islamic world as the Islamic "renaissance" or "golden age." Centuries before the Italian Renaissance, Baghdad attracted the best scholars from the Muslim world. Cairo, Damascus, Tunis, and Cordoba were also influential intellectual hubs. Islamic explorers traveled to the edges of the known world and beyond. Mecca served not only as a religious center, but also as a key intersection for multinational merchant traders coming from the far western regions of the Mediterranean to the far eastern reaches of India. This Islamic renaissance produced significant innovations, many of which are relevant today, including the underlying principles and ingredients of lipstick, suntan lotion, thermometers, ethanol, underarm deodorant, tooth bleaching, torpedoes, fireproof clothing, and charitable trusts.[5]

The Medici effect occurred in the Islamic and Italian renaissances, but it has also happened in modern times and in many places around the world. For example, Silicon Valley in the 1960s was anything but silicon. Yet, by the 1970s, all that had changed and technology innovation flourished during its renaissance decades of the 1970s, 1980s, and 1990s. Elsewhere in the world, countries and communities are actively attempting to create their own intersections of people with expertise in different fields to spark creative new ideas. China, for example, has bet substantial resources on its innovation future to the extent that the rest of the world believes that China is on track to become the world's most innovative country by 2020. In our work with the creative industries and social innovation sectors in China (like so many other sectors as well), we have found that they have dotted the land with artistic and social innovation incubators where ideas see not only the light of day, but the light of practice also.

The Medici effect also crops up in the many so-called "ideas conferences" that are flourishing—conferences such as the World Economic Forum Annual Meeting in Davos, Switzerland; the Aspen Ideas Festival; and TED (Technology Entertainment and Design) conferences, where diverse people join in a conscious attempt to cross-pollinate ideas and perspectives. Let's explore the power of TED. People go to these conferences to rub elbows and exchange ideas with extraordinary people—those who are well known and those who aren't. If you've never been to TED, take a look at its Web site to get a glimpse of how it creates a Medici effect year after year, and now in geography after geography (from TEDxTelAviv to TEDxRamallah to TEDxYourTown). A few of our personal TED favorites are Sir Ken Robinson questioning the foundation of educational systems, Kaki King experimenting far beyond what a guitar was originally intended to do, and David Gallo observing the incredible surprises of the deep sea (including the unexpected talents of squids). TED's underlying beauty springs from the intentional diversity of participants and presentations. This diversity forms the foundation for innovators to potentially connect the unconnected.

Innovators in our research not only frequented places like TED, but literally constructed a TED in their heads through an intentional depth and diversity of life experience, creating a *personal* Medici effect. For them, TED-like conferences were icing on a cake that they had already baked by actively questioning, observing, networking, and experimenting throughout their lives. This incredible foundation of deep and diverse experience fueled their associational thinking far beyond that of noninnovators. Look at PepsiCo chairman and CEO Indra Nooyi's life to get a glimpse of where her TED in the head comes from.

Nooyi was born to a middle-class family in Madras (now Chennai), where she often sat with her mother and sister "thinking big thoughts"; she played girls' cricket avidly and was lead guitarist in an all-girl rock band (it's no surprise that she still performs on stage at PepsiCo events). She finished a multidisciplinary undergraduate degree in chemistry, physics, and math before getting her MBA in Calcutta. Nooyi then worked in the textile industry (Tootal) and consumer products industry (Johnson & Johnson) before getting a master's of public and private management at Yale. After graduation, she shifted to the consulting industry (Boston Consulting Group) before doing a strategic stint in the electrical power industry (ABB), ultimately arriving at PepsiCo, where she became its first woman CEO.

Nooyi's diverse professional and personal experience convinced her that people, and especially CEOs, must "be willing to think disruptively." She did exactly that for the 2010 Super Bowl. Instead of spending $20 million on two sixty-second television ad slots, Nooyi took an entirely different approach, "Pepsi Refresh," emerging from a question she constantly asks: "How can we do better by doing better?" Pepsi Refresh invites people to submit ideas on how to "refresh" their communities, making them a better place to live. Each month, the Web site accepts a thousand ideas about arts and culture, health, education, and so on. Online voting produces winning ideas, with grants ranging from $5,000 to $250,000. In 2010 alone, PepsiCo allocated $1.3 million each month to Refresh projects based on over 45 million votes cast. Pepsi Refresh's Facebook numbers also topped 1 million by the end of 2010, and PepsiCo is now rolling out the program globally.

Associating: How It Works

To better grasp how associating works and why some people might excel at it more than others, it is important to understand how the brain works. The brain doesn't store information as a dictionary does, alphabetically with *theater* under *T*. Instead, while *theater* will associate with *T,* it will also associate with *all* of the other knowledge stored in the brain that the brain associates with it. Some associations with *theater* will seem logical, such as *Broadway, showtime,* or *intermission,* while others may be less obvious, such as *kissing, acting career,* or *anxiety* (perhaps due to a botched theater performance during high school). The more diverse knowledge the brain possesses, the more connections it can make when given fresh inputs of knowledge, and fresh inputs trigger the associations that lead to novel ideas. Scott Cook, founder and CEO of Intuit, describes these unexpected associations as "powerful and essential supplements to data" when working through a problem. Such analogies (or associations) are critical creative tools to help him generate strategic insights. When the brain is actively absorbing new knowledge, it is more likely to trigger connections between ideas (thus creating a wider web of neural connections) as it toils to synthesize novel inputs. Accordingly, the associating "muscle" can also be developed through the active practice of questioning, observing, networking, and experimenting.

In our research, every high-profile innovator excelled at associating (scoring at the seventieth percentile or higher on the innovator's DNA assessment), with process inventors showing slightly less associational skill than other inventors (yet still far more than noninnovators). (See figure 2-1.)

Why were all innovators so much better at associating than noninnovators? Our analysis found that the best predictor of excellent associating skills was how often people engaged in the other discovery skills—questioning, observing, networking, and experimenting. For example, Benioff got the initial idea for Chatter as he was asking, "Why isn't all enterprise software like Facebook and Twitter?" Research In Motion founder Lazaridis got the idea for the BlackBerry at a conference as he listened to someone talk about future trends in wireless data transfers. Starbucks founder Schultz got the idea for Starbucks as he was observing

FIGURE 2-1

Comparison of associating skills for different types of innovators and noninnovators

Sample items:

1. *Creatively solves challenging problems by drawing on diverse ideas or knowledge.*
2. *Often finds solutions to problems by drawing on solutions or ideas developed in other industries, fields, or disciplines.*

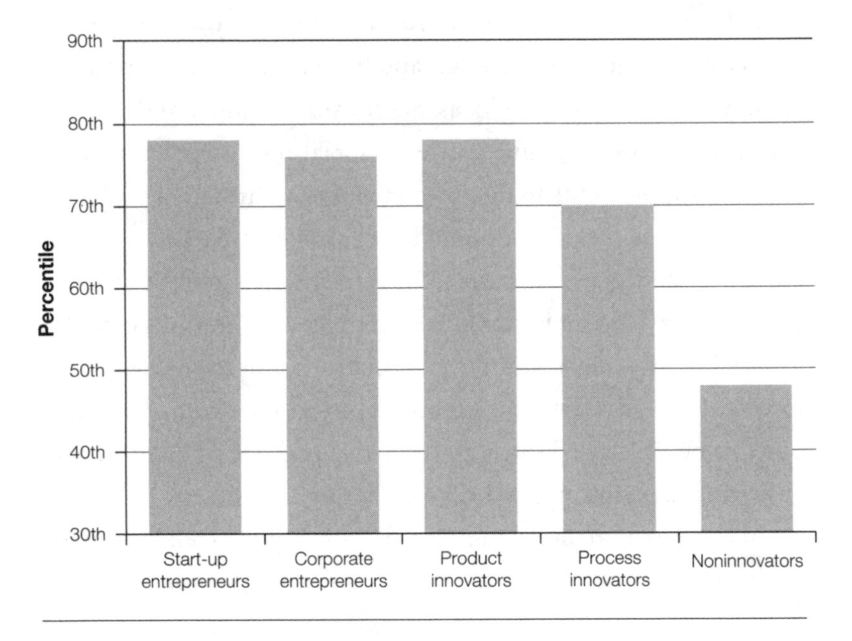

expresso bars in Italy. Disruptive innovators shine best at associating when actively crossing all kinds of borders (geographic, industry, company, profession, discipline, and so on) and engaging the other innovator's DNA skills.

Finding the right question, making compelling observations, talking with diverse people, and experimenting with the world usually delivers productive, relevant associational insights. In contrast, neglecting the other innovator's DNA skills usually *increases* the randomness (and often irrelevance) of a new association or insight, resulting in less impact on the marketplace. For an example similar to the identical twins scenario in chapter 1, consider two innovators independently attempting to surface valuable, new associations. The first person engages actively and regularly in a full range of discovery skills. The second does not. Which is most likely to get relevant, high-impact ideas? Obviously, the first, since she's been fully immersed in the world of real people facing real challenges *while* searching for a better solution. No surprise that her associational "ahas" are far more productive than her counterpart's relatively "random" connections, likely made from the safety and distance of an office chair.

On the Hunt for New Associations

In our work with disruptive innovators, we found several things that best described the dynamics behind their search for new associations. Creating odd combinations, zooming in and out, and Lego thinking allowed them to connect the dots across diverse experiences and ultimately deliver disruptive new business ideas.

Creating odd combinations

Neil Simon's successful Broadway play and subsequent TV series, *The Odd Couple*, centered on what life was like when two very different people—a prissy newsman and a sloppy sportswriter—lived together as roommates. The friction between opposite lifestyles often resulted in the most unexpected (and often creative) outcomes. Similarly, innovators often try to put together seemingly mismatched ideas to compose surprisingly successful combinations. They create odd couples, triplets, or quadruplets by consistently asking, "*What if* we combined this *with that*?" or

". . . this, this, and this *with* that?" They think different by fearlessly uniting uncommon combinations of ideas.

For Lazaridis, connecting ideas across disciplines was something he learned relatively early in life:

> When I was in high school, we had an advanced math program and we had a shop program. And there was this great divide between the two departments, and I was in both. And I became, inadvertently, the ambassador between the two disciplines, and saw how the mathematics we were learning in shop was actually more advanced than some of the mathematics we were learning in advanced math because we're using trigonometry, we're using imaginary numbers, we're using algebra, and even calculus in very real, tangible ways. So I was then tasked with *bridging the gap* and showing how math is used in electronics and how electronics is used in math.

Lazaridis noted that a teacher alerted him to the link between computers and wireless by telling him, "Don't get too distracted with computer technology because the person that puts wireless and computers together is really coming up with something special." And so the BlackBerry was born.

Likewise, Google cofounder Larry Page created an odd combination by connecting two seemingly unrelated ideas—academic citations *with* Web search—to launch Google. As a PhD student at Stanford, Page knew that academic journals and publishing companies rank scholars by the cumulative number of citations each scholar gets each year. Page realized that Google could rank Web sites *in the same way that academic citations rank scholars*; Web sites with the most links (that were most frequently selected) had more citations. This association allowed Page and cofounder Sergey Brin to launch a search engine yielding far superior search results.

Sometimes the world's most innovative leaders capture what seem like fleeting associations among ideas and knowledge, mixing and matching quite different concepts. In so doing, they produce the occasional outlandish ideas that may be catalysts for innovative business ideas. EBay founder Pierre Omidyar gave us a recent example of how he came up with a wild idea. He had spoken with consultants who were trying to solve the problem of how to get produce quickly from the farm to consumers in Hawaii before it spoils (the consultants explained that roughly one-third of the produce spoils). The first question Omidyar asked was, "What about the post office? Doesn't the post office go to everybody's house six times a week? Why don't we just mail the head of lettuce?" He then admitted: "It was probably an incredibly stupid idea and there are probably a dozen reasons why it won't work, but it's an example of how *I put two things together that haven't been put together before.* I understand the post office very well because eBay counts on shipping companies for the business model to work. The post office is an organization that visits every household six times a week! Do you know any other organization that does that? So using those assets in novel ways might be interesting."

Not everyone would consider putting "fresh produce" and "post office" together, but that's the kind of thinking that increases the probability of surfacing an innovative new business idea.

Zooming in and zooming out

Innovative entrepreneurs often exhibit the capacity to do two things at once: they dive deep into the details to understand the subtle nuances of a particular customer experience, and they fly high to see how the details fit into the bigger picture. Synthesizing these two views often results in surprising associations. Niklas Zennström (cofounder of Skype) explained this process of zooming in and out based on his own experience: "You have to think laterally. You know, seeing and combining certain things going on at the same time and understanding how seemingly unrelated things could have something to do with each other. You need the ability to grasp different things going on at the same time and then to bring them together. For example, I can look at the bigger picture and also have a very good feel for the details. So I can go between high-level things to really, really small details. *The movement often makes for new associations.*"

Steve Jobs has mastered zooming in and out to create excellent and often industry-changing products. At one point, when designing the original Mac computer, his team struggled to get the right finish on the plastic. Jobs unblocked the logjam by going to a department store and zooming in on the details of different plastic appliances. He discovered a Cuisinart food processor that had all the right plastic-case properties for producing an excellent case for the first Mac. In other instances, he visited the company parking lot to examine details of different cars to gain new insights about current or future product design challenges. One time, his parking lot excursion revealed a Mercedes-Benz trim detail that helped resolve a metal case-design dilemma.

Jobs is equally adept at zooming out to detect unexpected intersections across diverse industries. For example, as a result of buying and then leading Pixar for over a decade, he acquired a perspective on the entire media industry that was quite different from one he had gained earlier in the computer industry. This produced a powerful intersection of ideas when he returned to Apple. Years of personal negotiation with Disney executives about distribution rights and income for Pixar movies gave Jobs the insight and experience that later helped him create a workable solution to Internet-based music distribution—a solution that escaped senior executives at other computer and MP3 player companies. Jobs's Pixar experience provided the broad cross-industry perspective that has fueled the invention of several game-changing ideas like iTunes, iPod, iPhone, and most recently, the iPad.

Lego thinking

If innovators have one thing in common, it is that they love to collect ideas, like kids love to collect Legos. Nobel Prize winner Linus Pauling advised that "the best way to get a good idea is to get a lot of ideas." Thomas Edison kept over thirty-five hundred notebooks of ideas during the course of his lifetime and set regular "idea quotas" to keep the tap open. Billionaire Richard Branson is an equally passionate recorder of ideas, wherever he goes and with whomever he talks. Yet, absolute quantity of ideas does not always translate into highly disruptive ideas. Why? Because "you cannot look in a new direction by looking harder in the same direction," says Edward de Bono, author of *Lateral Thinking*. In other words, getting lots of ideas from lots of different sources creates the best of all innovation worlds. Innovators who frequently engage in questioning, observing, networking, and experimenting become far more capable at associating because they develop experience at understanding, storing, and recategorizing all this new knowledge. This is important because the innovators we studied rarely invented something entirely new; they simply recombined the ideas they had collected in new ways, allowing them to offer something new to the market. Questioning, observing, networking, and experimenting helped innovators slowly build larger, richer stocks of building-block ideas in their heads. The more building blocks they acquired, the better they were able to combine newly acquired knowledge to generate a novel idea.

To illustrate, think about a child playing with a set of Lego blocks. The more different kinds of blocks the child uses to build a structure, the more inventive she can become. But the most innovative structures spring from the novel combination of a wide variety of existing Legos, so as the child acquires different Lego sets (for example, combining a *Sponge Bob* set with a *Star Wars* set), she gets even better ideas for new structures. Similarly, the more knowledge, experience, or ideas you add from wide-ranging fields to your total stock of ideas, the greater the variety of ideas you can construct by combining these basic knowledge building blocks in unique ways. (See figure 2-2.)

People with deep expertise in a particular field, who can combine that knowledge with new concepts and ideas unfamiliar to them, tend to be more creative. This is why innovation design firm IDEO tries to recruit people who demonstrate a breadth of knowledge in many fields *and* a depth in at least one area of expertise. IDEO describes this person as "T-shaped" because the person holds deep expertise in one knowledge area but actively acquires knowledge broadly across different knowledge areas. A person with

FIGURE 2-2

Why boosting your diverse idea stock increases innovation

Conceptually, as innovators increase the number of building-block ideas, they substantially increase the number of ways they might combine ideas to create something surprisingly new. Combining this *with* that *creatively (building odd combinations) depends on how many unique* this *and* that *building blocks people have cached in their heads over time.*[a]

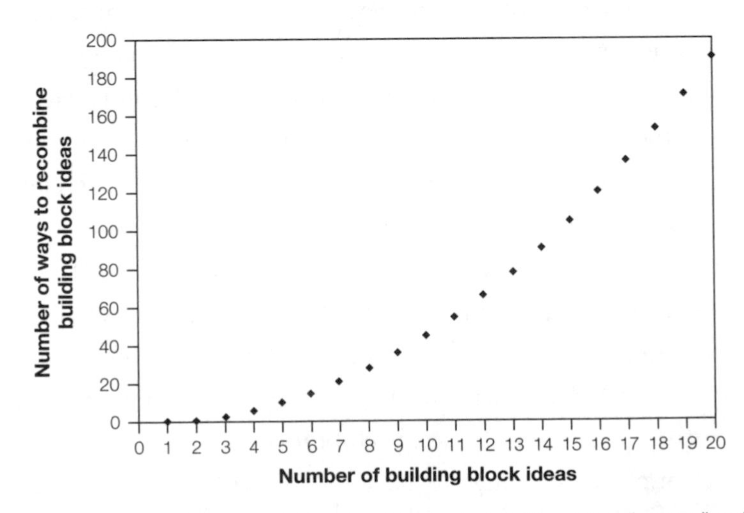

a. Mathematically, as the number of different building-block ideas (N) in our heads grows linearly, the potential ways to recombine those ideas grows even faster, or geometrically (by N(N–1)/2).

this knowledge profile typically generates innovative associations in two ways: (1) by importing an idea from another field into his area of deep expertise, or (2) by exporting an idea from his area of deep expertise to one of the broad fields he is exploring where he has shallow knowledge.

For example, a consultant with manufacturing expertise working at Bain & Company happened to visit with hospital administrators after the U.S. government implemented fixed-cost reimbursements to reduce health care costs. The hospital needed new ways to reduce costs, something it hadn't focused on when the government reimbursed for actual expenses *plus* a 10 percent profit markup. During the discussion, the Bain consultant—with deep expertise in the manufacturing sector—asked how the hospital managed patient throughput, minimizing the "touches" to the "product" (patient) and speeding its throughput through the "plant" (hospital). These manufacturing-sourced ideas were completely foreign to the hospital, where processes focused on keeping the patient longer to ensure quality care (and kept expenses and profits high). These new ideas from an entirely different industry delivered a dramatic redesign of hospital processes designed to get the patient through the hospital (like a plant) as quickly as possible. Within five years, Bain was working with over fifty U.S. hospitals applying these ideas to reduce costs.

A Safe Place for New Thoughts

After years of building a large stock of ideas through active questioning, observing, networking, and experimenting, innovators often make the most surprising associations. Sometimes an association or idea sparked at the very moment they were engaged in questioning, observing, networking or experimenting (as described in chapters 3 through 6). Equally often, innovators uncovered new ideas while in a relaxed state, without distractions, when they were not "trying" to solve a problem (researchers describe this as "defocusing their attention"). In other words, it rarely happened during a meeting when they were in a focused, convergent thinking mode searching for a solution to a particular problem. Instead, Diane Greene (cofounder of VMWare) told us that "the shower" is a great place to relax and think to get new ideas (a place frequently pitched by many innovators we interviewed, including David Neeleman [founder of JetBlue and Azul] and Jeff Jones [founder of Campus Pipeline and NxLight]). Innovators also unearth new ideas while walking, driving, on vacation, or in the middle of the night (as PepsiCo CEO Nooyi does). Benioff got the key inspiration for Salesforce.com when "swimming with the dolphins." In addition to hitting the shower, Greene gets some of her best new associations when sailing solo (which she has done since childhood). In short, Greene explained, "You get more creativity by giving yourself the space for ideas to simmer. Ideas come from having a longer time horizon about what you're thinking about and a broader view of where the idea might be going to go." The point is that you can sometimes spend too much time deliberately attacking a problem when some creative ideas will only emerge after putting yourself in a relaxed state with no distractions.[6] If all else fails when trying to figure out a problem, go to sleep. Yes, Harvard researchers have found that sleep is a consistent antidote to tunnel vision toward a problem. So when find yourself stuck in a thinking rut, give the problem extra time to percolate by adding some sleep into the mix. On average, that sleep will give you a 33 percent better chance of connecting the unconnected and getting a great new idea.[7]

The best innovators generally knew their safe places and times for generating new ideas. Do you? If not, look for places of transition or relaxation. Some folks find their best ideas early in the morning; others late at night. Whatever works best for you, make sure that you make the time to just meditate and think.

Disruptive innovators force themselves to cross borders (technical, functional, geographical, social, disciplinary) as they engage in the other discovery skills. If we do the same, placing ourselves in midst of bustling intersections of diverse ideas and experiences, exciting associations will naturally happen. The discovery skills of questioning, observing, networking, and experimenting will trigger surprising associations as we exercise them, over and over. Whether pursued out of the office or in a conference room, great associations are more likely to unfold when we create a safe place for them to happen. In time, your capacity to craft creative solutions to problems will become powerful, at work and beyond.

Tips for Developing Associating Skills

To strengthen your capacity to think different and weave together unexpected connections across ideas, consider the following short- and long-term exercises.[8] Most take relatively little time, but when done consistently, they can deliver positive results in generating new ideas. We have found that these exercises can work for creatively solving senior-level strategic problems as well as factory floor–level production challenges.

Tip #1: Force new associations

Innovators sometimes practice "forced associating" or combining things that we would never naturally combine. For example, they might imagine (or force) the combination of features in, say, a microwave oven with a dishwasher. This could deliver an innovative product idea, such as a dishwasher that uses some type of heating technology to clean and sanitize dishes that eliminates water completely. Or in the case of actual appliance companies, EdgeStar produced a countertop-size dishwasher, while KitchenAid went for an in-sink approach. Both are the size of a microwave oven, use limited amounts of water, and wash far faster than a full-size machine.

To practice forced associations, first consider a problem or challenge you or your company is facing. Then try the following exercises to force an association that you normally wouldn't make:

> Pick up a product catalog and turn to the twenty-seventh page. What does the first product that you see have to do with the problem you are thinking about? Does the way it solves a problem for a customer have anything to do with your problem? For example, what if you run across an iPad product in your random page flipping and your work challenge is figuring out how to increase herbal tea sales? Looking at an iPad might spur surprising syntheses, such as creating a novel iPad application to capture the interest of potential customers (or provide a means for current customers to become repeat customers).
>
> Or, open a completely random Wikipedia entry by choosing a random article from the Wikipedia Web menu. A random click might land on *boomerang*. Perhaps your organization hopes for more appealing product packaging. Bumping into the idea of a boomerang might suggest packaging a customer can return or a self-returning package after the product is used.

Now, back to the challenge you or your company is facing. Try one of these forced association exercises, identify an unrelated random item or idea, and take the time to reflect on what it has to do with your problem. The point is to randomly find things to associate with your problem and work your best to freely (even wildly) make associations, lots of them (remember, lots of associations can lead to great ideas). As you do so, table 2-1 might help organize your insights.

TABLE 2-1

Forcing new associations

Unsolved problem	Unrelated random item or idea	Potential associations

Tip #2: Take on the persona of a different company

Follow the lead of TBWA, which often holds a designated "disruption day" to get new ideas.[9] After defining a key strategic question or challenge, TBWA people haul out large boxes full of hats, shirts, and other things from some of the most innovative companies in the world, like Apple and Virgin. They put on the clothing and assume the persona of someone from that company to look at their challenge from an entirely different perspective.

Alternatively, write down a list of companies (in related and unrelated industries) on a stack of index cards (or randomly go down the list of the Fortune 500 or Inc. 100 companies). Use the card stacks to create random pairings of your company with another. Then creatively brainstorm ideas on how the two could create new value through partnership or merger. By combining the strengths of both companies, you may surprise yourself with new products, services, or process ideas.

Tip #3: Generate metaphors

Engage in activities that provoke an analogy or metaphor for your company's products or services (hopefully escaping from idea ruts), because each analogy holds the potential for seeing things from an uncommon perspective. To illustrate, what if watching TV were more like reading a magazine? (This is how TiVo has changed TV watching; you can start and stop when you want, skip over advertisements, and so on.) Or, what if your product or service could incorporate the benefits of some of today's hottest products like the Wii or iPhone? What might those new features or benefits be? (See table 2-2.)

TABLE 2-2

Generating metaphors

List of products ("what if" metaphor)	Possible new features/ benefits

Tip #4: Build your own curiosity box

Start a collection of odd, interesting things (e.g., a slinky, model airplane, robot, and so on) and put them in a curiosity box or bag (as people in the sixteenth and seventeenth centuries did when they used curiosity cabinets to store interesting objects from around the world). Then, you can pull out unique items randomly when confronted with a problem or opportunity (and if you're really daring, display them on your office shelves). When traveling (or even at home), visit local second-hand shops and flea markets in a new city to pick up surprising treasures (ranging from a Kuwaiti camel bell to an Australian didgeridoo) that might provoke a new angle on an old problem.

Interestingly, the global innovation design firm IDEO devotes full-time employee effort to finding new things for its "Tech Box." IDEO designers rely on Tech Box items (each box has hundreds of high-tech gadgets, clever toys, and a wide variety of items) when brainstorming for new ideas, because odd, unusual things often trigger new associations. It may sound silly, but seemingly silly things can provoke the most random associations, literally forcing us out of our habitual thinking patterns.

Tip #5: SCAMPER!

Try Alex Osborn and Bob Eberle's acronym for insight, SCAMPER: substitute; combine; adapt; magnify, minimize, modify; put to other uses; eliminate; reverse, rearrange. Use any or all of the concepts to rethink the problem or opportunity you are addressing (this is particularly useful when thinking of redesigning a product, service, or process). (Michael Michalko's *Thinkertoys* is a useful resource for more details about the SCAMPER method; see table 2-3.)

TABLE 2-3

The Scamper method

Scamper challenge	Invent a new type of wristwatch
Substitute	Use natural wood or rocks instead of steel material.
Combine	Create a space for easy, instant access to medications when the alarm goes off.
Adapt	Use the wristwatch as a reflective mirror when lost.
Magnify, **m**inimize, **m**odify	Make the wristwatch face large enough to be a cup holder.
Put to other uses	Frame the watch as a work of art.
Eliminate	Remove the internal workings of the watch and replace them with a sundial.
Reverse, rearrange	Change the watch hands to go counter-clockwise. Put the watch face on the inside of the wristband to make the back of the watch the focal point in terms of design and fashion.

3

Discovery Skill #2

Questioning

"Question the unquestionable."

—Ratan Tata, chairman, Tata Group

"ANY QUESTIONS?" MOST OF us have heard that phrase hundreds, if not thousands of times. Sometimes it comes at the end of a presentation or meeting, and most of us shuffle away because we don't really think it is an open invitation to question. But other times, you may have real questions—about why things are the way they are and how they might be different—but you don't ask them. You need to. If disruptive innovators occupied the same room, they would fill the empty space with thought-provoking questions. Why? Because questioning is how they do their work. It is the creative catalyst for the other discovery behaviors: observing, networking, and experimenting. Innovators ask lots of questions to better understand what is and what might be. They ignore safe questions and opt for crazy ones, challenging the status quo and often threatening the powers that be with uncommon intensity and frequency.

Take Orit Gadiesh, the famously inquisitive and inventive chairman of Bain & Company. As a child growing up in Israel, she was fascinated by many things and "always asking a hundred questions." Her parents also encouraged her to ask questions when called on in class, and she did. So much so that her eighth grade teacher wrote in her yearbook: "Orit, always ask those two questions, and even a third and a fourth question. Don't ever stop being curious." When reading this teacher's comment, Gadiesh realized for the first time that "asking questions was the true way to go." Later in life, she relied on the same approach to cocreate client insights at Bain, knowing that "asking clients lots of questions is key to generating powerful solutions to problems."

For example, in the early 1980s, Gadiesh was fresh out of graduate school and new at consulting. She was assigned to help a steel-manufacturing client cut its costs to stay competitive. During her first visit to the plant, she was warned by the over-sixty-year-old CEO that women were "bad luck in the industry." Undaunted, she pressed forward with the client, asking question after question about why it was doing what it was doing. At the time, there were two ways to make steel, the standard process of pouring it into ingots or, alternatively, continuous casting (then, a new technology), where you literally cast the steel continuously and cut it into slabs.

After reading about the continuous-casting process and sensing its potential, Gadeish visited Japan to observe continuous casting first-hand. She left the country convinced that the new process could create significant value for her client. But the client's executives and salespeople kept telling her that they couldn't do it because they had three hundred fifty different products for customers and it was impossible to continuous cast that many products when you have to add other materials to the steel simultaneously. "The client was stubborn, completely convinced that they couldn't make the change," she told us.

Here's where Gadiesh's questioning skills best tackled the client's problem. She went to visit customers and started asking questions, "Do you really need three hundred fifty products?" "Why do you need all three hundred fifty products?" Their initial autopilot answer was yes, but as she probed further with additional questions, it became clear that customers didn't fully grasp the cost advantages that continuous casting offered due to its unique capacity to add other (lower-cost) materials during the steel-casting process. Working with the client and customers, Gadiesh literally went through each of the three hundred fifty products asking, "Why do you have this? What is its core importance?" to fully grasp why they made each thing they made.

Based on the rich information gleaned from asking a series of simple questions about why each product existed, Gadiesh naturally moved from understanding what was to exploring in depth what might be. She moved deeper into disruptive territory by asking fundamental questions such as: "What if we shrink the existing product line by 90 percent?" "What if we cast steel continuously with that sharply reduced product line?" "How might we maximize the addition of cost-saving materials when casting the steel?" Before long, the steel company executives realized that reducing the number of products from three hundred fifty to thirty not only was possible but was the most profitable course of action because it would give them a competitive advantage in the product segments in which they did compete. This allowed them to add other materials like aluminum (thus reducing costs) through a new continuous-casting process, while still meeting most of their key customers' needs. The client (then a little over a billion-dollar enterprise) built a new production facility and quickly raced ahead of U.S. competitors.

Gadiesh's ability to generate new insights is largely based on her ability to ask her way into what's really going on and then push the edge with constant, provocative questions about what might be. At the core, she believes that "when you persist in asking questions throughout life—particularly challenging ones—it's central to who you are and how you lead." In fact, she shared with us that in a recent meeting with several heads of state and CEOs, she was curious as to why *they* weren't asking more fundamental questions about key policy issues. One CEO confided to her: "When you're in the room, I don't have to ask the fundamental questions because I know they're going to be asked." Her deeply rooted instinct to ask has helped her successfully guide Bain Consulting for almost twenty years. It's no wonder then that one of Gadiesh's key steel industry clients once gave her a hard hat engraved with the phrase "A little light will lead us," referring not only to her first name, Orit, which means "light," but also to her light-generating questions that helped transform their business.

What Is "Questioning"?

Questions hold the potential to cultivate creative insights. Einstein knew this long ago as he often repeated the phrase, "If I only had the right question . . . If I only had the right question . . ."[1] No wonder he finally concluded that "the formulation of a problem is often more important than its solution" *and* that raising new questions to solve a problem "requires creative imagination." In *The Practice of Management*, Peter Drucker grasped the same power of provocative questions, observing that "the important and difficult job is never to find the right answers, it is to find the right question. For there are few things as useless—if not dangerous—as the right answer to the wrong question."[2] Recent research by Mihaly Csikszentmihalyi confirmed these personal convictions by finding that Nobel laureates were far better at achieving breakthroughs once they found the right question to reframe their problem.[3] Our research also found that disruptors rely on crafting the right questions to accomplish their work.

Questioning is a way of life for innovators, not a trendy intellectual exercise. Our research found that not only do innovators ask more questions than noninnovators, they also ask more provocative ones. (Innovators who "strongly agreed" with survey statements such as, "I often ask questions that challenge the status quo," produced twice as many new businesses than innovators who simply "agreed.") Among the different types of innovators we studied, product inventors showed the highest reliance on questioning to deliver results, followed by start-up and corporate entrepreneurs and, finally, process innovators. (See figure 3-1.)

By asking lots of questions, A. G. Lafley, for example, helped change the game at Procter & Gamble (P&G). Lafley often began conversations or meetings with: "Who is your target consumer here? What does she want? What do you know about her? What kind of an

FIGURE 3-1

Comparison of questioning skills for different types of innovators and noninnovators

Sample items:

1. *Asks insightful "what if" questions that provoke exploration of new possibilities and frontiers.*
2. *Often asks questions that challenge the status quo.*

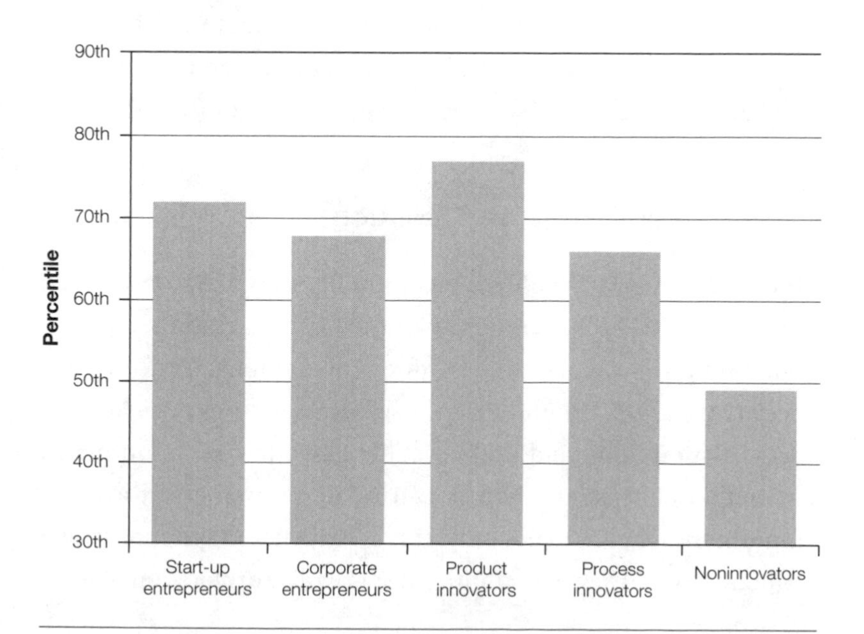

experience does she really want? What does she think is missing today?" Or when working within categories, Lafley often asked, "How well do you understand the different segments of consumers—not so much what we know about them demographically, but *psychographically*? What do we know about their biggest desires that aren't met today? What are they most unhappy about today?"

After searching for a deep understanding of what is, Lafley shifted lines of inquiry to powerful what-if questions to help deliver customer-centric innovations. For example, if talking to someone about science and technology or a product need, he asked: "What else is available in the world? Where else might we access what we need? Who across P&G—thinking across our business units or outside of P&G—could help us get what we need in the time frame and cost structure that we want?" Most of all, Lafley was constantly hunting for counterintuitive questions. Instead of asking, "How can we help consumers get floors and toilets clean?" he would query, "How can we give consumers their Saturday mornings back?" He found the latter question far more fruitful for surfacing rich insights about what might be in order to develop new products and services that consumers would want to "hire" to get their jobs done at home. No wonder Lafley's weekly question to himself is, "What will I decide to be curious about Monday morning?"[4]

How to Ask Disruptive Questions

Innovators constantly question common wisdom. Aaron Garrity, founder of XANGO (an innovative health and nutrition company), put it simply, "I am questioning, always questioning, with a revolutionary mind-set." Innovators' provocative questions push boundaries, assumptions, and borders. They leave few rocks unturned when they cultivate the garden. During interviews with disruptive innovators, we noticed not only a high frequency of questions but a pattern as well. They started with a deep-sea-like exploration of *what currently is* and then rocketed to the skies for an equally compelling search for *what might be.* Focusing on what is, they asked lots of who, what, when, where, and how questions (as world-class journalists or investigators do) to dig beneath the surface and truly "know the place for the first time" (as poet T. S. Eliot observed). They also invoke a series of what-caused questions to grasp the drivers behind why things are the way they are. Collectively, these questions help describe the territory (physically, intellectually, and emotionally) and provide a launching pad for the next line of inquiry. To disrupt the territory, innovators puncture the status quo with why, why-not, and what-if questions that uncover counterintuitive, surprising solutions. Whether descriptive or disruptive, innovators perpetually invoke powerful questions to help see beneath the surface of everyday action and discover what's never been.

Describe the Territory

Innovators treat the world as a question mark, rarely working on autopilot and constantly challenging the accuracy of their mental maps about the territory (whether products, services, processes, geographies, or business models). Suspended comfortably between a faith in and doubt of their maps, the best innovators remember that their views of the world are never the actual territory. Intuitively, they rely on a rich assortment of questions to develop a deep understanding of how things really are, before probing intensely into what they might be.

Tactic #1: Ask "what is?" questions

Disruptive innovators leverage a variety of what-is questions to surface unexpected subtleties. For example, Pierre Omidyar's work as a software architect (before founding eBay) sharpened his what-is questioning skills by focusing on user interfaces and trying to make software less complicated. (His first start-up was a pen-based computing application that attempted to make technology easier to use.) Using a blank-slate approach, Omidyar habitually watches others (for example, clients, customers, or suppliers) and wonders, "What are they *really* trying to do here?" He then follows up with all kinds of who, what, when, where, and how questions to dig beneath the surface.

Similarly, Dr. William Hunter, product inventor and start-up founder of Canadian-based Angiotech Pharmaceuticals, was intrigued by nontraditional ways that traditional drugs could be used. He ended up inventing the first surgical stent that was coated with a drug to reduce scar tissue (which causes up to a 20 percent failure rate compared to uncoated stents). His insight on coating stents came by changing the question traditional stent producers were asking, "How can we build a better stent?" to a more productive one, "What does the body do to these stents and why do they fail?" His relentless pursuit of the latter question ended up delivering a blockbuster product in the early 2000s.

In hot pursuit of *what is*, innovators inquire deeply for answers about what is happening right here and right now to gain understanding *and* empathy for others' experience. IDEO (and other successful design firms) employs diverse questions about the physical, intellectual, *and* emotional terrain to obtain a rich three-dimensional view of how end users actually operate. Intuit's Scott Cook also does this by asking fundamental questions such as, "Where is the real problem?" "What's the person trying to achieve?" "What's most important?" and ultimately, "What's the real pain point?" Innovators like Cook know their questions work when they reveal *what is* and build empathy for how it feels. Such empathic understanding produces the deep understanding behind better what-caused and what-if questions.

Tactic #2: Ask "what caused?" questions

The next step in understanding the way things are is to ask causal questions to gain insights into why things are the way they are. To illustrate, Mike Collins, founder and CEO of the Big Idea

Group (BIG) (a company that finds new product ideas through an inventor network and then launches them), shared an example of how inventors hunt down the real job to be done by understanding better what is really going on in their world. One inventor had pitched a fifteen-minute card game to Collins and his team for potential development and distribution by BIG. Collins felt that the game, as presented by the inventor, wouldn't crack a tough family-gaming market. But instead of turning the inventor away, Simon Cowell–style, he paused and asked, "What caused you to develop this game?" The inventor quickly replied, by answering a series of implicit who, what, when, where, and how questions, that he had three children (who?) and little time after work (when?) to spend with them at home (where?). He wanted to have fun in the evening with his children (what?), but there was no time for games like Monopoly or Risk. He was in search of a fifteen-minute game that would do the job of connecting him with his children for a quick and enjoyable few minutes at the end of the day.

From Collins's initial "what caused?" question, a series of answers to implicit who, what, when, where questions emerged that resulted in a successful line of "12 Minute Games" sold through Target. These games did the job many families needed at the end of a busy day or long week, and the insight to that job came by asking questions that gave simple, but critical, insights into what was really going on in the inventor's life.

Disrupting the Territory

After describing the territory well enough to thoroughly understand *what is,* innovators started their search for new, potentially disruptive solutions. They switched gears from descriptive questions to disruptive ones, like *why, why not,* and *what if.*

Tactic #3: Ask "why?" and "why not?" questions

Innovators persistently leverage why and why-not questions to acquire critical insights. Jeff Jones, founder of Campus Pipeline

Are You Willing to Look Stupid?

So what stops you from asking questions? The two great inhibitors to questions are: (1) not wanting to look stupid, and (2) not willing to be viewed as uncooperative or disagreeable. The first problem starts when we're in elementary school; we don't want to be seen as stupid by our friends or the teacher, and it is far safer to stay quiet. So we learn not to ask disruptive questions. Unfortunately, for most of us, this pattern follows us into adulthood. "I think a lot of people don't ask questions because they don't want to look stupid," one innovator told us. "So everyone sits around playing along as if they know exactly what is going on. I see this happen a lot—people go along because they don't want to be the one to question the emperor's nakedness [as in the story 'The Emperor's New Clothes']."

The second inhibitor is a concern about looking uncooperative, or even disrespectful. EBay's Omidyar admitted that others sometimes see him as being disrespectful when he questions their ideas or point of view. How can you overcome these inhibitors? One innovator gave the following advice, "I often preface my questions by saying 'I like to be the guy that asks a lot of dumb questions about why things are the way they are.'" He says this helps him to detect whether it is safe to ask basic questions (that could seem dumb) or to question the way things are (without seeming uncooperative). The challenge for all of us is that there is a basic element of courage here, in being brave enough to be the one who says. "Wait, I don't get it. Why are we doing it like this?"

Actually, the more powerful question behind our initial question, "Are you willing to look stupid?" really is, "Do you have sufficient self-esteem to be humble when you ask questions?" Over the years, we have found that great questioners have a high level of self-esteem and are humble enough to learn from anyone, even people who supposedly know less than they do. If this happens, they have learned to live the sage advice of Neil Postman and Charles Weingartner (early advocates of inquiry-based living and learning) where "once you have learned to ask questions—relevant and appropriate and substantial questions—you have learned how to learn and no one can keep you from learning whatever you need to know."[a]

a. Neil Postman and Charles Weingartner, *Teaching as a Subversive Activity* (New York: Dell, 1969), 23.

(a Web platform that helps universities securely integrate campus communication and resources) and NxLight (an IT tool for simplifying the management of complex intercompany transactions by easily and securely exchanging documents), grasps this fact well, concluding: "Once you discover that asking why in a different way and not being content with what the answer is, it's interesting what happens. You just have to go a little bit deeper asking questions one or two more times in a different way." This is exactly what disruptive innovators do to discover new business ideas.

Consider the example of Edwin Land, cofounder of Polaroid.[5] During a vacation with his family, Land took a picture of his three-year-old daughter. She could not immediately see the picture he had taken of her and wanted to know why. And, like most young children, probably asked why more than once. Her simple question pushed Land, an expert in photographic emulsions, to think deeply about the possibilities of "instant" photography. Why couldn't she see the picture immediately? What would it take for instant photography to be a reality? Within a few hours, the scientist developed the basic insights that would eventually produce instant photographs, a product that would transform his company and disrupt an entire industry. In effect, his child's naive question challenged industry assumptions and transformed Land's technical knowledge into a revolutionary product—the Polaroid camera. This industry-changing camera delivered incredible impact between 1946 and 1986, ultimately selling over 150 million units and an even higher volume of expensive film packs for use in the cameras.

Similarly, David Neeleman, founder of JetBlue and Azul airlines, says that one of his strengths "is an ability to look at a process or a practice that has been in place for a long time and ask myself, 'Why don't they do it this other way?' And sometimes I find myself thinking the answer is so obvious that I wonder, 'Why has no one else ever thought of this before?'" For example, Neeleman's first start-up was a charter airline called Morris Air. At the time, airline tickets were treated like money; if you lost your ticket, it was like losing cash. This created problems for travelers as they dealt with the challenges of lost tickets and for airlines as they tried to send tickets securely to travelers. One day, an employee was complaining about a ticket problem, prompting Neeleman to ask, "Why do we treat tickets like cash? Is there a better way?" This question sparked an idea, "Why not give customers a code when they buy a ticket that they could give us at the airport with their identification?" This idea led to the creation of e-tickets, an idea that eventually spread throughout the industry after Southwest Airlines purchased Morris Air.

In his most recent venture, Azul, Neeleman asked his senior team, "Why aren't more Brazilians taking advantage of Azul's low fares?" Azul's flights were cheaper than the competition, but his question surfaced the real challenge—getting price-sensitive customers to the airport. Then Neeleman asked, "How much does a cab cost for our typical customer to get to the airport?" The answer was "too much," potentially 40 percent to 50 percent of the airline ticket cost. So Neeleman searched for lower-cost bus or train alternatives, but they were either nonexistent or too infrequent. This prompted him to then ask, "Why not start our own free bus service to get customers to the airports?" (to take advantage of Azul's inexpensive fares). Today, passengers book (mostly online) over three thousand bus rides per day to the airport with Azul, the fastest-growing airline in Brazil.

In Asia, Taiichi Ohno, a former engineer at Toyota who is known as the chief architect of the Toyota Production System, put a five-whys questioning process—a technique for asking "what caused" questions—at the core of his innovative production system. The five-whys process requires that when confronted with a problem, one should ask *why* at least five times to unravel causal chains and come up with innovative solutions. Many of the world's most innovative companies have adopted variations of the five-whys process to push employees to ask why as they search for a better understanding of *what is* and new responses to *what might be.*

Tactic #4: Ask "what if" questions

Meg Whitman of eBay has worked directly with a number of innovative entrepreneurs and founders, including Omidyar (eBay), Niklas Zennström and Janus Friis (Skype and Kazaa), and Peter Thiel and Elon Musk (PayPal). When asked how these folks differ from typical executives, Whitman replied, "My experience is that they get a kick out of screwing up the status quo. They can't bear it. So they spend a tremendous amount of time thinking about how to change the world. And as they think and brainstorm, they like to ask, 'If we did this, what would happen?'"

Omidyar is a perfect example. As a systems analyst, he designs end-user interfaces from the ground up with no preconceived way of doing things. To do this, Omidyar probes deeply by asking a series of questions that work from a blank-slate perspective, such as, "What would be the cleanest way to solve it?" He sees himself as "the devil's advocate in the room saying things like, 'What if it really didn't work this way? Or what if we really did do the opposite of this? What would happen then?'"

In sharp contrast to disruptive innovators, delivery-driven executives in our research were far less likely to ask what-if questions that challenged their company's strategy or business model. Data from our 360-degree survey assessments of executives around the world revealed that most managers do not *regularly* question the status quo (though they often think they do). They prefer routine to rocking the boat and adhere to the adage, "If it ain't broke, don't fix it." But innovators actively look for things that are "broke" and activate a pattern of what-if questioning to surface new angles of inquiry. One technique that innovators use when imagining the future is to ask what-if questions that either impose constraints or eliminate constraints.

Ask "what if" questions to impose constraints. Most of us constrain our thinking only when forced to deal with real-world limitations, such as shrinking budgets or technology restrictions, but innovative thinkers do the opposite. Google's Marissa Mayer, vice president of search products and user experience, says: "Creativity loves constraint. People often think of it in terms of artistic work—unbridled, unguided effort that leads to beautiful effect. If you look deeper, however, you'll find that some of the most inspiring art forms—haikus, sonatas, religious paintings—are fraught with constraints. They're beautiful because creativity triumphed over the rules . . . Creativity, in fact, thrives best when constrained."[6]

Questions that artificially impose constraints can trigger unexpected insight by forcing people to think around the constraint. To initiate a creative discussion about growth opportunities at one company in our study, an executive asked this question: "If we were legally prohibited from selling our current products to our current customers, how would we make money next year?" This constraining question led to an insightful exploration of ways the company could find and serve new customers.

Variations of the same question can provoke surprising ideas. For example, you and your team might ask:

1. If the disposable income of our current customers (or our budget) dropped by 50 percent, how would our product or service have to change?

2. If air transportation was no longer possible, how would we change the way we do business?

Asking questions that place constraints on solutions forces out-of-the-box thinking because it ignites new associations. This is precisely what Apple did to come up with the iPod ("What if we created an MP3 player that could fit in a shirt pocket but hold five hundred to a thousand songs?") and highly successful experience-centered retail stores ("What if we used a regular-sized retail store to sell a very small number of Apple-only products?"

Likewise, Hindustan Lever (Unilever's business in India) wondered how it could reach millions of potential consumers in small Indian villages where severe constraints existed: no retail distribution network, no advertising coverage, and poor roads and transport. Collectively these constraints challenged its existing business model and produced a fundamental question: "How might we sell products in small villages *without* any access to traditional distribution networks, advertising, or infrastructure?" The answer ultimately surfaced from direct-selling business models (from companies like Avon). In close partnership with nongovernmental organizations, banks, and the government, Hindustan Lever recruited women in self-help groups across rural India to become direct-to-consumer sales distributors for its soaps and shampoos. The company also provided substantial training for them to succeed as micro-entrepreneurs. (By 2009, the innovative solution in a highly constrained country context produced over forty-five thousand women entrepreneurs selling Hindustan Lever products to three million consumers in a hundred thousand villages.[7]

Ask "what if" questions to eliminate constraints. Great questions also eliminate the constraints that we can unnecessarily impose on our thinking due to a focus on resource allocations, decisions, or technology limitations. To counter this tendency, one innovative CEO finds these questions key to eliminating unwanted sunk-cost constraints: "What if you had not already hired this person, installed this equipment, implemented this process, bought this business, or pursued this strategy? Would you do it today?" Jack Welch often posed the same kinds of questions during his two-decade tenure as GE's CEO. Questions like these quickly and effectively toss sunk costs (financial and nonfinancial) right out the window.

Another approach to relaxing constraints surfaces in this question: "What if X technology were available to every consumer? How would it change consumer behavior?" With a slight twist on this query, RIM's Lazaridis likes to look five years ahead. He persistently asks questions such as, "What CPUs will be available? What LCD technology? What keyboard? Mouse?" Once he gets the best answers possible to these questions, he then starts the more predictable graphical and industrial design work on the next generation of BlackBerry products.

After returning to Apple in the mid-1990s, Steve Jobs relaxed constraints by asking, "What would you do if money were no object?" prompting the creation of new products or services.[8] This kind of question assumes that the pursuit of excellence at Apple occurs independent of outside constraints, including customers' current preferences or the cost of providing exactly what customers might want. Now as a board member at Disney, Jobs pushes the same message further, admonishing people to "dream bigger" as they redesign Disney retail stores to now include one sales area labeled, "WWTD: What Would Tinker Bell Do?"[9]

Questioning Dilemmas for Senior Leaders

When it comes to status quo–challenging questions, leaders (particularly CEOs) face two key dilemmas. The first is that top executives are generally rewarded for generating better strategies or new business models, but they are also punished if they publicly question their firm's own strategy or existing business model. CEOs are expected to provide *answers*, not questions, to key external and internal stakeholders. One CEO told us, "If I openly question our strategy or key initiatives, this could create a crisis of confidence within the company. People don't like that kind of uncertainty." Senior executives know, as researchers David Krantz and Penelope Bacon do, that "to question an act, belief, or experience runs the risk of disrupting the activity."[a] When this happens, financial markets worldwide are generally unforgiving and punish such disruptions, at least in the short run.

The second dilemma for leaders is that it's difficult for people in the organization to ask the top boss questions that challenge the status quo. After all, the CEO may have reached his position by creating the status quo. So while CEOs may be in the best position to ask and respond to questions, they actually face major constraints in asking and receiving questions that challenge the status quo. As a result, it is no small feat for a CEO to create a culture that fosters the kind of questioning that produces innovative outcomes, particularly new businesses and business models.

Many innovative founders and CEOs address the first dilemma by cultivating an informal network of people whom they can question, and who will question them. For example, an innovative CEO at a major multinational firm told us that he

(continued)

has formed an informal, unofficial group of confidantes. "It's a fairly senior, fairly seasoned set of people who are comfortable throwing out ideas and then forgetting about them if these hunches or speculation aren't right," he said. "I can ask any question of these folks and they'll give me a straight answer."

Tackling the second dilemma is a little trickier as the challenge can be culturally sensitive. In some country—and company—cultures, you simply don't question the boss. For example, cross-cultural research suggests that eight in ten Japanese would agree with the following statement about the role of leaders: "It is important for a manager to have at hand the precise answers to most of the questions his or her subordinates may raise about their work."[b] The result is that Japanese leaders are expected to deliver answers to their people, not questions, particularly status quo–challenging ones. But a company or country culture that fails to encourage questioning sounds the death knell for disruptive innovation. Regardless of the cultural context, CEOs hoping to generate innovative ideas must make clear that leadership requires asking questions that challenge the way things are, even if such practices were established by the CEO on the way to the top!

a. D. L. Krantz and P. Bacon, "On being a naïve questioner," *Human Development* 20 (1977): 141–159.

b. N. J. Adler, N. Campbell, and A. Laurent, "In search of appropriate methodology: From outside the People's Republic of China looking in," *Journal of International Business Studies* 20 (1989): 61–74.

Questioning as a Potential Turbocharger

Questions are a critical catalyst to creative insights. Yet, *questions alone do not produce innovation. They are necessary, but insufficient.* In the absence of active observation, networking, or experimentation, theoretical innovators become what sportswriters in the United States might refer to as armchair quarterbacks. They ask clever questions from the sidelines and may naively believe that one or two magical questions will surface disruptive ideas, but they rarely, if ever, play in the real-life game of innovation.

We found that innovators were more likely to successfully launch innovative products, services, or businesses when they *combined* an ongoing instinct to formulate and ask the right questions *with* other innovator's DNA skills. In other words, leaders who ask questions *as* they observe discover more than those who don't. Leaders who ask questions *as* they network for new ideas discover more than those who don't. Leaders who ask questions *as* they experiment discover more than those who don't. Ultimately, questioning combined with the other discovery behaviors can truly turbocharge your innovation results.

Changing our questions can change the world. The key is constantly creating better questions to see that world through new eyes. When this happens, we will find ourselves living the profound observation that Jonas Salk (discoverer of the first polio vaccine) made that "you don't invent the answers, you reveal the answers" by "finding the right question."

We hope our framework for surfacing the right questions can help you along your innovation journey. Start by probing what is and then pursuing what if, particularly what-if questions that impose or eliminate constraints. But remember the framework is not the end, but the means. It is the first step to getting new ideas that might succeed, not a surefire prescription for successful ones. The next three chapters provide further insight into other concrete actions we can take to help improve the questions we ask and, in the end, reveal potentially disruptive solutions to difficult problems.

Tips for Developing Questioning Skills

Innovators not only ask provocative questions, but constantly work at asking better ones. For example, Michael Dell says that if he had a favorite question to ask, everyone would anticipate it, which wouldn't make it very good. "Instead, I like to ask people things that they don't think that I'm going to ask them," he told us. "I kind of delight in coming up with questions that nobody has the answer to quite yet." To consistently craft better questions, here are a few of our favorite tips.

Tip #1: Engage in QuestionStorming

A few years ago, we stumbled across an incredibly valuable questioning tool. We were teaching a graduate business school class and found ourselves stuck on a particular problem, unable to find any further insight through a typical brainstorming process. One of us suggested taking a time-out from the process and focusing our collective energies on only asking questions about the problem, instead of trying to construct another set of solutions. Much to our surprise, the questions-only approach dug much deeper into the fundamental elements of the challenge and opened everyone's eyes to a new understanding of the problem.

Since that first questions-only exercise, we have worked with individual executives and teams of executives over the years to develop a process we now call QuestionStorming.[10] We all know about brainstorming, a process in which you get together as a team and brainstorm solutions to a problem. QuestionStorming is similar, but instead of focusing on solutions, you brainstorm questions about the problem.

Here's how it works. First, as an individual or team, identify a personal, work unit, or organizational problem or challenge to solve. Then write down at least fifty questions about that problem or challenge. (If you're dealing with a work unit or organizational problem, it is preferable to generate these questions with a team and write all of the questions on a white board for everyone to see.) We suggest a couple of extra rules when doing this as a team: Generate only one question at a time. Have one person write the questions down so that everyone can see and reflect on each question being asked. No one can ask a new question until the last one is completely written down. This helps the group build on prior questions to generate better queries about the challenge. Prod each other to ask a full range of *what is, what caused, why* and *why not,* and *what if* questions during the exercise.

It's important to follow some other rules. When capturing the questions, discipline yourself or your team to simply ask the question without offering a long preamble as a setup. Ruthlessly facilitate the focus on questioning until you have at least fifty questions (in other words, don't tolerate answers; simply reinforce the importance of only asking questions about the problem or opportunity). After a possible stretch of initial silence (as your team might struggle to formulate new questions about the issue), most teams engage in an even deeper inquiry about the real root causes of the problem or dimensions of an opportunity to see them in a new light. After listing the questions, prioritize and discuss the most important or intriguing ones in your search for better solutions. You may want to assign an individual or team to attempt to answer the most important questions (probably through observing, networking, or experimenting) before having the group brainstorm solutions.

We have found that individuals who frequently engage in personal QuestionStorming about challenges facing their work unit, organization, industry, customers, suppliers, and so on are more likely to be viewed as creative, innovative, or strategic thinkers. One executive in a large pharmaceutical company started writing down questions for fifteen to twenty minutes each morning before work. Three months later, his boss told him that he had become the best strategic thinker in his business unit. Six months later, he was promoted. Practice does make perfect, or at least better, when it comes to questioning. So if your "questioning muscles have atrophied," as Ahmet Bozer (Eurasia and Africa Group president at Coca-Cola) recognized after a recent QuestionStorming workshop with his senior team, "it's time to start exercising those muscles."

Tip #2: Cultivate question thinking

When identifying problems or challenges, we often describe them as statements. In fact, we often ask groups of executives to identify their top-three challenges. As they wrestle with the task and identify these challenges, they typically frame them as statements. We then give the group an additional five to ten minutes to reformulate their top-three challenges into their top-three questions (about leading innovation effectively, for example). We have found that actively translating statements into questions not only helps sharpen problem statements, but also evokes more personal responsibility for the problems and moves them to take more active next steps in the pursuit of answers.

Tip #3: Track your Q/A ratio

Disruptive innovators we interviewed consistently displayed a high Q/A ratio, where questions (Q) not only outnumbered answers (A) in a typical interaction, but good questions generated greater value than good answers. To check your current Q/A ratio, observe and assess your questioning and answering patterns in a variety of contexts. For example, in the last work meeting you attended or directed, what percent of your comments were questions? Keep a record of your Q/A ratio (percent of comments made that fall into each category) during meetings you attend in the coming week. When reviewing self-observations, you might ask what was your personal Q/A ratio? How many questions did you ask? Work to increase your Q/A ratio by reflecting on what questions were asked and then asking yourself, "What are the questions that aren't obvious or are not being asked?"

Tip #4: Keep a question-centered notebook

To generate an even richer repository of questions, take time to capture your questions regularly. Richard Branson does this in notebooks "full of questions." Review the questions periodically to see how many and what kinds of questions you're consistently asking (or not asking). Table 3-1 can help you see what types of questions you might consider as you observe, network, and experiment to generate new ideas.

TABLE 3-1

Disruptive innovator's question check-up

	Describe the territory		*Disrupt the territory*	
Innovator's DNA skills	**What is?** **Who? What? When? Where? How?**	**What caused?**	**Why?** **Why not?**	**What if?** **How might?**
Observing				
Networking				
Experimenting				

As you keep your notebook, take a moment to reflect on the following:

- What are your questioning patterns? What kinds of questions do you focus on?
- What questions yield unexpected insights into why things are the way they are?
- What questions surface fundamental assumptions and challenge the status quo?
- What questions generate strong emotional responses (a great indicator of challenging the way things are)?
- What questions guide you best into disruptive territory?

4

Discovery Skill #3

Observing

"Observation is the big game changer in our company."

—Scott Cook, founder, Intuit

MOST INNOVATORS ARE intense observers. They carefully watch the world around them, and as they observe how things work, they often become sensitized to *what doesn't work*. They may also observe that people in a different environment have found a different—often superior—way to solve a problem. As they engage in these types of observations, they begin to connect common threads across unconnected data, which may provoke uncommon business ideas. Such observations often engage multiple senses and are frequently prompted by compelling questions.

Consider, for example, how Ratan Tata, chairman of India's Tata Group, gained a powerful insight that inspired the world's cheapest car, the Tata Nano. Throughout Tata's life, he had seen thousands of families riding scooters in India. On one very rainy day in Mumbai, India, in 2003, however, he noticed a lower-middle-class man riding a scooter with an older child standing in the front, behind the handlebars. The man's wife sat sidesaddle on the back with another child on her lap. All four were soaked to the bone as they hurried home. Tata saw with his eyes and listened with his heart to notice what he had previously failed to notice. He asked himself, "Why can't this family own a car and avoid the rain?" Or, put another way, he thought about a job that needed doing (in this case, the job was to create safe, affordable transportation for a family that could not afford to buy a car, but could buy a scooter).

This singular observation sparked several provocative questions about the possibility of creating an affordable "people's car." "The two-wheeler observation [with the family of four piled on the scooter] got me thinking that we needed to create a safer form of transport," Tata recalls. "My first doodle was to rebuild cars around the scooter, so that those using them could be safer if it fell. Could there be a four-wheel vehicle made of scooter parts?" Tata gathered a small group of engineers to design a low-cost vehicle with four wheels. The initial design had two soft doors with vinyl windows, a cloth roof, and a metal bar as a safety measure. But after seeing the initial designs, Tata and his group concluded that the market wouldn't want a "half car."

After several subsequent years of observation and experimentation by the Nano product development team, Tata's dream became a reality in 2009. Priced at $2,200, Nano was launched as the world's cheapest car. It generated two hundred thousand orders in the first few months after its launch, and its numerous innovations (including thirty-four patent applications) made it India's Car of the Year in 2010. Designed with a rear-mounted engine, the Nano can be assembled from kits at dealerships, much like motorcycles are in the United States. This approach may disrupt the entire automobile distribution system in India. And it all started one rainy day in Mumbai when Tata was actively observing on his ride home, rather than simply focusing on his destination.

Tata experienced what some people have referred to as *vuja de.* Déjà vu, of course, refers to a strong sense that you have seen or experienced something before, even if you haven't. Vuja de is the opposite—a sense of seeing something for the first time, even if you have actually seen it many times before.[1] Applying the principle of vuja de, Tata was able to "see" what had always been there before but had gone unnoticed or at least had not inspired anyone to act on it.

But Tata's initial observation—that many lower to middle-income Indians would benefit from being able to purchase an affordable car—is only the part of the story. Let's examine how Ratan Tata used customer observations to help Tata sell those $2,200 Nanos. As mentioned, he got the idea for the Nano by watching Indian families ride scooters in the rain. He knew that the rural villages of India were a large market for scooters, so he wanted to learn how Tata could sell the Nano in those villages to replace the scooters. So he sent a team out to observe how Indians in the rural areas purchased scooters. The team made some interesting observations that led to a very different way to sell cars in the villages.

First, the team observed that people did their major shopping on Sundays at farmers' markets or flea markets. There were no permanent scooter or car dealerships. Scooter dealers arrived in a big truck filled with scooters and just stuck them in rows on their allocated piece of ground at the market. People would buy a scooter, get a license, learn how to operate it, and then drive it home that same day. So the Tata team brought in forty Nanos and put them in the open-air market. They quickly found that customers didn't just walk up, buy a car, and drive it home. First, just as in urban areas, many customers needed financing, so Tata had to offer financing. But in order for people to drive away in a Nano, the team learned that the customer needed to have insurance available on the spot. So Tata had to offer insurance. Even more importantly, the team learned that most customers didn't have a driver's license, so Tata had to offer a driver's education class—and a way to get a license—right there at the market. So Tata ended up providing all these services in sequence so that within two to four hours a customer could pick out a car, have it insured and financed, receive training on how to operate it, get a driver's license, and finally register the car. Intense observation was the only way Tata could see how to fully meet the needs of a rural Indian who wanted to buy and drive a car.

A Framework for Observing: Look for the "Job" and a Better Way to Do It

IDEO's Tom Kelley, author of *The Art of Innovation*, has written that "the Anthropologist's role is the single biggest source of innovation at IDEO."[2] Why does he believe this? Anthropologists have developed techniques to study humans in their natural environments and learn from their behavior. Pretending that you are an anthropologist can be especially powerful when you watch someone in a particular circumstance trying to "do a job," to use Clayton Christensen's terminology in *The Innovator's Solution*. Christensen has argued that customers—people and companies—have "jobs" that arise regularly and need to get done. When customers become aware of a job that they need to get done, they look around for a product or service that they can "hire." When people have a job to do, they set out to hire something or someone to do the job as effectively, conveniently, and inexpensively as possible. Observing someone in a particular circumstance can lead to insights about a job to be done—and a better way to do it.

Tata's experience with the Nano illustrates this idea. Ratan Tata's initial observation of the Indian family on a scooter in the rain led him to realize that the scooter wasn't doing a very good *job* at transporting the family in a safe or dry manner. They needed a vehicle like a car that would provide more protection. This led to years of experimenting to create an affordable car that would be within reach of these middle-class families. But just being able to build an affordable car wasn't enough. To truly put Indian customers in the driver's seat, Tata needed to provide a set of complementary services that were critical to a customer's ability to buy a car, finance it, insure it, learn to operate it safely, and then drive it home. Tata's success was borne of two types of observations: one about the job to be done (transport families safely in a vehicle they could afford) and one about how to actually put a middle-class Indian in the driver's seat (take the cars to the village markets and provide the necessary services so the customer could operate the vehicle within a single day).

Understanding the Job to Be Done

Every job has a functional, a social, and an emotional dimension, and the relative importance of these elements varies from job to job. For example, "I need to feel like I belong to an elite, exclusive group" is a job for which consumers hire luxury-brand products such as Gucci and Versace. In this case, the functional dimension of the job isn't nearly as important as its social and emotional dimensions. In contrast, the jobs for which they might hire a delivery truck are dominated by functional requirements. Understanding the functional, social, and emotional dimensions of a job to be done can be quite complex, but may be key to an innovative solution.

(continued)

For example, we hire schools to educate young people in our society and often criticize them for not doing the job well. The question we typically ask is, "Why aren't schools performing as well as they should?" Perhaps a key reason we're dissatisfied with the state of public K–12 education is that we've been asking the wrong question. If we asked instead, "Why aren't students learning?" we might discover things that others do not yet perceive. A key reason why so many students languish unmotivated in school or don't come to class at all is that education isn't a job that they are trying to do. They mainly want to feel successful and to have fun with friends, meeting important social and emotional needs each day. No wonder some students drop out of school to hang out in gangs or cruise in cars with friends, since these activities often do the job better than school.

By understanding well the particular social and emotional needs of high school students (the jobs these students want done every day), the MET school, a charter school in Providence, Rhode Island, designed a project-based curriculum where students work together each day on various projects (containing elements of the Montessori method which provides "hands on" interactive learning experiences). This approach gives students an opportunity to have fun with friends while feeling a sense of accomplishment because they can see how their efforts move a project toward completion. They hardly realize they are developing new skills as they complete their tasks on the projects. By better meeting the students' social and emotional needs, the school motivates students to participate and learn. This illustrates how the jobs-to-be-done framework applies as much to services as to products and how important it is to look beyond the functional job to be done.

In similar fashion, Scott Cook founded Intuit, maker of the popular financial software Quicken and QuickBooks, based on two key observations. The first was a simple observation within his home. He hit on the idea for Quicken by watching his wife work on their finances and hearing her complain about how frustrating and time consuming it was. "She's got a good mind for math and is quite organized, so she handles the bills for us," Cook said. "But she frequently complained that it was a waste of time and bookkeeping was a hassle. So it was that observation combined with an understanding of what personal computers could do well and not do well that started Intuit."

What, we asked Cook, did he mean by separating out what computers "could do well and not do well"? His answer told us something about his observation skills and how he hit on a better way to do the job of managing personal finances. In 1981, he began watching what Apple was doing with its Lisa computer. "I got a buddy of mine who worked at Apple to show me the Apple Lisa before its launch," he recalled. "The Lisa wasn't trying to do financial software at all, but that graphical user interface [the mouse and drop-down menus] was amazing." Following the meeting, he drove to the nearest restaurant and sat down with a pad of paper. He wrote out the various insights that he'd gained from watching the concept of the graphical user interface.

Cook's observation convinced him that not only could the Lisa perform repetitious financial functions, but that its easy-to-use mouse and drop-down menus would allow the average person to use a computer. He was completely intrigued by the concept of making the items on a computer screen "work just like their real-world counterparts." (For example, a Quicken electronic check looks just like a paper check.) By building a software program that acted a lot like what people do in their daily lives, Intuit grabbed over 50 percent of market share the year after it was introduced.

Like Cook, we have found that observing is a key discovery skill for most innovators who tend to generate business insights from one of two types of observations:

1. Watching people in different circumstances who are trying to do a job and gaining insight about what job they *really* want to get done.

2. Observing people, processes, companies, or technologies and seeing a solution that can be applied (perhaps with some modification) in a different context.

Mike Collins (founder and CEO of the Big Idea Group) claims that successful product innovators always have their observation skills turned on. "Observation isn't just a one-'aha' day. Innovators are observing the world around them and asking questions all the time. It's part of who they are. For other people, it is an untapped skill." Collins knows what he is talking about. As founder of BIG, a company that uses the *American Idol* (or *Britain's Got Talent*) business model to screen the best ideas of inventors and then take them to market, Collins has worked with over a thousand inventors who are part of the BIG network. We found that product innovators boast the best observing skills among innovators, followed by start-up and corporate entrepreneurs, and finally process innovators. Innovators score at around the seventy-fifth percentile for observing, while noninnovators score at around the forty-eighth percentile. (See figure 4-1.)

How does someone develop the observing skill if it is currently untapped? To discover what innovators do, we asked them, "What makes someone a good observer? How can someone get better at observing?" We have found that observers are more successful at figuring out jobs to be done and better ways to do them when they: (1) actively watch customers to see what products they hire to do what jobs, (2) learn to look for surprises or anomalies, and (3) find opportunities to observe in a new environment.

FIGURE 4-1

Comparison of observing skills for different types of innovators and noninnovators

Sample items:

1. *Gets new business ideas by directly observing how people interact with products and services.*
2. *Regularly observes the activities of customers, suppliers, or other companies to get new ideas.*

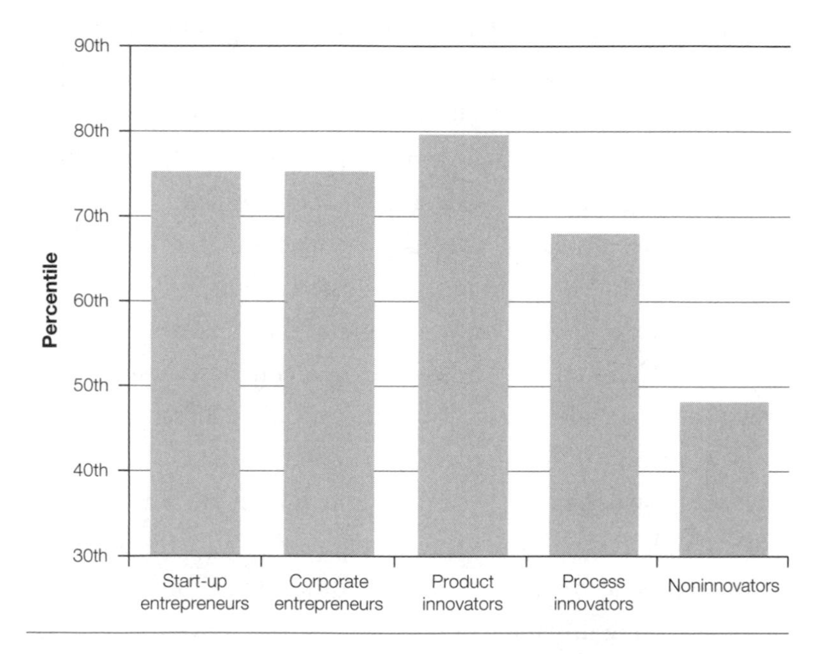

Actively Watch Customers—and Look for Workarounds

Perhaps the most obvious way to get business insights through observing is to actively watch people as they hire products to do jobs and then see what insights you can gain about the job to be done. For example, Gary Crocker, founder of the medical device firm Research Medical Inc. (acquired by Baxter International), got the idea for some "plumbing" devices that could help surgeons perform heart bypass surgery after observing them do what was very new surgery at the time. He noticed the cardiovascular monitoring catheters that were threaded into the heart to measure blood pressure, but he also noticed that there weren't any good "plumber tools," to manage the flow of blood. "There weren't really big catheters that would take all the blood out of the body and take it into the oxygenator when your lungs and heart are shut down during surgery," Crocker said. "There wasn't a well-structured plumbing line. So I thought I could create a product like that. That's a nice little niche."

So Crocker eventually left Baxter to start a company that created a variety of specialized devices to control the flow of blood during cardiac surgery. One device, Visuflo with Light Source, addressed the challenges of operating on bleeding sites in beating-heart surgery by blowing a stream of filtered, humidified air onto the suture site to remove unwanted blood flow that compromised the surgeon's visibility. The device also enhanced visibility by providing an ancillary light source that could be directed into the surgical opening. Without these devices, surgeons would come up with their own ways to get more light into a surgical opening (for example, have a nurse shine a separate light into the opening) or their own techniques to remove unwanted blood flow (for example, trying different suction devices to remove blood). The insights for Crocker's innovative devices came only after carefully observing the challenges that surgeons faced as they performed cardiac surgery and the workarounds they developed to solve those problems.

The term *workaround* originated in the IT world where programmers had to "work around" a particular problem in the system. The concept applies equally well to other domains. A workaround is an incomplete or partial solution to a particular job to be done. When you notice a workaround, pay attention, as it might provide clues for how to create an entirely new product, service, or business to do the job.

For example, OpenTable.com is a more comprehensive solution to the workarounds that we typically use when trying to have a great dining experience (the job to be done). The key elements include finding a restaurant that offers the desired quality of food and atmosphere, reserving a table at a convenient time without a wait, and getting a reasonable price for the meal. Finding the right restaurant often involves asking for referrals or reading restaurant reviews. After finding the right restaurant, you then call to make a reservation. If the restaurant doesn't take reservations or has no reservation available, then you start the process again. You might even simply go to the restaurant early—or possibly send someone to wait in line for you—in order to ensure you get a table or to minimize waiting time. If you are price sensitive, you might look for coupons online or in the newspaper to get a better price for your dining experience. All these activities take time and still don't ensure a great dining experience.

Chuck Templeton, founder of OpenTable.com, witnessed these workarounds firsthand in 1998 when his wife spent 3.5 hours trying—without any luck—to get reservations at a desirable restaurant when his in-laws visited them in Chicago. So Templeton launched an online app that is essentially your own restaurant concierge service: it allows customers to quickly and easily find a restaurant they might like (by providing insightful reviews and customer ratings), get a reservation at a convenient time (by allowing customers to see table availability and book their own reservation), and even have access to discounted meals (by giving points for meal discounts). Restaurants pay OpenTable $199 per month for the reservation service (to essentially rent a computer terminal and Internet connection) and a $1 fee for every diner who lands at their restaurant through the system. By doing a better job of helping customers have a great dining experience, OpenTable now dominates the dining reservation process in most large U.S. cities and in many others abroad (with over eleven thousand restaurants in its system worldwide).

While watching people trying to do a job to gain insights for new product or service offerings seems straightforward, most company managers spend little time in this simple, commonsense approach. But when companies uncover the hidden needs of the customer through observation (whether it be serendipitous observation, live-in immersion, or video observation), they gain insights that can prove extremely valuable. IDEO's Kelley reports that when designing a new kids' toothbrush for Oral-B, IDEO went out in the field to watch kids brush their teeth. What it noticed was that kids' toothbrushes were just smaller versions of adult toothbrushes, which proved to be a challenge for them to hold and maneuver because they lacked the dexterity of their parents. This led to an innovative design: big, fat, squishy toothbrushes that were much easier for kids to hold and use. The result? Oral-B had the best-selling kids' toothbrushes in the world for the next eighteen months.

Ten Questions to Ask While Observing Customers

Here are ten questions you should ask while observing customers to better understand the job they want done and how you can offer a product or service that will help them do it better.

1. How do customers become aware of a need for your product or service? Is there a way to make it easier or more convenient for them to find your offering?
2. What do customers really use your product or service for? What *job* is the customer hiring your product or service to do?
3. What does the customer ultimately consider as the most important features when selecting a final product or

service? (If the customer has a hundred points to allocate across all the features he considers important, how would he allocate them?)

4. How do consumers order and purchase your product? Is there a way you can make it easier, more convenient, or less costly?
5. How do you deliver your product or service? Can you do it faster, cheaper, in a completely different way?
6. How do customers pay for your product or service? Is there a way to make it easier or more convenient?
7. What frustrations do your customers have when trying to use your product? Do they use your product in ways you didn't expect?
8. What do consumers need help with when they use the product?
9. Do customers do things that hurt the longevity or reliability of your product or service?
10. How do customers repair, service, or dispose of your product? Are there opportunities to make this easier or more convenient (or teach the customer how to use the product so it requires less maintenance or to do self-maintenance)?

Look for Surprises

At Intuit, Cook asks his marketing and software engineers to observe customers in their homes as they load and attempt to use Quicken and QuickBooks software. As they watch customers use the product, he asks them "to savor the surprises"—the things that seem unusual or the times when people don't behave as they are supposed to. For example, Cook tells them: "When you see something unexpected, you need to ask, 'Why did you do that? Well, that doesn't make sense. I never expected that.'" Customers often have to find workarounds—meaning they may use the product in unintended ways—and these surprising workarounds often provide clues as to why the current product or service is an incomplete solution. Cook claims that *you have to consciously be looking for surprises*—the unexpected—because they are typically lost as our minds conform what we see to fit our preexisting beliefs. To battle that tendency, Cook says that "at Intuit we teach our people to ask these two questions as they observe: What is surprising? What is different from what you expected? That's where true learning and innovation starts."

The Value of Anomalies in Scientific as Well as Commercial Innovation

Many years ago, Thomas Kuhn, in his landmark book on the history of science, *The Structure of Scientific Revolutions*, essentially argued that scientific breakthroughs happen—and new and improved theories emerge—when a researcher observes the world well enough to identify and explain an anomaly.[a] The discovery of an anomaly—a surprise—gives scientists the opportunity to revisit a particular theory in an attempt to better understand it. This often leads to a modification or improvement of the theory by understanding and explaining the anomaly. For example, in research on the impacts of technological innovation on the fortunes of firms, early studies concluded that established firms, on average, do well when faced with incremental innovation, but stumble when confronted with radical change. But there were anomalies to this general conclusion. Some established firms successfully implemented radical technology change.

To account for these surprises, Michael Tushman and Philip Anderson (1986) offered a unique, new categorization: competency-enhancing versus competency-destroying technological changes.[b] This resolved many anomalies, yet subsequent researchers continued to uncover new ones that the Tushman-Anderson scheme could not explain. Rebecca Henderson and Kim Clark's (1990) categories of modular vs. architectural innovations; Clayton Christensen's (1997) categories of sustaining versus disruptive technologies; and Clark Gilbert's (2005) threat-versus-opportunity framing each surfaced and resolved anomalies that prior scholars' work could not account for. Understanding and explaining the anomalies yielded original insights for the researchers.

Kuhn's bottom line: scientific researchers who seek to reveal and resolve anomalies tend to advance their fields more productively than those seeking to avoid them. Thus, observing anomalies in scientific endeavors is as valuable as observing surprises in commercial endeavors is. Identifying surprises or anomalies—what isn't what you expected—may be the key to unlock the door to your innovation.

a. Thomas S. Kuhn, *The Structure of Scientific Revolutions* (Chicago: University of Chicago Press, 1962).

b. Michael L. Tushman and Philip Anderson "Technological Discontinuities and Organizational Environments," *Administrative Science Quarterly*, 31, (1986): 439–465.

Rebecca Henderson and Kim Clark, "Architectural Innovation," *Administrative Science Quarterly*, vol. 35, no. 1 (1990): 9–30.

Clayton Christensen, *The Innovator's Dilemma* (Boston: Harvard Business School Press, 1997).

Clark Gilbert "Unbundling the structure of inertia. Resource versus routine rigidity," *Academy of Management Journal*, vol. 48, no. 5 (2005): 741–763.

Noticing the unnoticed calls for a peripheral vision, where innovators habitually surface new ideas by noticing things at the edge of experience (or as an IDEO employee explained, "look for people on the extremes"). For example, Corey Wride founded Media Mouth Inc.—a company providing software that helps you learn to speak a new language by watching movies—after making what seemed to him a surprising observation during an extended trip to Brazil. Wride was conducting training sessions to prepare Brazilians for U.S. graduate school entrance exams like the GMAT. During these trips, he encountered a large number of Brazilians who were eager to practice their English on him to prepare for the TOEFL test. When he found people who were particularly good English speakers, he would often ask them how they learned the language. (He expected those with the best English skills to be individuals who regularly attended one of the many English-learning schools in Brazil. In fact, many of the better speakers did attend these schools, but he later learned that they were not the best speakers of English.)

One evening, he met Julia Trentini, a young woman in her twenties who spoke better English than anyone he had met. He asked her how she had learned English so well. To his surprise, he learned that she had not attended any English school. Instead, she learned by watching American television shows and movies, and then practiced by imitating the phrases and pronunciation of the actors. She watched shows like *Friends* just for fun and was later surprised to find that she could understand and talk to a group of Americans that she met on the streets of São Paulo. She hadn't formally studied English at all. Her newfound ability was a happy accident motivated by entertainment. Wride later observed that, like Trentini, other Brazilians with the best English skills also spent significant time watching and imitating American movies. (He learned that most Brazilians prefer to watch American movies in English even when Portuguese audio tracks are available. They prefer the authenticity of the actors' real voices.) This led to another question: why don't more Brazilians learn English by watching movies? The answer was that the actors spoke too fast, or used idioms or words that the Brazilians didn't know or understand.

So Wride, a software engineer by training, devised an ingenious program that would allow a Portuguese speaker to watch virtually any movie in English on her computer and then do four things: (1) slow down the speech of the speaker; (2) select words and hear them pronounced or defined, (3) identify idioms and their meaning in her native language, and (4) insert her own pronunciation into the mouth of the actor so she can hear whether she sounds the same as the actor (hence, the Web site name, MovieMouth.com). Wride's insight for his business emerged by observing that Brazilians who were supposed to be the best English speakers (those attending the best English training programs) were not the best speakers.

How else can you look for surprises? Leon Segal (an innovation psychologist and former IDEO employee) rightly noted that "innovation begins with an eye," but it certainly doesn't have to end there. It's critical to remember that observations frequently involve more than the eyes. Learning research repeatedly underscores the power of multisensory experience when it comes to seeing something new and making sense of the experience. The more senses we engage as we experience the world, the more we see and remember. As a result, looking for surprises can actually be listening, tasting, touching, and smelling something surprising as well. You may have never heard of Trimpin, but he's an accomplished musical innovator who has spent a lifetime asking the question, "How can we depart from the traditional orchestra?" He keeps his ears wide open in a constant hunt for new sounds. He says that "as soon as I see something, I hear it."[3] Trimpin sees the sounds of trolley cable sparks, earthquake-driven tympanis, and other surprising auditory phenomena to create award-winning innovations in the music world. Other innovators also engage a wide range of senses to uncover new business ideas. For example, Howard Schultz started down the path to founding Starbucks when first confronted with the intoxicating smell of Italian espresso bars, and Joe Morton, cofounder of XANGO, got the initial idea for a new health drink in part by tasting mangosteen fruit for the first time in Malaysia (more about this in chapter 5). In sum, remember to engage all your senses as you search the world for surprises.

Change the Environment

Think back to the first time you made a trip to a new country. Or reflect on the first few days that you started working for a new company. Do you remember noticing what was different from what you had seen or experienced before? When entering a new environment, we are far more likely to carefully observe what is going on around us because we automatically seek to understand what is new and different. People who put themselves in new environments and then intensely observe what is happening unearth new ideas.

For example, Starbucks founder Schultz engaged his sensory organs—his eyes, ears, nose, and mouth—when he hit on the idea for his coffee stores. Walking to a trade show in Milan, Italy, Schultz randomly observed what happened in a number of Italian espresso bars. He could tell that the customers were regulars and that the espresso bar "offered comfort, community, and a sense of extended family." As Schultz continued visiting Italian espresso bars, he had a revelation. "This is so powerful! I thought. What we had to do was unlock the romance and mystery of coffee, firsthand, in coffee bars. It was like an epiphany. It seemed so obvious," recalled Schultz. "If we could recreate in America the authentic Italian coffee bar culture, it might resonate with other Americans the way it did with me."[4]

Schultz stayed in Milan for about a week, visiting espresso bars just to observe. He then visited Verona where, losing himself in the streets of the city, he tasted café latte for the first time (he observed a customer order a café latte and, having never before heard of the drink, imitated the customer to see what it was). "Of all the coffee experts I had met, none had ever mentioned this drink. *No one in America knows about this,* I thought. *I've got to take it back with me,*" he recalls.

How many executives are willing, on a whim, to just take a week getting lost every day in an exploratory journey to observe something of interest and to see where the journey takes them? Without a willingness to actively observe in a new environment, Schultz would never have come up with the ideas that led to Starbucks's innovative coffee-retailing experience.

Not surprisingly, our research found that innovators were more likely to visit new environments, including traveling to new countries, visiting different companies, attending unusual conferences, or just visiting museums or other interesting places. A. G. Lafley, for example, told us what he learned from his regional assignment in Asia long before becoming CEO of P&G:

> Every time I traveled to China, I always went to stores to watch people purchasing our products. Then I went into homes. I always went in the evening because the woman almost always works outside the home. My routine was stores, homes, then the office. It gave me a current snapshot of what was going on. Of course, you can't generalize from a single qualitative experience, but over five years of doing this regularly, those experiences add up, combined with reading whatever you have access to, as well as the "harder" data. You develop a feel. You become more of an anthropologist because you can't understand the language. Your power is observation, your listening skills;

> your ability to read nonverbal cues gets a lot better. Your ability to observe increases. There are so many subtle things to read, understand, react to in a foreign country.

After returning to the U.S. P&G headquarters, he noticed how easy it was to "get lazy because everyone speaks English—you know what they're going to say and do next."

Innovators don't have to go to foreign countries for an immersion experience in a new environment. There is much to be learned by exploring exhibits, museums, zoos, aquariums, and nature. At Daimler, Dieter Gürtler, one of the company's top engineers, directed a team that focused on building a new aerodynamic concept car. To generate new ideas, he took the team members to a local museum of natural history to watch fish for a day. They were in search of insights that could break the automobile industry's assumptions about aerodynamics and found a surprising solution in the boxfish. Through direct observation of the fish, as well as conversation with the fish experts, his team worked on mimicking the size and skeletal structure of the boxfish. Ultimately, they produced a concept car that delivered unexpected reductions in weight as well as significant reductions in air drag. As Gürtler put it, "By looking at nature, you come up with ideas you could never have thought of on your own."[5]

Of course, it isn't always possible to put yourself in a new environment. Fortunately, a rich source for new ideas often resides right around us in the familiar world of people and places that we think we know well. The problem is that we sometimes miss the obvious new idea in the most obvious of places because we take things for granted and, as a result, we miss opportunities for innovation. As book and *New York Times* writer Peter Leschak has lamented, "All of us are watchers—of television, of time clocks, of traffic on the freeway—but few are observers. Everyone is looking, not many are seeing."[6] Acting on autopilot in everyday life automatically starves the brain's creative capacity.

Observation has the power to transform companies and industries. As Cook told us, "Basic observation is the big game changer in our company." Effective observation requires putting yourself in new environments. It involves watching customers to see what products and services they hire to help them do their jobs. It involves looking for workarounds—partial or incomplete solutions—that customers use to do those jobs. And it involves looking for surprises or anomalies that might provide surprising insights. As observers identify workarounds and anomalies, and dig deep to understand them, they increase their odds of uncovering an innovative solution to the problems they observe. We encourage you to develop and hone your observation skills and, in so doing, discover how they can be a game changer for you and your company.

Tips for Developing Observation Skills

Tip #1: Observe customers

Hone and sharpen your observing skills by scheduling regular observation excursions to carefully watch how certain customers experience your product or service. (This could be done in fifteen- to thirty-minute increments). Observe real people in real-life situations. Try to grasp what they like and hate. Search for things that make life easier or more difficult for them. What job are they trying to get done? Which of their functional, social, or emotional needs is your product or service not meeting? What is surprising about their behavior and different than expected? Ask the ten questions we suggested earlier in the chapter. In short, become an anthropologist and intensely observe a customer or a potential customer to experience an entire product or service life cycle.

Tip #2: Observe companies

Pick a company to observe and follow. Maybe it is a company you admire such as Apple, Google, or Virgin. It could be a start-up with an innovative business model or disruptive technology. Or it could be a particularly tough, innovative competitor. Treat the company as you would a business school case. Find out everything you can about what the company does and how it does it. If possible, figure out a way to schedule a visit to the company and examine firsthand its strategy, operations, and products to look for cross-pollination opportunities. As you learn new things about it, ask: "Are there any ideas that could be transferred, with some adaptation, to our company or industry? How is this strategy, tactic, or activity relevant to my job, my company, my life? Are there ideas here for a new *who, what,* or *how* in my industry?"

Tip #3: Observe whatever strikes your fancy

Set aside ten minutes each day to simply observe something intensively. Take careful notes about your observations. Then try to figure out how what you are seeing might lead to a new strategy, product, service, or production process. When you are out and about watching the world, jot down your key observations and thoughts on a notepad, and review your notes later, after a little time has passed. Keep a small camera (still or video) with you to take pictures of interesting things. The camera can remind you to observe and note what is going on around you. (Amazon's Bezos confided that he often takes pictures of "really bad innovations" to get ideas for things that might be done better.)

Tip #4: Observe with all your senses

As you observe customers, companies, or whatever, actively engage more than one sense (see, smell, hear, touch, taste). One structured way to do this is through Dialogue in the Dark (a practice developed by Andreas Heinecke) and Dialogue in Silence (a practice developed by Heinecke and his wife Orna Cohen). In these tours by visually or hearing-impaired guides, guests experience darkened or silent environments (ranging from permanent exhibitions to restaurants located throughout the world) and enter a completely different world of either darkness or silence. A less structured approach to engaging your senses is to simply and intentionally become aware of your wider range of senses. For example, pay attention to what you smell next time you're visiting with customers (as Schultz did in Italy) or eat your next dinner in slow motion, slowly savoring every bite and focusing only on the taste, texture, and smell of the food. Or notice how a product really feels as you touch it (when either using it or trying to understand how it works). As you learn how to observe, pay close attention to any creative insights the experience might trigger. Be sure to capture observations (sights, smells, sounds, touches, and tastes) in your idea journal and explore where the insights might lead you.

5

Discovery Skill #4

Networking

"What a person does on his own, without being stimulated by the thoughts and experiences of others, is even in the best of cases rather paltry and monotonous."

—Albert Einstein

THINKING OUTSIDE THE box often requires linking the ideas in your area of knowledge with those of others who play in different boxes, who are outside your sphere. Innovators gain a radically different perspective when they devote time and energy to finding and testing ideas through a network of diverse individuals. Unlike typical delivery-driven executives who network to access resources, sell themselves or their companies, or boost their careers, innovators go out of their way to meet people with different backgrounds and perspectives to extend their own knowledge.

Consider what happened when Michael Lazaridis, founder of a small technology company called Research In Motion (RIM), attended a 1987 trade show in search of new ideas. At the time, Lazaridis's fledgling company had one project: a contract from General Motors to provide technology that would allow large LED display signs on GM's assembly lines to scroll messages and updates to workers. Lazaridis knew his fledgling company needed more than just one contract and one kind of technology, so he set out to see what new ideas he could uncover.

During the trade show, a speaker from a company called DoCoMo described a wireless data system that it had designed for Coca-Cola. The technology allowed vending machines to wirelessly signal when they needed refilling. (This was early on in the life of personal computers and before people owned cell phones, so sending data wirelessly to a machine was cutting-edge technology.) "That's when it hit me . . . I remembered what my teacher had said in high school," recalls Lazaridis. "'Don't get too caught up with computers, because it's going to be the person that puts wireless technology and computers together that's going to make a big difference.'"

At this moment, Lazardis thought of creating an interactive pager, a product allowing people to wirelessly send data and information to each other. So RIM sold the rights to the LED display sign product to Corman Technologies and focused its full attention on the wireless technologies necessary to create interactive pagers—the precursor to RIM's blockbuster BlackBerry smartphone. "I realized that's what I wanted to do," Lazardis told us, "and since then, that's all we've done. Frankly we've never looked back."

Lazaridis's experience illustrates the value of talking and interacting with diverse people who can provide unique knowledge and a fresh perspective. What if Lazaridis had never attended the trade show and heard the speaker? Or what if he had not talked with his teacher, who told him to look for ways to put wireless technology and computers together? People who think outside the box often talk to people who play in a different box to get new ideas. Lazardis continues to use idea networking to design future versions of the BlackBerry, talking to all sorts of people to understand technology trends and get new ideas.

What Idea Networkers Do

Some of you may be thinking: "I'm a good networker. But I'm not particularly innovative." That may well be true. But it's probably because you are like most successful executives who are what we call resource networkers, rather than idea networkers. Most executives network to sell themselves, to sell their companies, or to build relationships with people who possess desired resources. In contrast, innovators are less likely to network for resources or career progression; rather, they actively tap into new ideas and insights by talking with people who have diverse ideas and perspectives. (See figure 5-1.) Our research on innovators revealed that start-up entrepreneurs and corporate entrepreneurs are

FIGURE 5-1

Networking differences between discovery- and delivery-driven executives

<u>Discovery-driven executives</u>

- **Why they network: Ideas**
  - Learn new, surprising things
  - Gain new perspectives
  - Test ideas "in process"
- **Whom they target:**
  - People who are not like them
  - Experts and nonexperts with very different backgrounds and perspectives

<u>Delivery-driven executives</u>

- **Why they network: Resources**
  - Access resources
  - Sell themselves or their company
  - Further careers
- **Whom they target:**
  - People who are like them
  - People with substantial resources, power, position, influence, etc.

slightly better at idea networking than product inventors are, and quite a bit better than process inventors and noninnovators. If you want to launch an innovative new venture, networking is a critical skill, not only for generating new ideas but also for mobilizing the resources to launch new ventures. Overall, innovators score at around the seventy-seventh percentile, whereas noninnovators score around the forty-seventh percentile. (See figure 5-2.)

The basic principle of idea networking—as opposed to resource networking—is to build a bridge into a different area of knowledge by interacting with someone with whom you, or people within your primary social networks, typically do not interact. EBay's Pierre Omidyar told us that he looks for insights in unexpected directions and from people who aren't experts (as well as experts). "I value ideas from unusual places," he said. "The cliché would be, rather than talking to the CEO, I would want to talk to someone in the mailroom, something like that. I really look for

FIGURE 5-2

Comparison of idea networking skills for different types of innovators and noninnovators

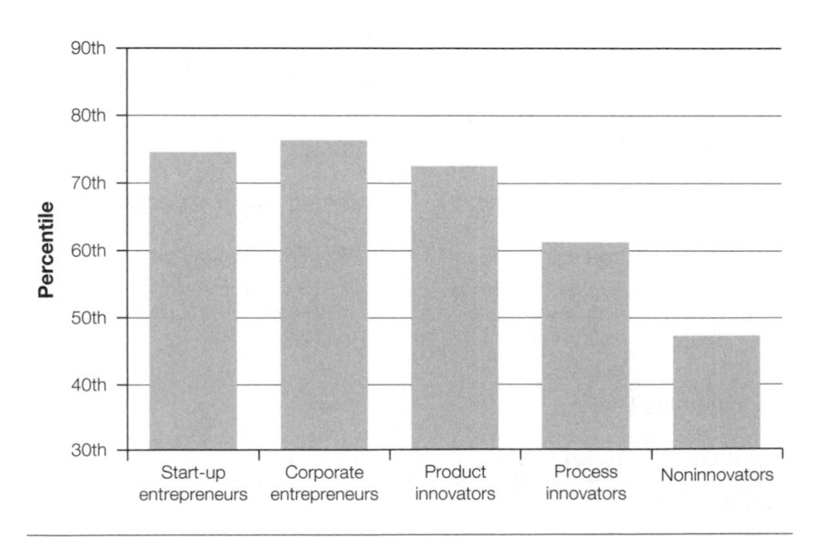

people that have diverse backgrounds, diverse ways of thinking about things; what I try to do is just be exposed to some different styles of thinking. And I get input from these different directions just in a very open-ended way, not in a directed way."

To this end, Omidyar and others like him make a conscious effort to meet people with different education backgrounds; who hail from different countries, industries, and business functions; and who are of different ages, ethnic backgrounds, and so forth. For example, Marc Benioff (Salesforce.com) told us about an interesting conversation he had with the State Oracle of Tibet, the official medium who, Benioff said, "was appointed by the Dalai Lama and is basically in charge of innovation for the Tibetan government." Few of Benioff's associates in the software industry have had the opportunity to get a different perspective from the State Oracle of Tibet. Innovators intuitively seem to understand that new ideas are often triggered through conversations with individuals who live in a different network of contacts.

University of Chicago sociologist Ron Burt has referred to this type of networking as bridging a "structural hole" or "gap" between different social networks. Burt studied 673 managers in a large U.S. electronics firm and found that those managers who had broader networks of contacts—contacts who were not connected to other managers in the organization—were consistently rated as generating more highly valued ideas.[1] "People with connections across structural holes [gaps in social networks] have early access to diverse, often contradictory, information and interpretations, which gives them a competitive advantage in seeing and developing good ideas," writes Burt. "People connected to groups beyond their own can expect to find themselves delivering valuable ideas, seeming to be gifted with creativity. This is not creativity born of genius; it is creativity as an import-export business. An idea mundane in one group can be a valuable insight in another." Burt also found that these "highly valued ideas" pay big dividends: managers with broad networks received more positive performance evaluations, had significantly higher salaries, and received more frequent promotions.

To illustrate how building bridges into different social networks can generate innovative new ideas, consider how Joe Morton, an entrepreneur in the health and nutrition industry, got a billion-dollar idea during a trip to Malaysia. (See figure 5-3.)

The figure shows Morton's direct connections to numerous individuals within the health and nutrition industry (depicted by line connections to circles). Morton also spent almost a year living in Malaysia, where he learned about health and nutrition products Malaysians use from folks like Mahathir. (Mahathir represents many people Morton spoke with.) "I had a number of Malaysians tell me about these two local fruits—durian, the king of fruit, which supposedly heated the body up, and mangosteen, the queen of fruit, which cooled the body down and brought it into balance," Morton told us. "I thought durian smelled horrible, even though

FIGURE 5-3

Bridging gaps in social networks to get new ideas

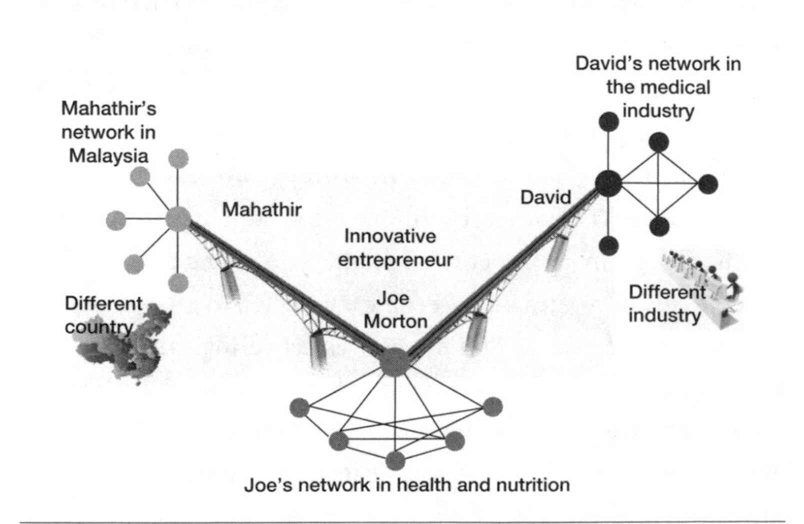

Southeast Asians love it. But the mangosteen was delicious. Locals said the husk offered numerous health benefits, including the ability to boost energy, reduce inflammations, and settle an upset stomach."

Even though Morton had significant experience in the health and nutrition industry, he was not aware of any products in the field using either durian or mangosteen. So he contacted his brother David, who was getting his PhD at the University of Utah medical school, to see if any scientific research had examined health benefits associated with durian or mangosteen. David searched for medical industry research studies about the fruits' health benefits.

Through David, Morton learned that while there were no medical studies on durian, there were numerous studies that indicated positive health benefits associated with xanthones, polyphenolic compounds found in abundance in mangosteen. These benefits included anti-inflammatory properties, as Mahathir and other Malaysians had suggested. Morton then used this information and his network of contacts in the health and nutrition industry (including cofounders Aaron Garrity and another brother, Gordon Morton) to found XANGO (pronounced "Zango") in 2002, a company that sells XANGO (mangosteen) juice. With a unique new product and an innovative network marketing approach, it took XANGO only six years to become a $1 billion company.

Morton would never have come up with the idea for mangosteen juice if he hadn't talked to Mahathir and other locals in Malaysia. Morton bridged a gap between two networks: his health and nutrition network of contacts in the United States and a network of locals in Malaysia who had knowledge of homeopathic herbs and fruits used there. The result: a very successful new product idea.

Like Morton, many innovators claim that by visiting, or preferably living, in a foreign country, they spawned a new idea by talking to a local. When we are in an environment (different country, company, industry, ethnic group, and so on) that is very different from our own, we are more likely to interact with people who are in different social networks. Being in a new environment allows us to ask dumb questions about how and why things work.

This type of networking often produces serendipity. In roughly half the cases we studied where new ideas came through networking, the lucky entrepreneur essentially stumbled onto the idea. We saw this happen with Chris Johnson, cofounder of Terra Nova Biosystems, a company that uses a type of bacteria to eat contaminants in soil, thereby allowing companies to clean up soil in an environmentally friendly way. While attending a July 4th neighborhood barbeque, Johnson met someone who told him about a microbial solution to pollution problems. He contacted the microbiologist who had developed the microbial solution and learned more about how bacteria could be used to eat pollutants. Johnson and his cofounders eventually developed a proprietary process that ensures fast, cost-competitive remediation of a wide range of contaminants in an ecologically safe manner. Johnson's purpose in attending the barbeque was to socialize, not look for new business ideas—and certainly not to learn about pollution-eating bacteria! But like many innovators, he takes advantage of every opportunity to talk to new people to see what he can learn. This habit produces the novel idea now and again through serendipity. But effective idea networkers also plan to find new ideas by regularly tapping outside experts for ideas, by attending networking events, and by building a personal network of creative confidants.

Tap Outside Experts

We found that purposeful networking was often effective when innovators attempted to reach out to experts in a different field of knowledge. To illustrate, consider the case of Norton,

Massachusetts-based CPS Technologies, one of the most innovative companies in the advanced materials industry. CPS has developed highly advanced and innovative ceramic composites, a class of materials superior to conventional ones in a number of ways, including improved thermal conductivity, increased stiffness, and lighter weight. Kent Bowen, founding scientist at CPS, made networking a priority when he hung the following credo in every office of his start-up:

> The insights required to solve many of our most challenging problems come from outside our industry and scientific field. We must aggressively and proudly incorporate into our work findings and advances which were not invented here.

One of Bowen's favorite questions when facing a technical challenge is, "Who else has faced or solved a problem like this before?" He actively looks for people in other fields and disciplines to understand what they do and what they know that might be relevant to his company's issues. As a result, scientists from CPS have solved numerous complex problems by talking with people in other fields.

For example, CPS's ceramic composites are made from uniform, submicron materials (aluminum oxide and silicon carbide) that are combined in slurries (an example of a slurry is a mixture like water and cement that eventually makes concrete). Dispersing these submicron materials in a uniform way is critical to making strong, defect-free ceramic products, but the chemistry for doing this had vexed some of the world's best colloid scientists. After Bowen discovered that photographic film manufacturers dispersed huge volumes of microscopic silver halide particles in very uniform films, CPS contacted a senior polymer chemist from Polaroid, the photographic film manufacturer. The chemist brought new knowledge that helped CPS solve the problem within a few weeks, thereby making the composite much stronger.

The CPS team solved another serious quality problem by talking to "sperm-freezing" specialists. CPS scientists observed that as their ceramic slurries were injected into molds and began freezing, ice crystals formed. These ice crystals were a serious problem because cracks in the composites would originate in the crystals, like cracks in concrete. In a scientific journal report, a CPS engineer discovered that biologists who do artificial inseminations routinely faced the same problem. Experts in sperm-freezing technology knew how to prevent ice crystal growth in cells during freezing. So CPS contacted them, learned their technique, and incorporated it into its manufacturing process. Collectively, these innovations were a stunning success, allowing CPS to produce some of the strongest and lightest ceramic composites ever made. Bowen's practice of actively seeking out people in other industries and disciplines has been critical to generating innovative ideas.

Despite all the positives of networking with experts in other fields, Intuit's Scott Cook cautions that sometimes talking to experts isn't the best way to generate innovations. "Some problems and new business ideas are such a paradigm shift that talking to people reinforces the current paradigm," cautions Cook. "Some paradigm shifts are, I find, better initiated by watching customers or watching things happen in the marketplace as opposed to talking to experts." The point is that while getting new ideas and perspectives from experts can lead to innovative ideas, experts are also indoctrinated with a particular perspective that may be incorrect. So remember to ask counterintuitive questions that challenge the so-called experts. Then listen carefully, with a healthy dose of skepticism.

Attend Idea Networking Events

In chapter 1, we noted that Frans Johansson has described cross-discipline connections as the Medici effect, referring to the explosion of creativity during the Italian Renaissance. Richard Saul

Wurman, the retired founder of the Technology, Entertainment and Design (TED) conferences, plays the same role as a modern-day Medici, creating a forum where experts in various fields can share cutting-edge ideas. In 1984, Wurman noticed the convergence of technology, entertainment, and design, and created an idea accelerator, where smart people from diverse backgrounds talked about the new projects they were working on. At the annual conference, the speakers and the audience members engage in the annual collision of ideas to create even better ones. TED conferences have evolved into a provocative forum for generating powerful new ideas, as smart individuals with diverse backgrounds connect in a common mind-set to change the world (as Bill Gates put it, "The combined IQ of the attendees is incredible"[2]).

Innovators are likely to frequent idea conferences such as TED, Davos (or other World Economic Forum events), and the Aspen Ideas Festival. Many innovators we interviewed are regular faces at these events (for example, Jeff Bezos regularly attends TED). Such conferences draw together entrepreneurs, academics, politicians, adventurers, scientists, artists, and thinkers from all over the world, who come to present their newest ideas, passions, and projects. Attending a conference that is designed for the exchange and debate of ideas from a variety of fields is likely to create a collision of concepts that can turbocharge your associating skill.

A conference on a topic outside your direct industry and field of expertise can also spark new ideas. One European transportation industry executive we interviewed happened to live next to a conference center in a large city. Even though he walked by the center each day on his way to work, he never ventured in. One day, he noticed a sign for a conference in a completely different industry: beekeeping. For some reason, this theme caught his attention and he wandered in. Much to his surprise, the experience proved invaluable as he applied an idea from beekeeping to come up with an innovative solution to one of his current work challenges. After that, he frequently dropped in on other conferences out of his field just to learn something entirely new.

David Neeleman, founder of both JetBlue and Azul airlines, detected and developed key ideas for JetBlue, such as satellite TV technology at every seat, at-home reservationists, and the hundred-seat JetBlue Embraer jet, through networking at conferences and elsewhere. Says Neeleman: "I always had this gnawing thought in my mind that 'I've got to do something in the seat-back pocket of each plane seat.' So I talked to a lot of people at a lot of companies about different entertainment options. Then one day, in the early days of JetBlue, I talked to someone who said, 'Look at this brochure on a company that can do live television on airplanes,' and I said, 'That's it. That's exactly what we want to do.'"

Not only did Neeleman follow up on the suggestion, he bought LiveTV, the company with the technology to provide satellite TV on airplanes. By purchasing the only company with such technology, he prevented competitors from offering satellite television to their passengers, thereby creating a competitive advantage for JetBlue. Until recently, any competitor who wanted to offer satellite TV to passengers had to purchase it from JetBlue.

When Neeleman was attending a small airline industry conference, someone alerted him to the capabilities of Embraer, an emerging, small plane manufacturer in Brazil. Neeleman immediately scheduled a trip to Brazil to visit Embraer and explore opportunities for JetBlue. During the visit, Neeleman saw the possibility of serving midsize cities with a new hundred-seat Embraer jet, one designed specifically for JetBlue. By offering satellite TV and large comfortable seats, the hundred-seat JetBlue plane would be far more desirable to passengers than the fifty-seat regional jets, and more economical than the larger Boeing and Airbus jets. As part of the deal, JetBlue purchased the Brazilian aircraft maker's hundred-seat plane-manufacturing capacity for two years. Later, the airline signed a contract with Embraer that prevented it from selling the jet at a price lower than JetBlue had paid.

In addition to attending conferences, some innovators create networking opportunities within their companies. For example, Richard Branson created an idea networking process when founding Virgin Music. He bought an old castle and transformed it into a conversation hub for diverse people from the entertainment industry, including musicians, artists, producers, filmmakers, and otherwise. Branson understands that creating networking opportunities within Virgin produces conversations between people that just might trigger innovative ideas.

Form a Personal Networking Group

We found that many innovators build a small network of people who are their "go to" folks when they want to find or test new ideas. For example, innovative entrepreneurs Jeff Jones (founder of Campus Pipeline and NxLight) and Eliot Jacobsen (RocketFuel Ventures) described how they liked to get together to jam (to use a music or jazz metaphor) to get new ideas. "I have a few people I like to get together with when I'm in need of a boost to my creative juices," Jones told us. "Eliot Jacobsen is one of my friends that I love to talk to because we just energize each other and build on each others' ideas." Jacobsen agreed, saying, "Jeff Jones is one of those people I like to talk to on a regular basis because we just connect in a creative way."

In similar fashion, we found that many innovators have a small group of creative confidants that they converse with whenever they need some fresh ideas—or someone to challenge their current ideas. Usually this network is relatively small (e.g., fewer than five people), but some innovators have actively created larger networks. One innovative executive told us that over the years he has cultivated a kitchen cabinet of twenty to thirty people from different industries who are his innovation advisers. At least once a year, he picks up the phone and asks his kitchen cabinet, "What's keeping you up at night?" He says, "Most of them either run companies or are involved in industries in a fairly senior way and they have very specific things to talk about . . . From these diverse conversations I try to piece together trends or directions. There are moments when the pieces just come together and new ideas form with amazing clarity."

As important as networking is, many senior executives face unique challenges when trying to talk candidly with others about new ideas. After all, intellectual property is at stake, and senior executives often have difficulty challenging the status quo in their organizations because they often created it. "As a CEO, there are few places where you can really publicly talk about fundamental concerns," one innovative CEO told us. "As a result, I've created an unofficial group. It's fairly senior, fairly seasoned people who are comfortable throwing out ideas and then forgetting about them if these hunches or speculations aren't right. One thing about being a CEO is that you've got to be very careful about what you say in public and whom you involve in these conversations. That's why networking for ideas, for me at least, is unofficial." For this reason, it's important to form a *trusted* network of confidants, since the issues under discussion are of critical and sensitive strategic value. Building a trusted and diverse idea network is often best accomplished throughout your career, because forming relationships with a diverse set of people takes time and experience. However, if done well, a small personal network of creative confidants can pay significant dividends.

Effective idea networking helps innovators create new processes, products, services, and even business models that deliver positive results. When multiple conversations abound in these networks, a new idea frequently emerges from the insights and refinements gained. Michael Dell put it this way: "I often have a hard time explaining how we innovate at Dell because we do it quite collaboratively, building on each other. Someone will say, 'Hey, what about this, how about that?' And by the time you're done, it's impossible to say, 'That's so-and-so's idea,' because you've got twenty-seven fingerprints all over the thing." In the end, idea ownership matters far less than development through the idea networking process.

Networking Sidebar: How Well Do You Take Rejection?

OK, so you've already heard about the importance of networking. But if you are like most people, you probably still don't have any sort of a plan to do it on a regular basis. Meeting new people is easier said than done. So what stops you? To be brutally honest, it may be a lack of confidence that prevents you from reaching out to people you don't know. You might get rejected. In fact you will get rejected, sometimes when making the pitch for a meeting or conversation, and sometimes after making the pitch. So what can you do to minimize the probability of rejection when making the pitch? Tell the person you want to engage that "I'm interested in your ideas. I'm interested in your perspective." This taps into his or her desire to help or be viewed as an expert. Most people derive satisfaction from being asked for their opinion and ideas. It's important to make sure they know you are only interested in their ideas, not their resources.

Once you get the opportunity to exchange ideas with someone, and if you want to keep the door open to future conversations, you have one goal: *be interesting*. What makes someone interesting? Two things seem to help. First, breadth of experience matters in a big way. If you've traveled widely

(continued)

(China, Australia, Italy), experienced widely (Broadway shows, scuba diving), read widely (novels, history, different subjects), or networked widely ("Yes, I know so and so; we met when . . ."), then you increase your chances of being interesting to someone. Second, make sure you perfect your elevator speech on the topic you want ideas about. If you can tell interesting stories about the problem or challenge you are trying to solve, that will spark an interest. Being able to tell short, interesting stories on a variety of topics increases your interesting quotient. Of course, it doesn't hurt to be funny or witty, but that really takes some practice.

Networking is most likely to spark innovative ideas when you initiate conversations with folks in different social networks. This means talking to people from different business functions, companies, industries, countries, ethnic groups, socioeconomic groups, age groups (eighteen-year-olds and eighty-year-olds), political groups, and religions. Diversity of network breeds diversity of ideas. Attending idea conferences such as TED can be a way to jump-start the diversity of your network. Moreover, when facing a particular problem, ask yourself, "Who else has faced a problem like this before?" and try to talk to those folks.

Tips for Developing Idea Networking Skills

We recommend the following activities to help you practice and strengthen your idea networking skills.

Tip #1: Expand the diversity of your network

List the top-ten people you would typically talk with if you were trying to get or refine a new idea. Go ahead. Make the list right now. How many of those people have a background or perspective that is likely to be very different from yours? For example, how many are teenagers, or how many are older than seventy-five? How many were born and grew up in a different country? How many are from a very different socioeconomic group than yours? If your current idea network either isn't very large or isn't very diverse, expand your idea pool by identifying and visiting with people who are the most different from you along some or all of the dimensions shown in table 5-1.

Tip #2: Start a "mealtime networking" plan

Plan to have a meal with someone from a different background at least once each week. Jacobsen, of RocketFuel Ventures, tries to schedule breakfast, lunch, or dinner with someone new every week. "I also frequently meet with people I know who are creative and who I've found are helpful in offering a different perspective," he says. "Networking is important to my success in coming up with new business ideas, and mealtime is for networking." For ideas on mealtime networking, see Keith Ferrazzi's book *Never Eat Alone*.

Tip #3: Plan to attend at least two conferences in the next year

Select one conference that is on a topic related to your area of expertise and one conference on a topic that isn't. Make an effort to meet new people and get to know what problems and issues they are facing; ask for their ideas and perspectives on problems and issues you are wrestling with.

Tip #4: Start a creative community

Identify a few founding members who you believe are open to discussing new ideas and who you think will stimulate your creative thinking. Decide on a creative place to meet where you can exchange ideas and develop new ones. Meet regularly (at least monthly) to discuss trends and new ideas.

TABLE 5-1

Diversify your idea network

Identify and have a dialogue with people most different from you.

Name	Country of origin	Industry	Gender	Profession	Organization level	Age (at least 20 years older *or* younger)	Political views	Socioeconomic status
1.								
2.								
3.								
4.								
5.								
6.								
7.								
8.								
9.								
10.								

Tip #5: Invite an outsider

Bring in a smart person with a different background (someone from a different function, profession, company, industry, country, age, ethnic group, socioeconomic group) to have lunch with you and your team once each week. Ask the person about your innovation challenges and get his or her perspective on your ideas. Or hold an open house for ideas, inviting two to four people from a variety of perspectives, including nonexperts who are new to a situation, to present their ideas and viewpoints.

Tip #6: Cross-train with experts

Find experts in different functions, industries, or geographic regions, and sit in on their training sessions and meetings to experience their work and world. (For example, marketing managers from Google and P&G traded jobs for a month to gain rich insights into each other's worlds as well as new ways to challenge fundamental assumptions in the other industry.)

6

Discovery Skill #5

Experimenting

"I haven't failed . . . I've just found 10,000 ways that do not work."

—Thomas Edison

WHEN MOST PEOPLE hear the word *experiment,* they think of scientists in white coats running experiments in a lab, or of great inventors like Thomas Edison. Like Edison, business innovators actively try out new ideas by creating prototypes and launching pilot tests. But unlike scientists, they don't work in laboratories; the world is their laboratory. And beyond just creating prototypes, they try out new experiences and take apart products and processes in search of new data that may spark an innovative new idea. Good experimenters understand that although questioning, observing, and networking provide data about the past (what was) and the present (what is), experimenting is best suited for generating data on what might work in the future. In other words, it's the best way to answer our "what-if" questions as we search for new solutions. Often, the *only* way to get the necessary data to move forward is to run the experiment. George Box, former president of the American Statistical Association, reinforces the power of experimentation in framing the future by noticing that, "the only way to know how a complex system will behave—after you modify it—is to modify it and see how it behaves." This is precisely what experimentation does for disruptive innovators. It provides key data on how well their ideas work in practice and helps them shape revolutionary business models piece by piece.

Experimenting with new business opportunities was, in fact, part of what Amazon.com founder Jeff Bezos did at D.E. Shaw, a Wall Street investment firm. In May 1994, Bezos was exploring the still-immature Internet in his thirty-ninth-floor office in midtown Manhattan. As Bezos was browsing, he came across a Web site that claimed to measure growth in Internet usage. Bezos couldn't believe his eyes. According to this site, the Internet was growing at a rate of 2,300 percent a year. "It was a wake-up call," he says. "You have to keep in mind that human beings aren't good at understanding exponential growth. It's just not something we see in our everyday life." What kind of business opportunity might this newfangled thing called the Internet represent?

Bezos began asking a series of questions: What would people buy remotely? What do they prefer to purchase by mail order rather than in a store? After researching the top-twenty mail-order products, Bezos decided that people would buy standard products via the Web—ones that people knew exactly what they were getting. Bezos didn't see books on the top-twenty list, which was a surprise because books seemed to meet the criteria of a standard product. After a bit of research, he discovered that there are so many books in print that it's impossible for one book catalog to contain information about them all. Such a catalogue would be far too large and expensive to mail. As Bezos saw it, the Internet was the ideal vehicle for offering such a catalog. He felt he had enough data to run the experiment to see if books could be successfully sold over the Internet.

Within the year, Bezos launched Amazon.com and dubbed it "Earth's Biggest Bookstore." Using book wholesaler Ingram to warehouse and ship books, Amazon offered the largest selection of books anywhere, without having made *any* investment in stores, warehouses, or inventory. But Bezos had bigger dreams than simply selling books. Even before Amazon became profitable, Bezos saw an opportunity for the company to become an online discount retailer, selling a full line of products from toys to TVs. So he made an incredibly risky bet. He decided to build a number of 850,000-square-foot warehouses around the country. The warehouses originally ran at 10 percent capacity. On the announcement, Amazon's stock tanked; analysts could not understand why the company was abandoning the original "no bricks and mortar" business model.

Today, of course, Amazon is positioned as the leading online discount store, with multiple product lines and efficient warehouse and fulfillment capabilities. More than anything else, Amazon is now a distribution company and virtual mall open to other vendor's products, a far cry from Bezos's original business idea. But Bezos isn't done experimenting with business models. In 2007, Amazon launched the electronic reader Kindle, an experiment that has successfully changed the company again. In addition to being a retailer of other companies' products, Amazon became the maker of a hot new electronic device (cornering 90 percent of the market until iPad's launch in 2010). Now Bezos is reinventing Amazon with its cloud computing services (Amazon EC2). Amazon rents data storage and computing power to businesses at extremely low prices by leveraging its huge investment in servers and computing equipment to run its online retailing business. By one estimate, 25 percent of small to medium-sized companies in Silicon Valley are now using Amazon's cloud computing services.

Where did Bezos's penchant for experimenting come from? Some of it clearly has its basis in genetics. His tinkering began early when, fed up with sleeping in his crib, he tried to take it apart with a screwdriver. As a twelve-year-old, Bezos desperately wanted a new device called the Infinity Cube, a set of small motorized mirrors that reflected off one another, so that it was like looking into infinity. Bezos was fascinated by this gadget, but it was very expensive. So he bought some mirrors and other parts, and, without any instructions to follow, he constructed his own version of the Infinity Cube. Beyond his natural inclinations to experiment, Bezos credits the annual summers on his grandparent's ranch for giving him time to hone and develop his experimenting skill. "I really gained confidence in my creative ability by helping my grandfather fix things on his ranch," he told us. "He often didn't have the money to fix things, so we'd have to improvise. One time I helped him fix a Caterpillar tractor using nothing but a three-foot-high stack of mail-order manuals. You learn that when one way doesn't work, you have to regroup and try another approach."

Bezos's experience has taught him that experimenting is so critical to innovation that he has tried to institutionalize it at Amazon. "Experiments are key to innovation because they rarely turn out as you expect, and you learn so much," Bezos told us. "I encourage our employees to go down blind alleys and experiment. We've tried to reduce the cost of doing experiments so that we can do more of them. If you can increase the number of experiments you try from a hundred to a thousand, you dramatically increase the number of innovations you produce."

Three Ways to Experiment

We found that innovators who start new businesses and those who invent new products are the best experimenters. (See figure 6-1.) This is not surprising, since start-up entrepreneurs and product innovators tend to launch something new to the market starting from ground zero (they also score much higher on risk taking). Of all the discovery skills, we found that experimenting was the best differentiator of innovators versus noninnovators, with noninnovators scoring in only the thirty-ninth percentile on experimentation. So if you want to find someone with a penchant for creativity and innovation, evaluating his or her experimenting skills is a great place to start.

FIGURE 6-1

Comparison of experimenting skills for different types of innovators and noninnovators

Sample items:

1. *Has a history of taking things apart to see how they work.*
2. *Frequently experiments to create new ways of doing things.*

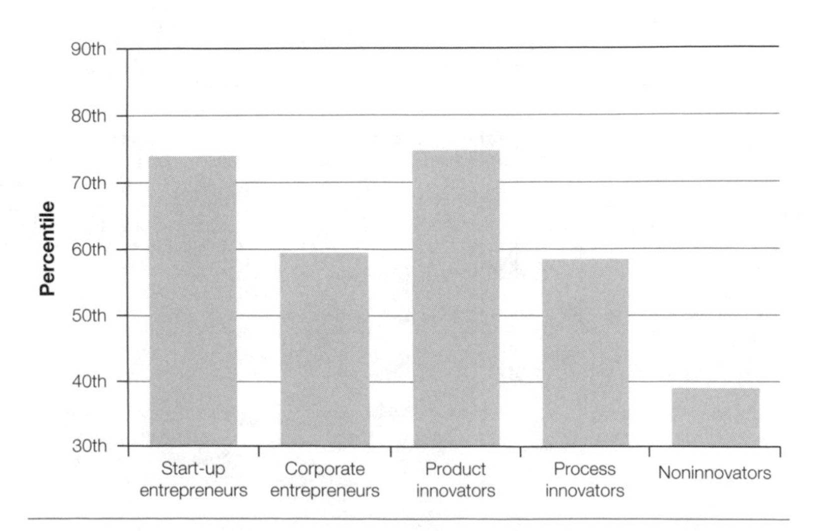

Most innovators in our study engaged in at least one of three forms of experimentation. (See figure 6-2.) The first is trying out new experiences through exploration, as Steve Jobs did when he stayed at an ashram in India or dropped in on calligraphy classes at Reed College. The second is taking things apart—either physically or intellectually, as Michael Dell did when, at age sixteen, he disassembled a personal computer (more about this later). The third is testing an idea through pilots and prototypes, as BlackBerry inventor Michael Lazaridis did when trying to construct a *Star Trek*-like force field in high school with wire, electricity, and chemicals. We found that innovators often generated their best ideas when engaged in one of the three different experimenting approaches.

We typically associate the word *experimenting* with the last of the three approaches. The classic laboratory approach to experimentation is to test an idea by creating a prototype to see if it will work, just as Edison did so often that he once famously said,

FIGURE 6-2

Three ways that innovators experiment

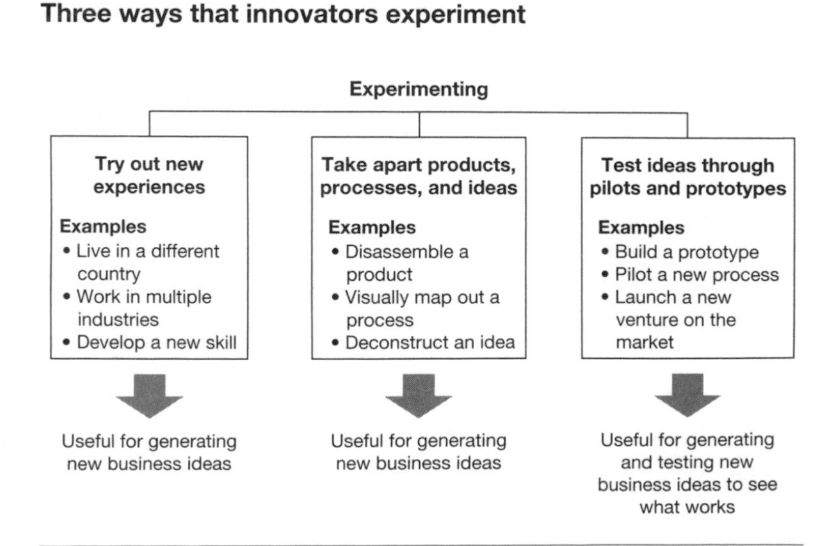

"I haven't failed . . . I've just found 10,000 ways that do not work." But we found that a much broader interpretation of experimenting better reflects how innovators cultivate new ideas. For example, when simply trying out a new experience, you have no explicit intention to test an idea. It's simply an exploratory journey to see what you can learn. The same can be said for taking things apart, either physically or intellectually. When Dell disassembled his first personal computer, he wasn't looking to create a new computer or company; he just wanted to see how it worked. Experimenting can also involve launching a pilot or prototype, and then modifying it as you go along. Bezos's online bookstore didn't stay where it was after its initial success; it morphed into an online discount retailer, selling a full line of products from toys to consumer electronics. Virgin started out as a record company, but Richard Branson experimented with all types of new businesses, from Virgin Records to Virgin Atlantic to the starry-eyed Virgin Galactic, which plans to carry megarich customers into space. And Apple hasn't stayed solely a computer company, launching successful products in music (iPod), phones (iPhone), and books (iPad), as well as unsuccessful ones in PDAs (Newton) and digital cameras (Apple QuickTake). The argument that innovators are experimenters is certainly not new; everyone knows that. But what isn't well understood is the different ways that they experiment to ignite new ideas.

Try Out New Experiences

Many executives view trying out new experiences as a waste of time if the experience is not directly linked to a desired learning outcome. Delivery-driven executives focus on efficiently solving the problem at hand. So if an activity doesn't have a clear connection to a current deliverable, then they view it as a waste of time. By contrast, discovery-driven executives grasp the idea that trying out new experiences means engaging in interactive learning experiences that may not have any obvious practical application. Indeed, *from net present value logic (e.g., the size of the investment made discounted by the time horizon), the return on time invested when using any discovery skill produces a payback that is not only further into the future but also less likely to ever materialize.* Jobs never expected that spending time in calligraphy classes would have any practical application or payback. But the calligraphy experience turned out to be a major differentiator for the first Macintosh computer by allowing it to produce documents with beautiful typography.

Innovators understand that diversity of experience allows you to engage in divergent thinking, as you draw on a broader set of ideas when associating. "Of course, it was impossible to connect the dots looking forward when I was in college," Jobs says. "But it was very clear looking backward ten years later. So you have to trust that the dots will somehow connect in your future . . . believing that the dots will somehow connect down the road will give you the confidence to follow your heart even when it leads off the well-worn path. And that may make all of the difference."[1] Trying out new experiences may prove worthless from a financial standpoint, but it also might make all the difference when searching for disruptive ideas.

Take, for instance, the example of Kristen Murdock, an entrepreneur who literally figured out how to turn cow pies (manure) into money. Murdock has done this by offering an interesting, if rather disgusting, new product that's caught interest inside and outside the United States: Cow-Pie Clocks. Not surprisingly, Murdock didn't just wake up one day and say, "I think I'll take a bunch of desert-baked cow pies, cover them with glaze, insert a clock in them, and sell them to people who want a truly unique clock." Rather, while watching her sons ride motorcycles in the desert areas of southern Utah, she stepped over some "interesting looking old petrified cow pies. So I picked one up, smelled it, and it didn't smell bad; it was really baked," she said. "I started collecting them and brought them home and put them in the garage. It kind of freaked my kids out." She had no idea what she would do with them; she just thought they were interesting.

Within a few days, some of them started to disintegrate. So to keep them intact, she applied a glaze and liked what she saw. They were like shiny, petrified pieces of wood, and she thought they were pretty due to the color variations or the interesting rocks embedded in them. Then one night while lying in bed, she hit on the idea to insert a clock into the petrified cow pie and give it away as a gag gift. So she started inserting clocks into the cow pies and giving them to girlfriends with funny sayings, like: "You Dung Good," or "For all you do, this crap for you." "None of my girlfriends liked them," she says. "They hated them . . . they thought it was so sick." Her big break came after she gave a clock to a relative, who was a friend of entertainer Donny Osmond. Murdock said Osmond called her wanting a clock for himself, so she made one for him. A few weeks later, her relative called and said, "Turn on *Donny and Marie,*" Osmond's daily talk show. There, Murdock saw Osmond showing off her clock to a nationwide audience. The calls started to flood in. She quickly set up an Internet business. Each cow-pie clock comes with a display stand and a saying attached such as, "Happy Birthday, You Old Poop." Murdock will provide whatever saying the customer wants. She has lists of suggestions to choose from, with more coming in continually from customers and friends.

But she didn't stop there. She kept all of the funny sayings people sent her and created a cow-pie greeting card line. She hired a graphic designer to create a signature cow and cow pie and sold a line of cow-pie greeting cards to Hallmark. The business has been extremely profitable because she gets paid a royalty for the ideas and cow-pie brand, but she doesn't have to actually print the cards.

As in Jobs's experience with calligraphy, Murdock had no way of knowing that collecting cow pies could lead to any practical application in her life. It all started because she was curious enough to collect a few cow pies while wandering in the desert. Murdock jokingly sums up her success saying, "I'm an entre-manure."

Innovators like Bezos and Murdock seem to intuitively understand the value that can come from trying out new experiences in new environments. Our research on innovators revealed that one of the most powerful experiments innovators can try out is living and working in different cultures. The more countries someone lives in, the more likely he or she is to leverage that experience to deliver innovative products, processes, or businesses. Individuals who live in a foreign country for at least three months are 35 percent more likely to start an innovative venture or invent a product (each additional country brings additional benefit, though there are diminishing returns after living in two countries). Moreover, if managers try out even one international assignment before becoming CEO, their companies deliver stronger financial results than companies run by CEOs without such experience, roughly 7 percent higher market performance on average.[2] And part of that performance premium comes from the innovation capability that a CEO has acquired by living overseas.

P&G's A. G. Lafley, for example, spent time as a student studying history in France; later on, he ran retail operations on U.S. military bases in Japan. He eventually returned to Japan as head of P&G's Asia operations before becoming CEO. His diverse international experience served him well as the leader of one of the oldest and most innovative companies in the world. Similarly, innovator Reed Hastings's experience working for the Peace Corps in Swaziland continues to influence his innovative strategy and leadership (as founder and CEO) of highly successful Netflix.

In similar fashion, the more industries or companies someone works in, the more likely he or she is to be an innovator. Each additional industry offers an even bigger boost to innovation than living in a foreign country. Working in different company environments helps you develop deep experience with a variety of people, processes, and products. You also learn various ways to solve problems, since each company and industry tends to have distinctive approaches. P&G (led by Lafley) and Google (led by founders Larry Page and Sergey Brin) understand the value of seeing how things work in diverse company environments, which is why these companies orchestrated a three-month swap of employees to see how a very different, but highly successful company operates (more on this in chapter 9). These types of experiences boost a person's capacity to look at a problem from a variety of angles and perspectives.

Finally, taking the opportunity to learn new skills in different arenas—as Jobs did when learning calligraphy—can boost your innovation capability. For example, Nate Alder (inventor of the Klymit vest) decided to pick up scuba diving during a trip to Brazil. During the scuba certification, he learned about argon gas as an insulator to keep dry suits warm. He thought, "Hey, that's a cool idea. I wonder if I could put argon gas in a snowboard jacket to keep me warm?" (Alder was a snowboard instructor at the time.) This experience was the catalyst for the creation of the Klymit vest (insulated with argon gas) and a variety of other products using argon gas. As described in chapter 2, innovators tend to be T-shaped in terms of their expertise, with deep knowledge in at least one area and some expertise in a wide variety of knowledge areas. Developing new skills in new areas is a great way to build diversity of knowledge in your head.

In summary, living in a different country, working in a different industry, and learning a new skill are three ways to try out new experiences and boost your creativity. Experimenters seek these types of experiences because they expand the diversity of their knowledge and increase their capacity to innovate.

Take Apart Products, Processes, and Ideas

In 1980, Michael Dell looked forward with great anticipation to his sixteenth birthday. However, he was most excited because his parents had finally agreed to let him purchase his own computer—an Apple II. On the day the computer arrived, Dell was so anxious to get his hands on it that he made his dad drive him down to the UPS office to pick it up. What he did next both shocked and dismayed his parents, but it also proved to be instrumental in his discovery of the "direct from Dell" business model. "After we pulled into my driveway," Dell recalled, "I jumped out of the car, carried the precious cargo to my room, and the first thing I did was take my new computer apart. My parents were infuriated. An Apple cost a lot of money in those days and they thought I had demolished it. But I just wanted to see how it worked." Dell's desire to understand what made his Apple II tick led to a variety of experiments designed to make his computer work better and faster. He bought a variety of components and add-ons to enhance his personal computer, like more memory, disk drives, faster modems, and bigger monitors. He soon learned how to make some money from his "hobby." "I would enhance a PC the way another guy would soup up a car. Then I would sell it for a profit and do it again," says Dell. "I was soon going to distributors and buying PC components in bulk to reduce the costs. I remember my mother complained that my room looked like a mechanic's shop."

Dell soon gained enough familiarity with the cost of PC components that he acquired an important insight. At the time, an IBM PC sold in a store for around $2,500 to $3,000. But the exact same components could be purchased for $600 or $700, and IBM didn't own the technology. Dell told us that this raised a critical question in his mind: "Why does it cost five times more to buy a PC in the store than the parts cost?" He realized that he could buy the latest components, assemble them in the exact configuration a customer wanted, and deliver it for far less than the retail price in a store. Thus, the "direct from Dell" business model was born.

Like Dell, many innovators hit on an innovative idea while taking something apart—a product, a process, a company, a technology. For example, Google's Page is also a tinkerer who likes to deconstruct things. Page's brother gave him a set of screwdrivers when he was nine years old, which he used to completely take apart every power tool his family had in the house. In similar fashion, Page tinkered with various ideas related to efficiently searching the Web, eventually hitting on the page-ranking idea that searched the Web in a way that was very different from the other search engines at the time. Another experimenter, Albert Einstein, took apart Newton's theory of time and space intellectually, rather than physically, to come up with his innovative theory of relativity. Einstein is reported to have generated his insights "based purely on thought experiments—performed in his head rather than in a lab."[3]

In summary, experimenters love to deconstruct—products, processes, ideas—to understand how they work. In the process of taking things apart, they also ask questions about why things work the way they do. This often triggers new ideas for how things might work better.

Test New Ideas Through Pilots and Prototypes

Max Levchin, cofounder of PayPal, majored in computer science during college, where he developed an intense interest in security and encryption technology. In the summer of 1998, Levchin moved to Silicon Valley to pursue his dream of starting a company offering security software. One hot summer day, he decided to drop in on an encryption technology lecture at Stanford University to see if he could spawn any ideas to further his dream. Only six people attended the lecture, so it wasn't hard to start up a conversation with Peter Thiel, a hedge fund manager who was interested in using encryption technology to secure financial transactions. The two immediately hit it off and decided to start a company based on security software for handheld devices like the Palm Pilot.

The initial idea was to turn the Palm Pilot into a wallet, in which users could secure private information like credit card numbers or passwords. They launched the product with great anticipation but soon learned that the market was quite small, limited to those few users of Palm Pilots who cared about securing private information. So they decided to try out a different business idea: provide software that would allow a Palm Pilot to store money that could be beamed from one Palm Pilot to another.

So Levchin and Thiel developed software that could beam money from one Palm Pilot to another. This business idea caught the attention of some leading venture capital companies in Silicon Valley, leading to PayPal's first round of financing at Buck's restaurant, a favorite restaurant for many venture capitalists. PayPal's investors showed up with $4.5 million preloaded on a Palm Pilot that they beamed to Levchin and Thiel's Palm Pilot. PayPal seemed to be on its way.

PayPal's initial growth was rapid, but the market leveled off rather quickly because it was limited to the roughly 3 million handheld (PDA) users in the United States. It didn't take long before Levchin and Thiel realized another problem with the business model. "The initial idea of beaming money between Palm Pilots was basically a bad idea," Thiel told us. "I mean, if you have to meet face to face to exchange money, which you had to with the Palm Pilot idea, you could just hand the other guy a check. But in the course of building out this idea, we made midcourse changes that were really interesting." These midcourse changes were prompted in part by customers who wanted to sync their Palm Pilots to their computers and send money through the Internet to someone else with a computer and Palm Pilot. "We came up with the idea of attaching money to an e-mail," Thiel recalled. "Since there were 120 million e-mail users in the United States, this made it much more viral. You didn't have to meet face to face."

Today, PayPal is the world's largest processor of e-mail payments, but this never would have happened if its founders hadn't been willing to constantly experiment and launch earlier versions of the product. Just as the security wallet experiment was a "failure," the original Palm Pilot experiment also fell on its face. But these critical experiments generated the data necessary for PayPal's ultimate success.

The PayPal experience is not atypical for innovative entrepreneurs. They realize the importance of experimenting with prototypes and pilots to see what they can learn. Because of their bias for action, they tend to launch products or businesses as quickly as possible, almost as an experiment, to see what the market's response will be. They like to throw new product, process, and business ideas against the wall to see what will stick. PayPal's experiments were essentially launched as products to the market, and they generated important data when the products failed to gain traction.

While some innovators seem prone to quickly launch their prototypes directly to the market, others more carefully test and compare competing prototypes to see what works best. Jennifer Hyman and Jennifer Fleiss did this before launching Rent the Runway, a Netflix-type business model for renting designer dresses. During a trip home to New York City, Hyman noticed her sister, Becky—an accessories buyer at Bloomingdale's—struggling over what to wear for an upcoming wedding. Her sister wanted something stunning, but even though she had a decent salary, every designer dress was too expensive and out of reach. As Hyman watched her sister agonize over what to do, she wondered, "If the Beckys of this world can't wear a designer dress, what hope is there for the rest of us?" She also thought that designers had a problem as well. "If designers can't get their pieces into the hands of young, fashionable women," she thought, "they are going to have a difficult time building their brands." Hyman's simple observation of a common ritual (finding a dress for a special occasion) in a familiar place (home) with a familiar person (her sister) produced an uncommon insight. Why not modify the Netflix business model and apply it to high-end fashion? Instead of purchasing designer dresses, women could rent the designer dresses online for that special occasion, for only one-tenth the cost.

So Hyman and Fleiss set up some experiments to test their idea. They bought a hundred dresses from designers like Diane von Furstenberg, Calvin Klein, and Halston and ran three experiments. The first was on the Harvard University campus; they rented dresses to Harvard undergrads, letting young women try on the dresses first. The pilot was an unqualified success. Women not only rented the dresses but returned them in good condition. This experiment demonstrated that there was a market for renting dresses and that renters would return them in good shape. But would women rent dresses they couldn't try on? To answer that question, they set up another experiment, this time on the Yale campus, allowing women to see the dresses before renting, but not allowing them to try them on. Although fewer women rented, the pilot proved successful. Finally, they took photos of dresses and ran a test in New York City where women rented a dress only from PDF photos and descriptions of how they fit. This experiment would tell them whether they could truly use a Netflix model of renting over the Web, or whether they must open stores where women could see and try on dresses. The final experiment showed that roughly 5 percent of women looking for special occasion dresses were willing to try the service, enough to demonstrate the viability of renting over the Web. And that's how Rent the Runway launched. It has proved very successful, with over six hundred thousand members and roughly fifty thousand clients trying the service in the first year. Trying different experiments was critical to designing a successful business model. As Hyman told us, "Our revenue growth is amazing. This is a dream come true."

As we studied innovators and their experiments, one thing we noticed was that the amount of experimenting required to gain new insights is almost the inverse of the amount of prior questioning, observing, and networking they had done. In other words, if you haven't done much questioning, observing, or networking (or haven't done them well), then you will have to run more experiments to gain the insights required to move forward. For example, Rent the Runway's experiments were able to be carefully crafted to generate the right data because of years of observations that Hyman, in particular, had made of the needs of young women attending special events. (Hyman had worked for years at Starwood Hotels where she launched programs to meet the needs of wedding parties and honeymooners; she also worked at WeddingChannel.com and IMG, one of the world's top firms for female models.) As a result, she had a deep knowledge of the needs of fashion-oriented young women, special events, and designers and designer clothing. This allowed her and Fleiss to design better experiments to test their ideas.

The bottom line is that if you ask salient questions, observe salient situations, and talk to more diverse people, you will likely need to run fewer experiments. And the experiments you do run will be better designed to generate the data you need to take the next step. Random experimentation occurs when you know very little from your questions, observations, and networking conversations.

In the end, we've learned that even when you've effectively questioned, observed, and networked, persistent experimentation is likely to be important for generating disruptive insights. Virtually every disruptive business that we studied evolved over time—through a series of experiments—into a business model that changed an industry. Some experiments were accidental. For example, Herb

Kelleher of Southwest Airlines told us that the original low-cost airline entrant stumbled onto its quick-turnaround capability when financial pressures forced the company to service its routes with three planes instead of the four it had originally planned to use. It had to either cancel flights or figure out a way to fly a four-plane schedule with three planes. This led management to develop a new set of practices for turning the plane around as quickly as possible, eventually leading to a fifteen-minute plane turnaround. This innovation completely changed Southwest's strategy and business model, as well as its bottom line.

Similarly, IKEA never intended to have knockdown kit furniture (disassembled furniture in flat parcel boxes) as a central feature of its low-cost furniture retailing model. A serendipitous experiment early on in the company's history yielded an important insight. After completing a photo shoot for a furniture catalog, a marketing manager found not all the furniture fit back into the trucks. When a photographer suggested that they take the legs off the table and then slide the table into the truck, the lights went on: Ikea could knock down almost all its furniture to reduce shipping costs and make the customer the final assembler. This small experiment was critical to IKEA's business model as a global furniture retailer.

Innovators engage in three types of experimenting to generate data and spark new insights: trying out new experiences, taking things apart, and testing ideas by creating prototypes and pilots. Although questioning, observing, and networking are excellent for providing data about the past and present, experimenting is the best technique for generating data on what might work in the future. In other words, it's the best way to answer what-if questions. Innovators also understand that by asking salient questions, observing salient situations, and talking to the right people, you will likely need to run fewer experiments. This reduces the cost and time associated with experimenting. Finally, innovators understand—and accept—that the majority of their experiments will not turn out as planned (and indeed may turn out to be a colossal waste of time), but they know that experimenting is often the only way to generate the data required to ultimately achieve success.

Tips for Developing Experimenting Skills

To strengthen your experimenting skills, you will need to consciously approach your work and life with a hypothesis-testing mind-set. We recommend the following activities to practice and strengthen your experimenting skills.

Tip #1: Cross physical borders

Visit (or even better, live in) a new country or some other new environment, such as a different functional area within your company or a new company in a different industry. Acquire a passport mind-set to break free of common routines. Explore the world by engaging in new activities. Join new social or professional activities beyond your normal sphere, attend a lecture by someone whose work you're unfamiliar with, or visit an unusual museum exhibit. When you try out these new activities, ask yourself questions to help produce new insights from the experience, such as: "If my work team were here, what could we learn from this experience that would lead us to do something new? If I were going to replicate one thing (product, process, and so on) from this environment in my everyday environment, what would it be?" Work to cross one border at least once every month.

Tip #2: Cross intellectual borders

Take out a new annual subscription to a newspaper, newsletter, or magazine from an entirely different context (or to help save trees, intentionally and regularly search the Web for country, industry, or profession information about areas distant from your own). If you live in the United States or France, consider reading a publication from China, India, Russia, or Brazil. If you work in the oil and gas industry, read a publication from the hospitality industry. If you are trained in marketing, read a publication related to engineering or operations.

Tip #3: Develop a new skill

To gain new perspectives, create a plan to develop some new skills or acquire new knowledge. Look for opportunities in your community to take classes in acting or photography, or get some basic training in mechanics, electronics, or home building. Try out new physical activities like yoga, gymnastics, snowboarding, scuba diving, or even sky diving (if you are brave enough). Check out the menu of courses at your local university and sign up for classes that sound interesting to you, ranging from history to chemistry to calligraphy. Or closer to home, identify another function in your company, whether it be marketing, operations, or finance, and see if you can learn how that function works in your company.

Tip #4: Disassemble a product

Look through your house for something that no longer works, or go to a junkyard or flea market to buy a few things that you can easily take apart. (This is especially fun to do with your kids.) Search for something that you've always been interested in but have never taken the time to explore. Set aside a block of time to take the objects apart piece by piece and search for new insights into how they were designed, engineered, and produced. Draw or write about your observations in a journal or notebook.

Tip #5: Build prototypes

Identify something that you would like to improve. What would it look like if you changed it? Build a prototype of your new, improved invention from random materials in your house or office, or go on a shopping spree to obtain odd things that might work well in the prototype. Play-Doh (the children's modeling clay) is a great medium for creating prototypes. If you are feeling adventurous and want to splurge, you may even want to buy a three-dimensional printer that produces objects on demand (according to your design).

Tip #6: Regularly pilot new ideas

Gordon Moore, the cofounder of Intel, once recalled that, "most of what I learned as an entrepreneur was by trial and error." Engage in frequent pilot tests (small-scale experiments) to try out new ideas and to see what you learn from doing something differently than you've done before. You, too, can become an experimenter when you embrace learning through trial and error, but you must have the courage to fail and learn from your failures. Make up your mind to plan and carry out a pilot test of an idea you have at work during the next month.

Tip #7: Go trend spotting

Actively seek to identify emerging trends by reading books, articles, magazines, Web links, blogs, and other sources that specifically focus on identifying new trends. Read material written by individuals you believe excel at identifying trends and seeing what's next. Try reading the work of Kevin Kelly (executive editor of *Wired* and author of *New Rules for the New Economy*), Chris Anderson (editor in chief of *Wired* and author of *The Long Tail* and *Free*), or another author who is looking into the future. Then think about how these trends might lead to an interesting experiment with regard to a new product or service. Figure out a way to creatively conduct that experiment.

PART TWO

The DNA of Disruptive Organizations and Teams

7

The DNA of the World's Most Innovative Companies

"Fast-growth companies must keep innovating. Companies are like sharks. If they stop moving, they die."

—Marc Benioff, founder and CEO, Salesforce.com

IN THIS BOOK'S first six chapters, we described how innovative *people* think differently and act differently to generate creative ideas for new products, services, processes, and businesses. Now we shift our attention to answering the question: how do *companies* comprising many people build the code for innovation? Without a doubt, executives worldwide face this critical question as they try to build innovation capabilities within their companies to generate growth opportunities. Before addressing this question, though, let's look at two other equally important ones. First, which companies are truly the most

TABLE 7-1

BusinessWeek list of most innovative companies (2005–2009)

Business Week rank*	Company name	Innovation premium rank	Company name	5-year innovation premium
1	Apple	1	Amazon	57%
2	Google	2	Apple	52%
3	Microsoft	3	Google	49%
4	Toyota	4	Procter & Gamble	35%
5	General Electric	5	Starbucks	35%
6	Procter & Gamble	6	Microsoft	29%
7	IBM	7	Nintendo	26%
8	Nokia	8	Reasearch In Motion	20%
9	Sony	9	Cisco Systems	19%
10	3M	10	Hewlett-Packard	19%
11	Amazon	11	3M	18%
12	Samsung	12	General Electric	10%
13	BMW	13	IBM	8%
14	Honda	14	Southwest	7%
15	Research In Motion	15	eBay	7%
16	Hewlett-Packard	16	Target	7%
17	Nintendo	17	Walmart	5%

Business Week rank*	Company name	Innovation premium rank	Company name	5-year innovation premium
18	Starbucks	18	Intel	4%
19	Target	19	Dell	4%
20	Intel	20	Nokia	–16%
21	Dell	21	BMW	–26%
22	Cisco	22	Toyota	–26%
23	eBay	23	Honda	–27%
24	Walmart	24	Sony	–28%
25	Southwest	25	Samsung	–29%

*5-year average rank; excludes private companies: Virgin at 16 and Tata at 25.

innovative and should serve as models of innovation? Second, does having an innovation capability (and a reputation for innovation) turbocharge a company's market value?

In 2005, *BusinessWeek* began creating a list of the world's one hundred most innovative companies. It based this list on a Boston Consulting Group survey of executives who voted on the companies. (See table 7-1 for the *BusinessWeek* top twenty-five innovative companies from 2005 through 2009.) A quick look at the list shows Apple at number one and Google at number two. OK, intuitively that sounds right. But based on the methodology, the list is largely a popularity contest based on *past* performance. Do General Electric, Sony, BMW, and Toyota really deserve to be on the list of most innovative companies today?

To answer these questions, we decided to develop our own list of innovative companies based on expectations of *future* innovations. We thought the best way to do this would be to see whether investors—voting with their wallets and purses—could give us insight into which companies they believe are most likely to produce new products, services, or markets.

We teamed up with HOLT (a division of Credit Suisse that had done a similar analysis for *The Innovator's Solution*) to develop a methodology for determining what percentage of a firm's market value could be attributed to its existing products, services, and markets. If the firm's market value was higher than the cash flows attributed to its existing businesses, then the company shows an *innovation premium.* This is the proportion of a company's market value that cannot be accounted for from cash flows of its current products and businesses in its current markets. Investors give this premium because they expect companies to come up with profitable new products or markets (for details on how to calculate the premium, see the endnote).[1] It is a premium that every executive and every company would like to have.

So how does the *BusinessWeek* top twenty-five stack up using our methodology? Our analysis reveals a different ranking order. (See our ranking in table 7-1 based on the average innovation premium over five years.)[2] Our research puts Amazon at number one (with a premium of 57 percent), Apple at number two (a premium of 52 percent), and Google at number three (a premium of 49 percent)—results that are reasonably similar to the *BusinessWeek* list. But take a look at the bottom five. Samsung (–29 percent), Sony (–28 percent), Honda (–27 percent), Toyota (–26 percent), and BMW (–26 percent) generate cash flows from existing businesses that are actually higher than their current market value. In other words, investors are not anticipating growth from new innovative products or services and, worse, they're expecting that these firms' existing businesses will likely shrink or have profit levels drop.

As we analyzed these results in greater detail, we realized that investors not only cared about whether companies could produce innovations, but also cared about whether they could generate profits from new products and services. For example, Sony (number nine on the *BusinessWeek* list) and Samsung (number twelve on the list) have historically produced innovations in the consumer electronics industry, but recently investors haven't seen large profits from them and don't expect to in the future. However, competitor Nintendo (number seventeen on the *BusinessWeek* list) has an innovation premium of 26 percent, which means Nintendo not only has done a better job of generating profits from past innovations (such as the Wii), but is expected to do so in the future, giving it a much higher ranking on our list. Automakers BMW, Toyota, and Honda rank low on our list not because they won't innovate going forward, but because they will face severe challenges generating any profits from their innovations. Not only will these companies continue to fight emerging existing competitors (such as Korea's Hyundai and China's Chery), but a slew of brand-new competitors coming into the market, including battery-powered carmakers Tesla and Coda.

Given the differences described, we decided to generate our own list of most innovative companies based on their innovation premium. (See table 7-2.) We focused on large public companies (more than $10 billion in market value), since the *BusinessWeek* list likewise focused on large companies. Our ranking revealed that, looking into the future, Salesforce.com is ranked number one (Benioff's disruptive cloud computing company, featured in chapter 2), followed by Intuitive Surgical (makers of the da Vinci system of surgical robots, which we will describe later). These companies are right up there with Amazon, Apple, and Google, which ranked three, five, and six, respectively. Do Salesforce.com and Intuitive Surgical deserve to be at the top of the list? Investors seem to think so. Salesforce.com not only has led the charge with cloud computing but has also introduced the AppExchange—which *Forbes* called the "iTunes of Business Software" and which won awards from the Software & Information

TABLE 7-2

The world's most innovative companies (ranked by innovation premium)

Innovation premium rank	Company name	Industry/key businesses	5-year innovation premium
1	Salesforce.com	Cloud computing software for businesses (e.g, CRM)	73%
2	Intuitive Surgical	Da Vinci system robots for robotic-assisted surgeries	64%
3	Amazon.com	Online discount retailer, Kindle, cloud computing	57%
4	Celgene Corp.	Pharmaceuticals	55%
5	Apple	Computers, software, music devices, phones, etc.	52%
6	Google	Software, primarily for information retrieval (e.g., search)	49%
7	Hindustan Lever/Unilever Heavy Electricals	Household products	47%
8	Reckitt Benckiser Group	Household products	44%
9	Monsanto Co.	Seeds, genetically modified seeds, crop protection	44%
10	Bharat Heavy Electricals	Electrical equipment	44%
11	Vestas Wind Systems	Electrical equipment	43%
12	Alstom SA	Electrical equipment	42%
13	CSL Limited	Biotechnology	40%
14	Beiersdorf AG	Personal products	38%

Innovation premium rank	Company name	Industry/key businesses	5-year innovation premium
15	Synthes Incorporated	Health care equipment and supplies	38%
16	Activision Blizzard Inc.	Online and console game publisher	37%
17	Alcon Incorporated	Health care equipment and supplies	37%
18	Procter & Gamble	Consumer products (e.g., Downy, Gillette, Pringles, Dawn)	36%
19	NIDEC Corporation	Electronic equipment, instruments, and components	36%
20	Colgate-Palmolive	Consumer products (e.g., Colgate toothpaste, Palmolive soap)	35%
21	Starbucks	Restaurant and retail coffeehouses	35%
22	Ecolab Inc.	Hygiene chemicals, food safety, pest control	34%
23	Keyence Corporation	Electronic equipment, instruments, and components	34%
24	Essilor International Societe Anonyme	Health care equipment and supplies	34%
25	Hershey Co.	Chocolate, candy manufacturer	32%

Source: HOLT and The Innovator's DNA LLC.

Industry Association, *SD Times*, and others. The AppExchange offers more than a thousand applications for businesses in much the same way that the iPhone offers a multitude of applications for consumers. Moreover, Salesforce.com recently unveiled Chatter, a new social software application seen as "Facebook for businesses."

Chatter takes the best of Facebook and Twitter and applies it to enterprise collaboration (as we describe in chapter 2).

Intuitive Surgical (number two) is an equally impressive innovator, having introduced robotic-assisted surgery to the world. For many surgeries—like prostate surgery—Intuitive's da Vinci system has become the modus operandi in most operating rooms. But someday it could also play a major role in military surgical units. A surgeon in London could use it to operate on an injured soldier in any of the world's military hot spots. The $1.5 million da Vinci system allows surgeons to operate using three-dimensional visualization and four robotic arms that work with a precision that most surgeons cannot duplicate. This results in smaller incisions, fewer mistakes, shorter recoveries, and reduced hospitalization costs.

India's Hindustan Lever (number seven) not only has been a consumer products innovator but, as described in chapter 3, has also used an innovative network-marketing approach to sell its products through thousands of underprivileged rural women throughout India. This has allowed Hindustan Lever to sell in over 135,000 villages and become the most trusted Indian brand—used by two out of three Indians. The U.K.'s Reckitt Benckiser Group (number eight) has been an innovation powerhouse with roughly 40 percent of revenue in recent years coming from innovations launched in the prior three years. Many ideas come through networking with outsiders via its IdeaLink Web site where it lists jobs that need to be done and requests solutions. The company is currently hunting for "methods for detection of parasites and other parasite eggs" among other things. Denmark's Vestas Wind Systems (number eleven) recently won the "Innovation Cup" as the country's most innovative company. It is the world's leading supplier of wind power solutions and has spawned a number of innovations, including floating foundations for wind power stations at water depths of over thirty meters.

We believe our list better identifies the *current and future* innovators and is consistent with A. G. Lafley and Ram Charan's argument that: "An innovation is the conversion of a new idea into revenues and profits . . . In fact, there is no correlation between the number of corporate patents earned and financial success. A gee-whiz product that does not deliver value to the customer and provide financial benefit to the company is not an innovation. Innovation is not complete until it shows up in the financial results."[3]

If you agree with this statement, you probably prefer our ranking to *BusinessWeek*'s.

The DNA—People, Processes, and Philosophies—of Innovative Companies

Drawing on a sample of companies that lead both lists, we dove deeply into the practices of some of the world's most innovative companies. We relied on both lists as models of innovation and emphasized those that appear in each (e.g., Amazon, Apple, Google, P&G) and those on the innovation premium list that may not be as well known globally for innovation (e.g., Salesforce.com; Intuitive Surgical; Hindustan Lever; Reckitt Benckiser).

We started by asking innovative founders at some of these firms, like Amazon's Bezos or Salesforce.com's Benioff: What makes your firm so innovative? What happens inside your firm that results in innovative new products, services, processes, or businesses? The first insight to emerge from these interviews is that founder innovators typically imprint their organizations with their own innovator's DNA. To illustrate, Bezos described how he surrounds himself with *people* at Amazon who are inventive. He asks all job candidates: "Tell me about something that you have invented." He adds, "Their invention could be on a small scale—say, a new product feature or a process that improves the customer experience, or even a new way to load the dishwasher. But I want to know that they will try new things." When the CEO asks all job candidates whether they've ever invented anything, it sends a powerful signal that invention is expected and valued. "I also look for people who believe they can change the world," Bezos told us. "If you believe the world can change, then it's not a stretch to believe you can be a part of it."

He also talked about the importance of experimentation *processes* (as we described in chapter 6), stating that, "I encourage our employees to experiment. In fact, we have a group called Web Lab that is charged with constantly experimenting with the user interface on the Web site to figure out improvements for the customer experience." Finally, he discussed the importance of culture, saying that most company's big errors are "acts of omission" instead of acts of "commission." "It's the opposite of sticking to your knitting. It's when you shouldn't have stuck to your knitting and you did," says Bezos. So he encourages people at Amazon to ask "why not?" when considering whether to launch something new. "It's very fun to have a culture where people are willing to take these leaps. It's the opposite of the 'institutional no.' It's the institutional yes. People at Amazon say, 'We're going to figure out how to do this.'"

To sum up: Bezos looks for people with an inventive attitude like his. He personally experiments as a way to generate innovative ideas, so he's created processes at Amazon that encourage and support experimenting by others. And he asks why not and is willing to take leaps (as he did leaving D.E. Shaw to start Amazon; he certainly did not "stick to his knitting" when he made that career decision). Not surprisingly, this philosophy has become part of the culture at Amazon in which others are also expected to ask why not and take leaps.

Our observations at Amazon and other highly innovative companies confirm insights about the genesis of organizational culture made by MIT's Edgar Schein in his classic work *Organizational Culture and Leadership*. Schein argues that organizational culture arises during the early stages of an organization when it faces particular problems or must accomplish particular tasks. For example, the challenge might be: "How do we develop a new product?" or "How do we deal with this customer's complaint?" In each instance, organization members responsible for resolving the problem sit down and decide on a method for resolving it. If the method works successfully, the organization likely uses it again and again when faced with similar problems and it becomes part of the organization's culture (a taken-for-granted way for how the organization addresses certain problems). If it does not work well, the organization's leaders will devise a different method for solving the problem and continue to search until a method successfully solves it. As any particular method for solving a problem is profitably used over and over, it becomes part of the culture. Not surprisingly, Schein observes that a company founder has a significant influence on the methods chosen to solve the organization's early challenges. Ultimately, if the founder's methods for reaching solutions work reliably and successfully, they come to be taken for granted for accomplishing particular tasks in the company. It is through the repeated, successful application of the founder's initial solutions that they become embedded in the organization's culture.

The point, of course, is that the DNA of innovative organizations likely reflects the founder's DNA. As we talked to innovative founders about creating innovative organizations and teams, they repeatedly discussed the value of populating the organization with *people* who are like them (in other words, innovative), *processes* that encourage the innovative skills they depended on (e.g., questioning, observing, networking, experimenting), and *philosophies* (a culture that encourages everyone to innovate and take smart risks). Our observations of other companies on our most innovative list revealed the same thing. This led us to develop a set of *working hypotheses* about the DNA of innovative organizations that we put into a 3P framework of innovative organizations.

People

First, we found that innovative companies were often led by founder entrepreneurs, leaders who excelled at discovery and who were not bashful about leading the innovation charge. In fact, key leaders of these companies showed a higher discovery quotient than leaders of less innovative companies (more on this in chapter 8). We also found that highly innovative companies had stronger discovery skills in all management levels and each functional area of the organization. They also monitored and managed the appropriate mix of decision makers' discovery and delivery skills throughout the innovation process (from ideation to implementation). Finally, they often had created a senior-level position focused on innovation, which is what Lafley did when he hired Claudia Kotchka as vice president for design, innovation, and strategy. Put simply, these companies were filled on average with far more people who excelled at the five discovery skills described in chapters 2 through 6, and they were wiser than less innovative companies about the strategic use of discovery-driven people.

Processes

Just as inventive people systematically engage their questioning, observing, networking, and experimenting skills to spark new ideas, we discovered that innovative organizations systematically develop processes to encourage these same skills in employees. Most innovative companies construct a culture that reflects the leader's personality and behaviors. For example, Jobs loves to ask "what if" and "why" questions and so do Apple employees. Lafley has devoted hundreds of hours to observing customers, just as anthropologists observe tribes, and has put specific processes in place for observing customers at P&G. Benioff is a great networker, and at Salesforce.com he introduced Chatter and other networking processes to help employees network both inside and outside the company for unusual ideas. As an exceptional experimenter himself, Bezos has tried to institutionalize experimentation processes at Amazon that allow employees to go down blind alleys in pursuit of new products or processes. By creating organizational processes that mirror their individual discovery behaviors, these leaders have built their personal innovator's DNA into their organizations.

Philosophies

These organizational discovery processes are supported by four guiding philosophies that imbue employees with the courage to try out new ideas: (1) innovation is everyone's job, (2) disruptive innovation is part of our innovation portfolio, (3) deploy lots of small, properly organized innovation project teams, and (4) take smart risks in the pursuit of innovation. Together, these philosophies reflect the courage-to-innovate attitudes of innovative leaders. They believe innovation is their job, so they constantly challenge the status quo and aren't afraid to take risks to make change happen. To illustrate, the most innovative companies don't relegate R&D to one unit. Instead, virtually everyone, including the top management team, is expected to come up with new ideas, which results in a democratization of innovation efforts. The notion that everyone should innovate and challenge the status quo is supported by a risk-taking philosophy, such as IDEO's "fail soon to succeed sooner." The remarkable companies we studied not only show a tolerance for failure; they see failure as impossible to avoid and a natural part of the innovation process. Moreover, since they believe that everyone can be creative, they work hard to keep units small so that each employee feels empowered and responsible for innovating (Amazon's Bezos employs a "Two Pizza Team" rule, meaning that teams should be small enough—six to ten people—to be adequately fed by two pizzas).

FIGURE 7-1

People, processes, and philosophies in the world's most innovative companies

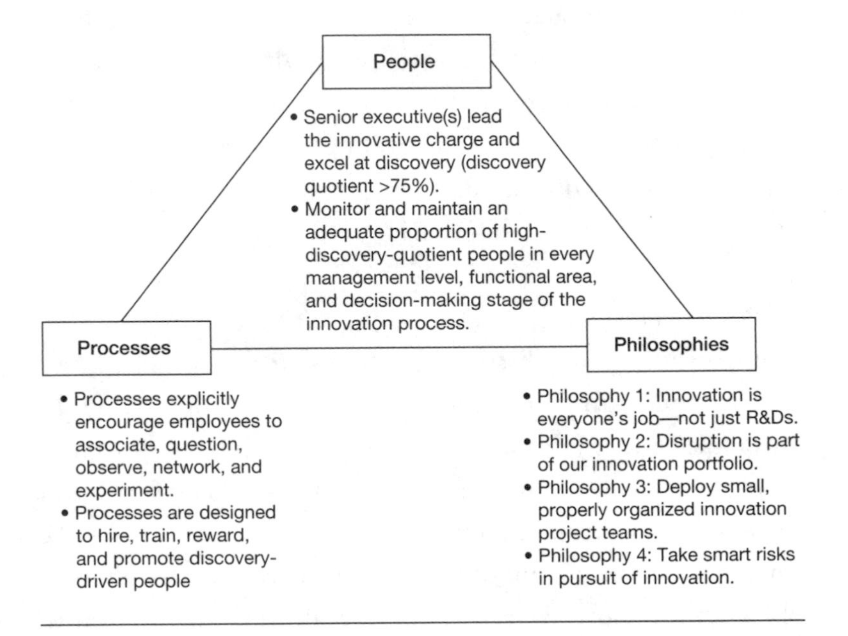

In sum, our interviews and observations revealed that innovative companies build the code for innovation right into the organization's *people, processes,* and guiding *philosophies* (the 3P framework that comprises the DNA of innovative organizations.) (See figure 7-1.)

Of course, the devil is in the details in making the 3P framework real to employees. Many organizations *say* that they have innovative people and that they encourage innovation through the company's processes and guiding philosophies. But they can be clueless about how to embed them deeply into the organization's culture. In this chapter, we have identified some of the world's most innovative companies and provided a framework to help you see how creative organizations do it.

How Innovative Is Your Organization or Team?

To get a quick snapshot of your organization or team's innovation profile, take the following short survey (1 = strongly disagree; 2 = somewhat disagree; 3 = neither agree or disagree; 4 = somewhat agree; 5 = strongly agree). Remember to answer based on the people, processes, and philosophies that *actually* exist within your organization or team, not what you would like them to be.

People

1. Our organization or team has leaders with a well-known track record for generating innovative ideas for new processes, products, services, or businesses.
2. Our organization or team actively screens for creativity and innovation skills in the hiring process.
3. Evaluating an employee's creativity or innovation skills is an important part of the performance appraisal process within our team or organization.

Processes

4. Our organization or team frequently engages in brainstorming to generate wild or very different ideas by drawing analogies from other products, companies, or industries.
5. Our organization or team encourages team members to ask questions that challenge the status quo or conventional ways of doing things.

6. Our organization or team cultivates new ideas by giving people frequent opportunities to observe the activities of customers, competitors, or suppliers.
7. Our organization or team has instituted formal processes to network outside the company to find new ideas for processes or products.
8. Our organization or team has adopted processes to allow for frequent experiments (or pilots) of new ideas in search of new innovations.

Philosophies

9. Our organization or team expects everyone to offer creative ideas for how the company should change products, processes, and so on.
10. People in our organization or team are not afraid to take risks and fail because top management supports and rewards risk taking.

To score your survey:

Add up your total score for all ten questions. Your team or organization scores very high on the innovator's DNA if the total score is 45 or above; high if the score is 40–45; moderate to high if the score is between 35 and 40; moderate to low if the score is 30–34; low if the score is below 30. The short survey is drawn from a more systematic organization or team assessment available from the authors; for more information, see http://www.InnovatorsDNA.com.

As we mentioned at the beginning of this chapter, chapters 2 through 6 focused primarily on how individual innovators do their work. In this chapter, we've suggested that the innovator's DNA has some clear organizational analogs and applications. We think there are equally compelling applications to teams at work (where the principles apply as they do with individuals and organizations). We believe this because the boundaries between what an organization is and what a team is are becoming increasingly blurred in our fast-paced world where organizations like Vodafone start entirely new business units with twelve people. Is that an organization or a team? We see it as a classic case of both, since an organization is a collection of teams, and the innovator's DNA works well in each. In the three chapters that follow, we describe in detail how innovative organizations and teams build the code for innovation into their people, processes, and philosophies.

8

Putting the Innovator's DNA into Practice

People

"Innovation distinguishes between a leader and a follower."

—Steve Jobs

EVERY DAY, your executive actions may be the most powerful signal to your organization and team that innovation truly matters. Our interviews with dozens of senior executives of large organizations revealed that in most cases, they *did not feel personally responsible* for coming up with innovations. They only felt responsible for "facilitating the process" to make sure someone in the company was doing so. But in the world's most innovative companies, senior executives like Jeff Bezos (Amazon), Marc Benioff (Salesforce.com), and A. G. Lafley (Procter & Gamble) didn't just delegate innovation; their own hands were deep in the innovation process.

As we showed in chapter 1, leaders of highly innovative companies scored around the eighty-eighth percentile in discovery skills (an overall discovery quotient of 88 percent), but only around the fifty-sixth percentile in delivery skills. When asked about their lower delivery-skill scores, innovative executives typically responded that they didn't have the time or didn't want to spend the time on execution tasks. Their focus was innovation, so they actively engaged in questioning, observing, networking, and experimenting, which had a powerful imprinting effect on their organization and team. Because innovators excelled at the innovator's DNA skills, they valued them in others, so much so that others within the organization felt that reaching top executive positions required personal innovation capability. This expectation helped foster an innovation focus throughout the company.

By contrast, a sampling of top executives *without* a personal innovation track record revealed that, on average, they scored at

FIGURE 8-1

Discovery-delivery skills matrix

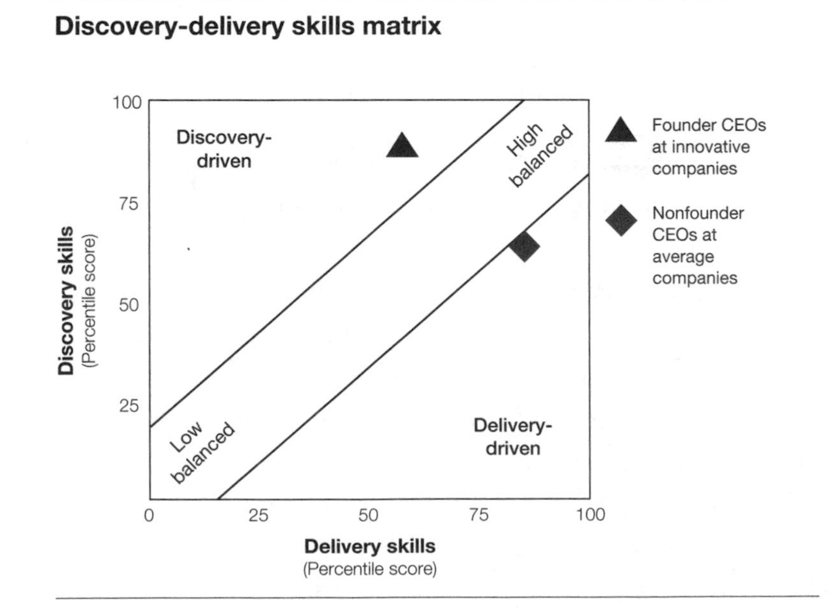

around the sixty-eighth percentile in discovery skills, but roughly the eightieth percentile in delivery skills. (See figure 8-1.) They were clearly above average in discovery, but it wasn't their distinctive competence. Basically they were delivery-driven executives who had moved up the management pyramid by executing and delivering results. Since they were role models for advancement, others marching up the management ladder were selected for a similar skill set. As a result, the entire management team of less innovative organizations displayed a lower discovery quotient.

Apple's performance under Jobs, compared to other leaders, powerfully illustrates this concept. (See figure 8-2.) From 1980 to 1985 during Jobs's initial tenure at Apple, the company's innovation premium was 37 percent. However, during the 1985–1998 period without Jobs, Apple's innovation premium dropped to an average of –30 percent. Apple quit innovating and investors lost confidence in Apple's ability to innovate and grow. When Jobs returned and restructured his senior management team with more discovery-driven capacity, Apple started to innovate again. It took a few years

FIGURE 8-2

Innovation premium for Apple Inc.

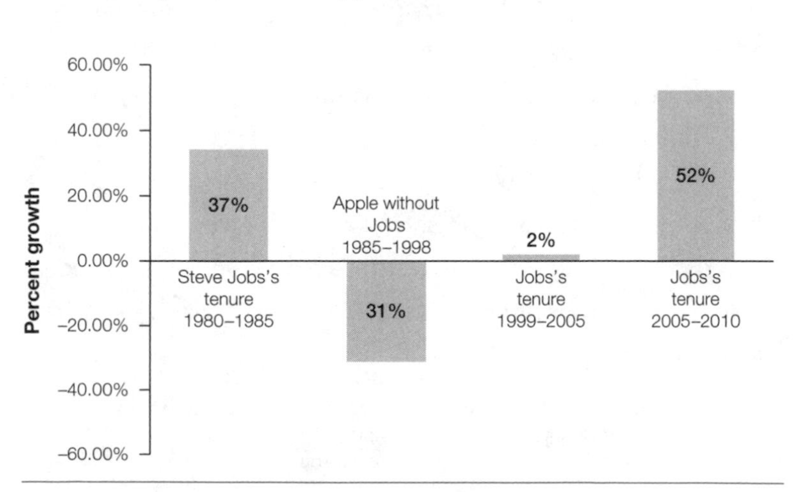

Why Innovative Leaders Make a Difference

In chapter 1, we described how Jobs got key ideas for the Macintosh computer (mouse and GUI interface) during his pivotal visit to Xerox PARC. He recalled "being shown a rudimentary graphical user interface. It was incomplete, some of it wasn't even right, but the germ of the idea was there. Within ten minutes, it was so obvious that every computer would work this way someday."[a] Jobs was so impressed that he took his entire programming team on a tour of PARC and returned to Apple laser-focused on developing a personal computer that incorporated and improved on the technologies they saw at PARC. Jobs assembled a team of brilliant engineers, gave them the needed resources, and infused the Macintosh team with a vision of what was possible. That's what an innovative leader does.

In stark contrast, the executive team at Xerox lacked the discovery skills necessary to exploit technologies developed in their own company. As PARC scientist Larry Tesler observed, "After an hour looking at demos, they [Jobs and Apple programmers] understood our technology and what it meant more than any Xerox executive understood after years of showing it to them."[b] Jobs agreed with Tesler, saying, "Basically they were copier heads that just had no clue about a computer or what it could do. And so they just grabbed defeat from the greatest victory in the computer industry. Xerox could have owned the entire computer industry today."[c] No wonder Tesler left PARC and joined Apple. Innovators want to work with and for other innovators. Moreover, companies with innovative leaders are much more likely to devote the resources required to pursue potentially revolutionary ideas.

a. "1994 *Rolling Stone* Interview of Steve Jobs," http://holykaw.alltop.com/1994-rolling-stone-interview-of-steve-jobs
b. Robert X. Cringely, *Triumph of the Nerds*, PBS documentary, New York, 1996.
c. Ibid.

to get back on track, but between 2005 and 2009, Apple's innovation premium jumped to 52 percent.

In similar fashion, P&G performed well as an innovative company before Lafley became CEO in 2000, as evidenced by the 23 percent average innovation premium from 1985 to 2000. However, Lafley's innovation focus boosted P&G's innovation capability and delivered a 35 percent innovation premium, on average, during his 2001 to 2009 tenure. (See figure 8-3.)

Lafley, and other innovative leaders we studied, very consciously set the example by modeling innovation behaviors to help make them matter to others. "Lafley always gets out in marketplaces and wants consumer interactions," says Gil Cloyd, a member of his top management team and former chief technology officer. "He's genuinely curious about it. This becomes important because it's not just role modeling of something you'd like, but it's an infectious curiosity to discover how we can provide an ever more delightful experience for our consumers, improving lives in

FIGURE 8-3

Innovation premium for Procter & Gamble

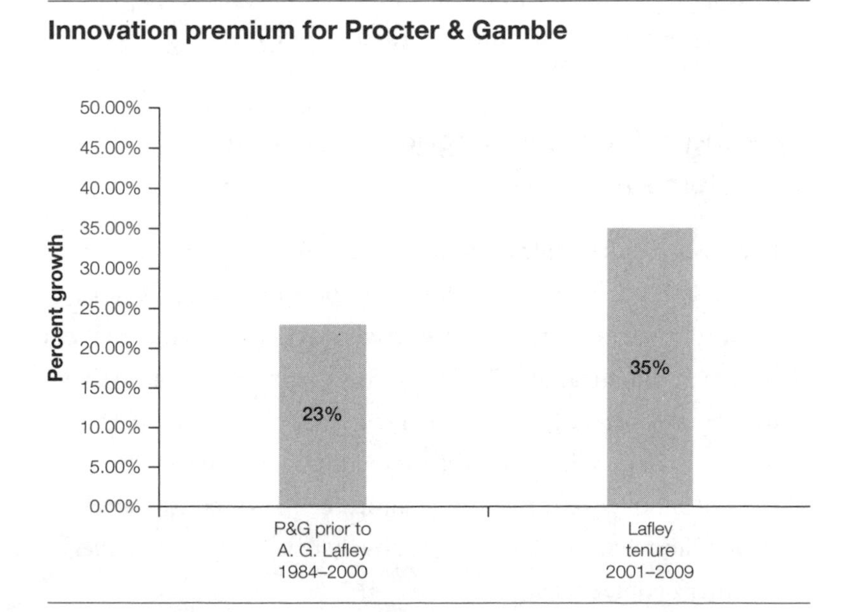

yet another way." By simply watching Lafley's everyday actions and noticing how much time he personally spent generating new ideas, his team (and organization) "got it" about innovation. Lafley also demonstrated that innovation is just not an individual game but, in the end, a powerful team effort. "You remember the times when nobody knew what to do and you came through with something that people didn't think you could come through with or when you create something that people didn't think could be created," Lafley observed. "When this happens in our company, it's never one person. It's always a group . . . Getting everybody in the same boat, rolling in the same direction, that is really what's fun. Especially when you win."

These innovation premium data on CEO impacts at Apple and P&G reflect a key finding in our research that if top executives want innovation, they need to stop pointing their fingers at someone else and take a hard look at themselves. They must lead the innovation charge by understanding how innovation works, improving their own discovery skills, and sharpening their ability to foster others' innovation. Moreover, they must actively populate their team and organization with enough high-discovery-quotient individuals to truly make innovation a team game.

Building a Team and Organization with Complementary Skills

While ensuring that your organization is populated with folks who are good at the five discovery skills is important, we don't want to leave the impression that discovery-driven people are all that matters in a team or organization. The fastest way for an organization to die is to stop executing. Discovery-driven leaders need the delivery-driven skills of people who excel at execution. Not only do effective leaders of innovative teams understand their own constellation of discovery and delivery skills, they actively balance their *weaknesses* with other people's strengths.

Complementary Discovery Skills Can Boost Innovation

We accidently discovered something about the composition of highly innovative teams after Ross Smith, director of Windows Core Security at Microsoft, and Dan Bean, a member of the Microsoft Defect Prevention (DP) team, called us to discuss team innovation. Smith was managing roughly seventy teams (ranging from four to eight people) working on various issues related to Window's security. He had observed that one of those teams, the six-person DP team, had been the most innovative for the past five years. The team had pioneered a number of innovations, but perhaps the most valuable were clever "productivity games" for enticing users to give feedback on key Microsoft products.

For instance, the DP team members created whimsical games that presented each of the Windows dialogues in a different language for native speakers. To get feedback, they sent the game to the thousands of Microsoft employees who spoke a language other than English, from Chinese to Slovakian. When playing the game, users received a colored electronic pen for highlighting language errors and dragging them to a "no good" bucket (for which they gained extra points). They could also type in comments when dragging errors to the bucket. "These productivity games had huge impact," Smith told us. "We saved millions of dollars and improved quality to a level that we've never seen before."

Smith wanted to better understand why this particular team showed greater innovation results than some other teams staffed with equally talented software engineers. One answer, Smith believed, was that the DP team had developed a high level of mutual trust through active, focused effort. Another important ingredient—first noticed by team member Bean—was

(continued)

that team members seemed to possess complementary discovery skills. We tested and confirmed Bean's hypothesis with our 360-degree innovator's DNA assessment.

Specifically, we found that each team member excelled at a different discovery skill. Smith excelled at associating, Bob Musson at questioning, Bean at questioning and observing, Joshua Williams at networking, and Harry Emil at experimenting. Thus, *the team displayed a collective discovery aptitude that was extremely high, thanks to team members' complementary discovery skills*. In short, the team achieved higher synergies in discovery because team members brought different novel inputs to the team through different discovery skills. "All I know," says Bean, "is that the discussions we have in this team are the most creative and stimulating I have run into at Microsoft. And that makes it really fun to work in the team." It also didn't hurt that team leader Smith, according to team members, is someone who "trusts his people," "encourages folks to come up with new ideas and take risks," "values independent thinkers," "encourages and inspires new ideas," and "evangelizes the work of others and has a tendency to downplay his own contribution." In short, Smith has done exactly what a good leader does to create a safe space for others to innovate (more on this in chapter 9).

Beyond Microsoft, we noticed similar patterns in other highly innovative teams. When complementary discovery skills exist, the rich skill diversity increases the team's overall ability to innovate. Thus, the team's capacity to generate new ideas consistently outstrips the ability of either any individual team member or another team when team members excel at the same discovery skill (e.g., networking is the primary source of new ideas for all team members). Moreover, when different team members shine at different discovery skills, they can learn more from each other, creating further innovation synergies.

For example, during the highly successful 1990 to 2005 run at Dell Computer, Michael Dell engaged in a frequent tug of war between discovery and delivery with then president Kevin Rollins. Dell recalled:

> I gave Kevin a Curious George stuffed animal. The Curious George is for Kevin to ask questions, to be a little more inquisitive. Kevin responded by giving me a toy bulldozer driven by a little girl with a huge smile on her face. Sometimes I'll get really excited about an idea and I'll just start driving it. Kevin put the bulldozer on my desk, and it's a signal to me to say "Wait a second, I need to push it a little more and think through it for some others and kind of slow down on this great idea that I'm working on." We don't use them that much, but they're subtle little jokes between us.

Rollins acknowledged that Dell and he played different roles, telling us, "Michael simply owns more of the entrepreneurial juice stuff. He has an idea a day, an hour. In big companies, you can't do an idea a day. I'm the governor of the innovation engine."

Similarly, eBay's Pierre Omidyar was aware that he was strong at discovery but weak at execution. Identifying this need for stronger execution skills on his team, he invited Jeff Skoll, a Stanford MBA, to join him. "Jeff and I had very complementary skills," Omidyar told us. "I'd say I did more of the creative work developing the product and solving problems around the product, while Jeff was involved in the more analytical and practical side of things. He was the one who would listen to an idea of mine and then say, 'OK, let's figure out how to get this done.'" Omidyar grasped the power of complementary skills when building a top management team at eBay.

The takeaway from these stories is that successful innovation as a team requires the ability to generate novel ideas *and* the ability to execute those ideas on the team. Both skills sets are necessary. Smart leaders know this and consciously think about team composition, making sure the team is balanced enough in terms of discovery and delivery skills. Figure 8-4 shows discovery and delivery skills temporarily "in balance" on a team. But remember that perfect balance is not necessarily the perfect solution.

Sometimes discovery skills should weigh more heavily on a team or throughout an organization (particularly during the founding stage of an organization or if the team is charged with product development, marketing, or other business development tasks). At other times, delivery skills are relatively more important, and those skills should be given greater weight on the team (during growth or the mature stage of a business, or in functional areas related to operations and finance). In figure 8-5, we show the *average* desirable team profile for different types of high-performing teams in organizations (assuming each team averages about the seventieth percentile across both skill sets).

People in product development and marketing teams should score, on average, higher on discovery than delivery skills (though having some team members who excel at execution might work best). In contrast, people on finance and operations teams should

FIGURE 8-4

Balancing discovery and delivery skills in a team or company

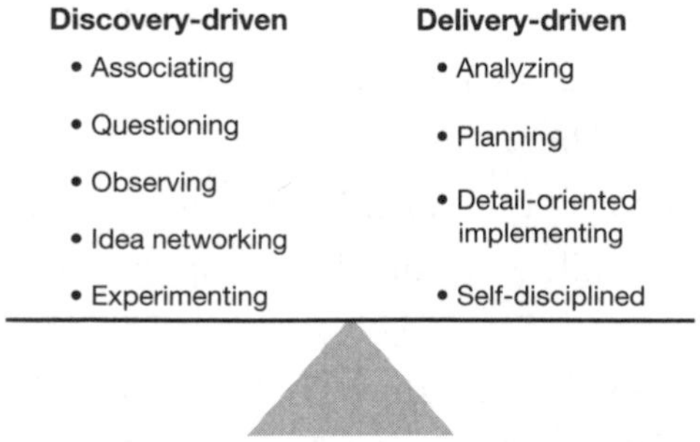

FIGURE 8-5

Desired skills composition in different types of teams

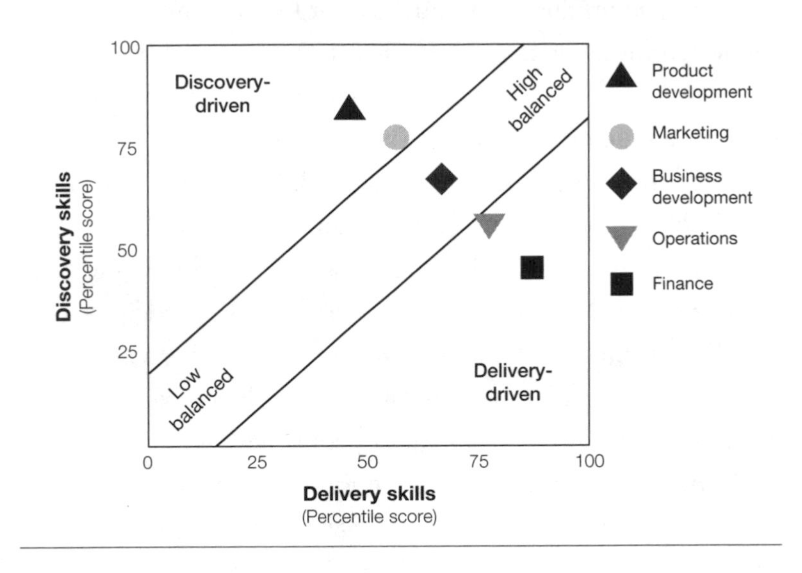

score, on average, higher on delivery than discovery skills (again, it's not a bad idea to have a few folks strong at discovery in the mix). The trick is first knowing who has what skills and then figuring out how to combine complementary strengths within a team to generate ideas with impact.

The relative importance of discovery and delivery skills on a particular team also varies with the team's particular role in the innovation funnel (or innovation cycle). For example, at BIG, a company that uses the business model of the *American Idol* TV show to find inventors and bring their products to market, CEO Mike Collins wants a different mix of discovery and delivery skills at each stage of the innovation funnel.

Stage one at BIG is "idea generation," when his organization actively looks for innovative ideas from inventors around the world. His company engages in "big idea hunts" through road shows in different cities, Internet and newsletter solicitations, and connections with professional inventor groups. Over time, BIG has developed a network of professional inventors that it taps not only for their own product ideas, but also for BIG's clients. BIG makes money from taking inventor's ideas to market and by using its inventor network to come up with new product ideas for specific clients wanting new product ideas from outside their companies. In effect, companies outsource new product development to BIG just as they outsource innovative product designs to IDEO.

During stage two, called "winnowing," Collins invites (and pays) individuals with strong discovery skills to participate on a panel to listen to inventors' ideas and evaluate whether a new product idea shows market potential. Over time, he's learned that the panel works best when it includes people with strong discovery skills, because they see beyond the initial idea in search of ways to improve it. "On one occasion, we were evaluating ideas for new toys, and we asked a senior merchandising executive from a major toy retailer to participate on the panel," Collins told us. "But he was useless because all he could do was analyze why an idea wouldn't work. He was all about execution, and at the idea stage, you need people who can find creative ways to make an idea work." Collins's experience suggests that the first two stages of the innovation funnel need people very strong at discovery, but these skills become less critical in stages three and four.

Stage three is the "refinement" stage when the idea is tested to see whether it works in the marketplace. Designers and engineers collaborate to help design and build product prototypes. Marketers assess whether a sizable market exists for the product. Manufacturing specialists (often in China) analyze the product's cost at different unit volumes. These tasks require stellar execution skills first and foremost. However, even at this stage, Collins and others with strong discovery skills serve a critical role in searching for innovative adaptations to the product, making it even more desirable to customers.

Stage four is the "capture value" stage when the product launches to the market. While this stage centers mostly on delivery in terms of manufacturing, marketing, distributing, and selling the product, discovery skills can still generate value as BIG searches for innovative ways to manufacture, market (brand), distribute, and sell (price) the product. "You can find ways to innovate at any stage of the innovation process," says Collins. In fact, BIG is quite innovative in this final stage of the innovation funnel, using a wider variety of distribution channels for its inventor-produced pipeline of products than a typical company.

To illustrate, BIG's early search for new product ideas was in the product category of toys. Once BIG had gone through the first three stages of sourcing and developing a new toy idea, it then would face the question: what is the best way to capture value from this product (e.g., manufacture, market, sell)? Some new toy products fit well with Toys "R" Us, the retailer you would normally think about as the best way to distribute new toys. In these cases, BIG might source production from China and let Toys "R" Us take it from there. However, rather than just rely on Toys "R" Us or Walmart (the big-box toy retailers in the U.S.), BIG found that some new toy ideas were better suited for the Learning Company, Basic Fun, the *National Geographic* catalog, QVC, Brookstone (toys for adults), or numerous other channels. It also licensed toy ideas to Hasbro, Mattel, or other toy manufacturers that were better positioned to take a particular toy to market due to their particular resources and processes. In short, BIG was far more innovative in the final stage of the innovation funnel compared to a toy company like Mattel, which basically took all its toys to big-box retailers like Toys "R" Us or Walmart. The point is that, while you might need more discovery skills at the early stages of the innovation process, you should deploy (or at least sprinkle) people with strong discovery skills throughout every team in the organization—and at every stage of the innovation funnel.

The Value of Complementary Human, Technical, and Business Expertise

Making sure that innovative teams possess complementary discovery and delivery skills matters, but making teams multidisciplinary—comprised of individuals with deep expertise in different disciplines—also matters in company innovation. To illustrate, consider how IDEO, the hottest innovation design firm in the world (it has won twice as many Industrial Design Excellence Awards as any other firm) staffs innovation design teams. These are teams explicitly charged with creating an innovative product design or new service concept.

In general, IDEO works to create multidisciplinary teams comprised of individuals who are T-shaped in terms of expertise: deep in one area of expertise with shallow expertise in multiple areas of knowledge (as described in chapter 2). Of course, as a design firm, all IDEO teams have a team member with significant design expertise. However, IDEO teams also search for individuals with expertise that falls in one of three domains: "human factors" expertise (to determine the *desirability* of an innovative idea), "technical factors" expertise (to assess the technical *feasibility* of an innovative idea), and "business factors" expertise (to evaluate the business *viability* and profitability of an innovative idea).

First, IDEO includes a human-factors expert on the team, someone with a background in one of the behavioral sciences such as anthropology or cognitive psychology. This person provides insight into the desirability of a new product (or service) from the user's perspective. The human-factors person orchestrates in-depth observations of customers to understand the job to be done and to acquire deep user empathy. For example, when designing a product or service for people in wheelchairs, the human-factors person might make sure that people on the team spend one day experiencing the world as someone in a wheelchair would. By gaining insight and empathy into the user experience, the human-factors person brings insight

A Lack of Business Innovation May Stifle Technology Innovation

A few years ago, Clayton Christensen received a visit from a few technology executives at 3M who expressed frustration that innovations weren't getting to market because of a lack of innovation on the business side. 3M has long been known for innovation, and Christensen knew the company well as a result of several onsite visits to grasp how innovation works there. During his visits, he found that 3M's research and development arm applied the innovation principles described in this book. It hired people with deep and varied expertise, connected discovery-driven people with varied technology expertise, and had philosophies that encouraged innovative behavior.

So what was the problem the 3M team brought to Christensen? They showed him a gift bag that was unlike anything he had ever seen. If you looked at the bag straight on, it was a beautiful purple color. If you looked at it at a different angle, it was pink. Inside it was bright white. By using technologies that allowed polymers to absorb or repel wavelengths, the team created a gift bag that could literally change colors. This seemed remarkable, but the team was far from elated. "The corporation doesn't want to take it to market," they said. "The market's not big enough."

From Christensen's view, this was an amazing gift bag. The market for these types of bags must be huge. Indeed, the world market for gift bags and boxes is in the billions, but profit margins in the gift-bag segment are only 30 percent, he was told. 3M's typical profit margins are 55 percent, and the treasury didn't typically fund product launches with lower margins. This led to the question, what if the team just raised the price on the bags to reach the target margin of 55 percent? The response was

(continued)

that if the price increased, the market would shrink so much (to a small niche) that it wouldn't be big enough for 3M to pursue.

The challenge was finding a way to profitably take this innovative product to market. But 3M didn't pursue innovation on the business side as much as it did on the technology side. It had created rules about launching products and didn't expect innovation on the business side of how it decided to fund or not fund the launch of a new product.

We've observed this challenge elsewhere. Companies relegate innovation to the R&D unit where people should innovate, but those on the business side should just execute and skip the same innovation challenge. The result (in 3M and other companies) is that a lack of business innovation can easily stifle technology innovation. Not surprisingly, this can deflate folks in the R&D side of the business. Moreover, the company can miss disruptive opportunities that it wouldn't miss if it could only innovative a bit more in how it manufactures, distributes, markets, prices, or allocates resources to a product.

into the *desirability* of an innovative new design. This perspective is particularly important in early stages of designing a new product or service.

The technical-factors person brings deep expertise in various technologies that the team might employ in the design of a new product or service. This person likely comes from an engineering or science background. This expertise is important in order for the team to grasp what technologies are *feasible* for use in a particular new product or service design. Technical expertise is particularly critical after the team has clearly identified the user's needs (the job to be done) and then is searching for and deciding on technologies to provide the optimal solution.

Finally, the business-factors person brings the expertise necessary to figure out whether an innovative new product or service design will prove *viable* in the market. This person likely has a business background, such as a master's degree in business administration (MBA) with expertise in operations, marketing, or finance. Naturally, this expertise becomes more relevant in the later stages of the innovation process when a team must determine the optimal way to manufacture, distribute, promote, and price the product for profitability.

By staffing teams with complementary expertise, IDEO can better look at problems from a variety of angles and discover a new product or service that is *desirable, feasible,* and *viable*. No wonder it generates so many successful innovations.

Like IDEO, Apple spurs innovation by filling its ranks with people who possess various different types of expertise. "Part of what made the Macintosh great was that the people working on it were musicians, and poets, and artists, and zoologists, and historians, who also happened to be the best computer scientists," says Jobs. "The reason Apple is able to create products like the iPad is because we always try to be at the intersection of technology and liberal arts, to be able to get the best of both."[1] The key point is that innovative companies select a mix of people who possess not only complementary discovery and delivery skills, but also different expertise and diversity of backgrounds to look at problems through multiple lenses.

In summary, the most innovative companies in the world have leaders who understand innovation at a deeply personal level. They lead the innovation charge with a high discovery quotient and regularly contribute innovative ideas to the company. As one executive with a delivery-driven boss complained to us, "you can't be all about execution and expect people to be innovative. It just doesn't work that way." Innovative companies find novel ways to hire discovery-driven people who have a track record of innovation and a strong desire to change the world. Having a larger number of discovery-driven people lays the foundation for strong innovation synergies as discovery- and delivery-driven folks interact well enough to learn from and support each other. Innovative teams (and companies) perform best when discoverers honestly appreciate the pivotal role of those with strong execution skills (and vice versa), especially in teams staffed with folks possessing complementary skills. Finally, innovative companies hire and staff teams with people who possess different types of expertise (preferably with a T-shaped profile) so that the team or organization can view and solve problems from very wide angles.

9

Putting the Innovator's DNA into Practice

Processes

"We don't care if you give us a toothbrush, a tractor, a space shuttle, a chair; we want to figure out how to innovate by applying our process."

—David Kelley, founder, IDEO

OUR RESEARCH ON THE WORLD'S most innovative companies reveals that the DNA of innovative organizations mirrors the DNA of innovative individuals. Just as inventive people systematically engage in questioning, observing, networking, and experimenting to trigger new ideas, innovative organizations develop processes that encourage these same skills in employees. They also rely on systematic processes to find people with strong discovery skills who thrive in environments that embrace their use of those skills. As described in chapter 7, organizational processes reflect a response to recurring tasks that when used frequently become taken-for-granted recipes to solve particular problems. However, for processes to help organizations generate innovations (e.g., new process, product, service, or business ideas) systematically, they must be widely understood and employed throughout an organization (not just by an innovative founder or a small number of highly innovative people). In this chapter, we first discuss how innovative organizations find people who excel at discovery, and then we examine the processes that encourage—even require—employees to question, observe, network, and experiment.

How Innovative Organizations Find Discovery-Driven People

Leaders of highly innovative organizations understand the critical need to attract creative people if the company hopes to build a cadre of innovators at all levels. "In most things in life, the dynamic range between average quality and the best quality is, at most, two-to-one." Steve Jobs discerned. "But, in the field that I was interested in—originally hardware design—I noticed that the dynamic range between what an average person could accomplish and what the best person could accomplish was 50 or 100 to 1. Given that, you're well advised to go after the cream of the cream. That's what we've done. A small team of A+ players can run circles around a giant team of B and C players. That's what I've tried to do." So how do highly innovative companies find employees that rate A+ for innovation? They look specifically for people who:

1. Show a track record that demonstrates strong discovery skills (for example, they have invented something).
2. Possess deep expertise in at least one knowledge area and show breadth in a few others (for example, the T-shaped knowledge profile of innovators we discussed in chapter 2).

3. Display a passion to change the world and make a difference.

Clearly, if companies want innovative ideas from employees, they should screen for innovation potential in the hiring process. Most companies rarely do it but highly innovative ones do. They explicitly screen candidates for creativity and innovation skills as part of the new-hire process. For example, at Virgin (number sixteen on the *BusinessWeek* list), Richard Branson has made innovation one of six key characteristics the company evaluates when screening new employees. To get hired at Virgin, you must demonstrate a "passion for new ideas," you must "make your creativity apparent," and you must show "a track record of thinking different." Virgin describes its people as "easy to spot. They act in unusual ways, as it's the only way they know how. But it's not forced—it's natural. They are honest, cheeky, questioning, amusing, disruptive, intelligent, and restless." By looking for people who are cheeky, questioning, amusing, disruptive, intelligent, and restless—and show a track record of thinking different—Virgin increases the probability of having a crew of innovators at every level.

Google (number two on the *BusinessWeek* list; number six on our list) has developed a variety of innovative techniques to find job candidates both bright and curious. To illustrate, Google came up with a Google Labs Aptitude Test (GLAT), a twenty-one-question test that is a somewhat tongue-in-cheek way of screening for new employees. Some questions focus on evaluating quantitative ability (one question: "How many different ways can you color an icosahedron with one of three colors on each face?" Hint: the answer is 58,130,055). Others are designed to test for creativity and a sense of humor: "In your opinion, what is the most beautiful math equation ever derived?" Another says: "This space left intentionally blank. Please fill it with something that improves on emptiness." People who lack the patience for such frivolity do not apply. People who both understand the question and find it amusing and challenging are exactly the kind of people Google wants to hire.

Another innovative technique for finding qualified and creative job candidates is Google Code Jam. Launched in 2003, Google Code Jam is a timed problem-solving contest (tournament) where all participants compete online to solve the same problems under the same time constraints. The prize for winning? $10,000 and a job offer from Google. In fact, in Google's Code Jam 2006, it awarded jobs to the top twenty finalists. Of course, being a top-twenty finalist is no small feat, considering twenty-one thousand people from all over the world competed in the contest. Through use of the tournament, Google effectively screens twenty-one thousand worldwide applicants for jobs in a matter of days with a format that is almost entirely automated. The fact that winners of Code Jam have come from Russia, Poland, and China shows that Google is attracting global talent (entrants for Code Jam 2010 came from 125 countries). While the early qualifying rounds largely test an individual's speed in solving computer programming problems, the final challenge phase, conducted with the a hundred finalists at Google's headquarters, asks the participant to demonstrate more innovative thinking; each contestant attempts to crack the programming code of the other participants. This process has been very successful at helping Google find highly talented programmers who are passionate about programming and about wanting to work for Google.

A consistent theme within the most innovative companies was hunting for people who had invented something, held deep expertise in a particular knowledge area, and demonstrated a passion to change the world through excellent products and services. Amazon sends a powerful signal to any potential new hire that it expects and values invention by questioning them about something they have invented. IDEO (frequently in Business Week's top 25 most innovative, but not on our list because it is a private company) looks for people with deep expertise, whether in psychology, anthropology, design, engineering, or whatever, in part because it demonstrates that they are passionate about something. Apple looks for A+ talent by explicitly looking for people with a demonstrated track record of excellence. "We wanted entrepreneurs . . . high energy contributors who defined their previous role in terms of what they contributed and not what their titles were," said Sharon Aby, a former recruiter at Apple. "The main quality: expectation of excellence . . . As recruiters, we didn't settle. I fought with some managers who wanted to fill a role quickly to get a project moving, but if it took six months to find the best, they'd have to wait. We looked for people who were excited to create new things. Our motto was, 'Surprise me.' "[1]

Processes That Mirror the Discovery Skills of Disruptive Innovators

Highly innovative companies have a culture that reflects the leader's personality and behaviors. In other words, innovative leaders often imprint personal behaviors as processes within the company. Here are some examples of how innovative leaders institutionalize processes to encourage questioning, observing, networking, and experimenting throughout their organizations.

Discovery Process #1: Questioning

By now, virtually anyone working in a manufacturing environment has heard of lean manufacturing or, as it is known in the automobile industry, the Toyota Production System (TPS). The now-famous system was a leapfrog innovation over the mass-production techniques pioneered by Henry Ford. While Toyota (number four on the *BusinessWeek* list) certainly stumbled on quality in 2009, the original innovation propelled Toyota to become the global

Processes Can Turn "B" Players into "A" Players (and Vice Versa)

Jobs says Apple always goes for A+ players. Great advice—but doesn't every company try to do this? What if you can't attract A+ players though? And even if you can get them, does this ensure that they will perform? An intriguing study by Harvard's Boris Groysberg, Ashish Nanda, and Nitin Nohria provides some interesting answers to these questions.[a] They studied the performance of stock analysts over time, particularly "star" performers who moved to a different company. Star stock analysts were identified by rankings provided by *Institutional Investor* (rankings based on criteria such as earnings estimates, stock selection, and written reports). Analysts with higher rankings delivered more accurate stock forecasts, and their reports produced bigger stock price impacts. The same star analysts who moved to an investment firm with less effective processes and resources though, experienced an immediate decline in performance that persisted for at least five years. Star analysts who moved between two firms with *equivalent* processes and resources also exhibited a performance drop, but only for two years. Thus, a firm's resources and processes play an important role in star analysts' performance. The researchers found that some firms, like Sanford Bernstein, were far more successful at growing stars because of key processes established to train, mentor, and support analysts. These findings are consistent with a study of 2,086 mutual fund managers that reported that 30 percent of a mutual fund's performance could be attributed to the individual and 70 percent was due to the manager's institution.

Most of us possess an instinctive faith in talent and genius, but it isn't just people who make organizations perform better. The organization—its processes and philosophies—can also make people perform better. Companies can turn B people into A performers—or worse, A people into B performers—depending on its innovation processes and resources.

a. Boris Groysberg, Ashish Nanda, and Nitin Nohria, "The Risky Business of Hiring Stars," *Harvard Business Review* (May 2004).

automotive leader in both revenues and profits for decades. Taiichi Ohno, a former engineer at Toyota who is known as chief architect of TPS, put a five-whys questioning process at the core of his innovative production system. Many of the world's most innovative companies have adopted variations of the process.

The five-whys process requires that when confronted with a problem, ask yourself *why* at least five times to unravel causal chains and spark ideas for innovative solutions. To illustrate, in 2004, Bezos was visiting an Amazon fulfillment center with his leadership team. During the visit, he heard about a safety incident when an associate had seriously damaged his finger on a conveyor belt. When Bezos learned of the incident, he walked to the whiteboard and began to ask five whys to get at the problem's root cause:

Question 1: Why did the associate damage his thumb?

Answer: Because his thumb got caught in the conveyor.

Question 2: Why did his thumb get caught in the conveyor?

Answer: Because he was chasing his bag, which was on a running conveyor.

Question 3: Why was his bag on the conveyor and why was he chasing it?

Answer: Because he placed his bag on the conveyor, but it then turned on by surprise.

Question 4: Why was his bag on the conveyor?

Answer: Because he used the conveyor as a table for his bag.

Question 5: Why did he use the conveyor as a table for his bag?

Answer: Because there wasn't any place near his workstation to put a bag or other personal items.

Bezos and his team determined that the likely root cause of the associate's damaged thumb was needing a place to put his bag but not having one around he used the conveyor as a table. To eliminate further safety incidences, the team provided portable, lightweight tables at the appropriate stations and additional safety training to alert associates about the dangers of conveyor belt work. While this innovation was minor, one Amazon member, Pete Abilla, said it was a transforming experience "that I carry with me to this day." Abilla went on to describe several things that he learned.

1. "Bezos cared enough about an hourly associate and his family to spend time discussing his situation.
2. He properly facilitated the five-why exercise to arrive at a root cause: he did not blame people or groups (no finger pointing allowed).
3. He involved a large group of stakeholders, demonstrated by example, and arrived at a root cause (solution).
4. He is the founder and CEO, yet he engaged in the dirt and sweat of his employees' situation."

"In that simple moment, he taught all of us to focus on root causes," says Abilla. "He demonstrated by example the importance of questioning."[2] If Bezos were the only one to use the five-whys method, then it wouldn't be a process at Amazon that consistently contributes to innovations. Instead, Amazon teaches the five-whys questioning process in training programs, and employees frequently rely on it when problem solving.

Our observations of Apple (number one on the *BusinessWeek* list; number five on our list) suggest that while it isn't formalized, you could almost say the company uses a five what-ifs process as it brainstorms ways to wow customers. The iPad might never have been created had it not been for Jobs and his leadership team asking effective what-if questions. If they had asked, "How can we build a better e-book reader for the iPhone?" the innovative iPad might never have been created. Instead, Jobs reportedly asked, "Why isn't there a middle category of device, in between a laptop and a smart phone? What if we build one?"[3] The what-if question sparked a discussion about a middle category that would have to be far better than either a smartphone or laptop in doing some key tasks like browsing the Web, enjoying or sharing photographs, and reading e-books. Consistently asking what-if questions is a key part of the culture at highly innovative companies.

Discovery Process #2: Observing

One company that turned keen observations into gold is medical robot maker Intuitive Surgical (number two on our list). Fred Moll, a surgeon turned entrepreneur, used his firsthand observations as a surgeon to develop robots that can perform surgery. Moll licensed some technology from SRI, a company that had worked on a Pentagon-funded project to bring the operating room to the battlefield without putting surgeons in harm's way. The key was to ensure that robots could precisely mimic what surgeons wanted robots to do.

To refine the da Vinci robot prototype, Moll and Robert Young (an electrical engineer and founder of Acuson, a maker of ultrasound devices) mounted forty sensors along the joints of the flexible "master" joysticks. The sensors register the surgeon's hand movements, which are conveyed as digitized information to a computer and recalculated as wrist, shoulder, and elbow positions thirteen hundred times a second. Those movements are transmitted electromechanically to robotic arms and then to the "slave" handles that manipulate the surgical instruments. Moll's intent was for the robots to be precise, but he knew that surgeons lack perfect hand control. So the computer filters out hand tremors, making the da Vinci robot extremely precise. Even more important, Intuitive Surgical's product developers continue to observe surgeons to create new da Vinci system tools, allowing medical robots to assist in doing more and different types of surgeries.

Keyence Corporation (number twenty-three on our list), a Japanese company that specializes in factory automation devices such as electronic sensors, makes sure that 25 percent of the devices it sells every year are new products and more advanced than anything rivals can offer. New product ideas surface mostly from the hands-on experience of seven thousand salespeople who proactively head to the production floors of some fifty thousand customers. Salespeople are required to spend hours observing customer manufacturing lines to gain insights into their problems. By watching the production lines of instant noodle makers, Keyence learned that noodle quality was compromised because they were manufactured at variable thicknesses. So Keyence developed laser sensors that could measure noodles to 1/100th of a millimeter. Instant noodle makers now depend on these sensors to keep noodle thickness consistent. Each year, thousands of observations like these by salespeople lead to hundreds of new factory automation devices for customers.

Beyond observing customers, our leading innovators also find ways to observe other companies' practices to spark new ideas. For example, in 2008, Google and P&G (number six on the *BusinessWeek* list; number eighteen on our list) did an employee swap to spur innovation, despite the fact (or perhaps *because* of the fact) that the companies are quite different (P&G is a consumer products giant that spends $9 billion on advertising each year but very little online, whereas Google is an online search giant that makes most of its money through online advertising). Roughly two-dozen human resource and marketing employees spent weeks sitting in on each other's training programs and meetings where business plans got hammered out. The initiative allowed for up-close observation of each other's practices—with some interesting results.

For example, when Google observers watched P&G launch an ambitious new promotion for its Pampers line (using actress Salma Hayek), they were stunned to learn that Pampers hadn't invited any "mommy bloggers"—women who run popular Web sites about child-rearing—to attend the press conference. "Where are the bloggers?" Google staffers asked in disbelief. In response, Pampers invited more than a dozen mommy bloggers to visit P&G's baby division, where they toured the facilities, met diaper executives, and got a primer on diaper design. The bloggers claimed to have drawn anywhere from a hundred thousand to 6 million visitors to their Web sites.

Another result of the swap was an online campaign inviting people to make spoof videos of P&G's "Talking Stain" TV ad and post them to YouTube. The original ad for Tide to Go stain-removing pens, aired during a Super Bowl, shows a job candidate being drowned out by a talking stain on his shirt that babbles nonsense every time he tries to speak during the interview. Spoof campaigns can be risky because people might post something rude about your product or not participate at all. But with guidance from Google, P&G provided prospective spoofers a tool kit of official logos. In the end, 227 spoofs turned up, and a few were good enough to air on TV. The campaign was so successful that Tide plans to use more consumer-generated content in the future.

IDEO's David Kelley best summed up the importance of observing processes: "Asking questions of people who were there, who should know, often isn't good enough. It doesn't matter how smart they are, how well they know the product or opportunity. It doesn't matter how many astute questions you ask. If you're not in the jungle, you're not going to know the tiger."

Discovery Process #3: Idea Networking

Not surprisingly, innovative companies, like innovative people, are also great idea networkers. They develop formal and informal networking processes to facilitate knowledge exchanges both outside and inside the company.

Internal Networking

Most companies have processes for sharing ideas among employees, but innovative companies take it to the next level. One popular internal networking process at innovative companies comes from the *American Idol* model for finding new ideas. Basically, this process involves challenging employees to generate and submit innovative ideas, which a panel of judges screens and selects. For example, Google holds an "Innovator's Challenge" four times each year. In this competition, employees submit ideas for top management review; winning ideas receive the resources necessary to maintain momentum. Google also has a process for sharing new ideas internally that facilitates networking. Marissa Mayer, director of consumer products and a champion of innovation at Google, holds regular brainstorming sessions during which engineers have ten minutes to pitch new ideas. Mayer and a group of a hundred others discuss the idea. These sessions try to build on the initial idea with at least one new complementary idea per minute.[4] They have an established process for deciding which projects are refined enough to present to the company founders (though they do not reveal the process).

Innovation at Google is very democratic; it lets market forces determine which ideas move forward and which don't. Once projects and ideas post to an internal electronic idea board, individuals throughout the company rate the ideas and provide feedback. Employees can also choose to spend 20 percent of their time working on projects of their own choosing. Google executives believe that the market forces inside the company are strong enough to reward good ideas and punish bad ones, much as the "real" market would if the ideas were actually developed and launched. Google also facilitates internal networking through free food. Google Cafe provides tasty, healthy, free lunches and dinners (prepared by the Grateful Dead's former chef Charlie Ayers) to employees. "The free food at Google serves an important function beyond giving employees access to good, healthy food," Gagan Saksena, a former software engineer at Google, told us. "It's totally possible for you to be sitting by someone who has been working in an area that you were not interested in. And then suddenly a discussion with that person may trigger some new ideas for both of you."

External Networking

Over the last few years, companies have increasingly looked outside their own walls for new ideas. The term *open market innovation* has been used to describe this phenomenon. When Lafley became CEO in 2000, he established a goal of increasing the percentage of P&G's new product ideas through external sources from 10 percent to 50 percent. By 2006, 45 percent of new product ideas came from external sources, and P&G had reduced its R&D from 4.8 percent of sales to 3.4 percent of sales, while launching hundreds of products based on externally sourced ideas. The company experienced this growth in external idea generation through its Connect + Develop (C&D) initiative. Through C&D processes, P&G teams work with independent researchers, other companies, and sometimes even competitors to generate ideas.

P&G employs a number of different processes to gather ideas from these external sources. For example, the company uses

NineSigma and InnoCentive, third-party matchmakers that link companies like P&G with outside technology. These companies help P&G prepare technical briefs describing problems it is trying to solve and then anonymously sends these briefs to thousands of researchers around the world. The process brings P&G into contact with people providing solutions on a contract basis. C&D has helped P&G develop many new products such as Swiffer WetJet, Olay Daily Facials, Crest Whitestrips, Iams Dental Defense, Mr. Clean AutoDry, and Max Factor Lipfinity.

Consumer products giant Reckitt Benckiser (RB) (number eight on our list) has seen similar results using its IdeaLink Web site where it lists its "most wanted" jobs that need to be done and requests solutions. For example, RB launched Finish Quantum, a new dishwasher detergent designed to provide maximum clean and shine. The driving force behind Quantum's "clean and shine" performance is three highly active chemical agents that are normally incompatible. The challenge was to combine them in a single product but hold them apart. Working closely with external experts, RB developed an innovative polymer system and processing technique to create a dissolvable shell with three chambers that separate each agent until it's needed.

Beyond networking for solutions to particular technical problems, RB also networks with entrepreneurs to help launch entirely new products using RB brands. RB does this by actively licensing its brands to entrepreneurs or companies with access to sales channels or product competencies that RB believes will add value to the equity of its brands. If an entrepreneur has a good new product idea, RB promises to complete the evaluation process and give a decision on licensing within three months. Through processes like these, RB's innovation pipeline is so full that a new product launches or a product formula changes every eight hours. No wonder CNBC named CEO Bart Becht the European business leader of the year in 2009.

Discovery Process #4: Experimenting

Companies with high innovation premiums also institutionalize experimentation. For example, Monsanto's (number nine on our list) premium results from creating genetically engineered seeds that make crops drought resistant and immune to herbicides and insects. It's even working on making a lettuce with the crunch of iceberg and the nutrients of romaine, and heart-healthy soybeans with omega-3 (fish) oil. Its biotech crops come out of the same genetic engineering revolution that produced companies like Genentech and Amgen.

How does Monsanto do it? One secret is innovative software that allows for digital experimentation with seed genetics. Monsanto uses software, which it calls the "molecular breeding platform," to accelerate plant production to bring higher yields and herbicide resistance. This custom software—with the help of robotics and data visualization capabilities—tracks terabytes of information about plants down to the genotypes of individual seeds. Instead of spending years in planning and trial and error, Monsanto can use these digital planting experiments to predict good and bad crops and quickly get the information to researchers. Experimentation has been key to producing innovative seeds that have captured 90 percent of the U.S. soybean crop and 80 percent of corn and cotton crops.

Like Monsanto, Beiersdorf Group (number fourteen on our list), maker of Eucerin and a host of other skin-care products, invests considerable resources in experimenting with new products—and has done so since 1911 when it first launched Nivea facial creme. Beiersdorf develops most products at its Hamburg research center, the largest and most advanced of its kind in Germany (and perhaps the world). The research center's work is symbolized by the unusual architecture of the auditorium—known by resident researchers as the "philosopher's stone"—that is modeled on the structure of a skin cell.

The Hamburg research center incorporates a test center where it tries out the effectiveness and tolerance of new skin products on some six thousand volunteers every year. The test center contains dozens of bathrooms and examination rooms with technology that can measure even the smallest changes in skin-cell structure. This facility enables testers to use products under real-life conditions, and Beiersdorf researchers to carefully monitor and document the effectiveness of various products. In one case, Beiersdorf discovered that testers weren't getting the necessary UV protection from sunscreen because they weren't applying it properly and, in most cases, they applied far too little. By experimenting with customers using sunscreen (and by using an innovative method by which the amount of UV protection on the skin is made visible and can be measured), Beiersdorf researchers made adjustments in consumer education and the products themselves to help customers achieve optimal protection.

Of course, customer experiments happen only after Beiersdorf runs its own experiments. It tests each raw material and each combination of substances—including full cosmetic formulas—using special methods to ensure that they pose no health threat and are compatible with skin. It does this by testing cell cultures, as opposed to animal testing (typical in other companies). Beiersdorf's experimenting processes help it launch between 150 to 200 new products and apply for 120 to 150 new patents each year.

Amazon's Bezos also imprinted his penchant for experimenting on his company. "You need to do as many experiments per unit of time as possible," says Bezos. "Innovation is part and parcel with going down blind alleys. You can't have one without the other. But every once in a while, you go down an alley and it opens up into this huge, broad avenue . . . it makes all the blind alleys worthwhile." One way Amazon conducts small experiments is by offering a pilot product or service to half of its customers and compares their response to the other half. In similar fashion, Google has institutionalized experiments by using "beta" labels to release products early and often for public trials, allowing Google to quickly get direct customer feedback. It pursues innovation by having hundreds of small teams pursue—and pilot—new projects simultaneously. No wonder Google creates so many innovative new product and service offerings.

Combining Discovery Processes to Produce Innovations

Although we can deploy innovators' DNA skills as separate processes to spark new ideas within teams or organizations, we can also use them in a connected way as a system. Innovation design firm IDEO does just that in teams. Kelley attributes IDEO's success at innovating to its team processes. "We're experts on the process of how you design stuff," Kelley says. "We don't care if you give us a toothbrush, a tractor, a space shuttle, a chair; we want to figure out how to innovate by applying our process."[5] So what processes does IDEO rely on to innovate? IDEO teams start with a questioning process, move to observing and networking processes to gather data about their initial questions, and conclude with an experimenting process where innovative ideas emerge and evolve through rapid prototyping. In 1999 the late-night news show *Nightline* highlighted how IDEO used these processes to completely redesign a shopping cart in five furious days. Today, IDEO takes the same approach in its quest for more innovative products and services with a variety of clients. For example, the processes formed the core of IDEO's recent work with Zyliss, a maker of kitchen products, to completely redesign its kitchen gadget line, from cheese graters to pizza cutters to mandolines (slicers).

Process #1: Questioning

The IDEO project team began its quest for an innovative cheese grater (or pizza cutter, or mandoline) by asking a series of diverse questions to better understand the problems associated with using traditional cheese graters. What are the problems with cheese graters? What don't people like about existing cheese graters? How important is safety? What other things do people want to grate with a cheese grater? Who are the "extreme users" of cheese graters (highly skilled and highly unskilled users) and how do their needs differ? As far as kitchen gadgets go, extreme users are cooks and chefs (those using kitchen gadgets for hours each day) as well as first-time or rare users of kitchen gadgets, such as college students, children, or the elderly.

While IDEO teams didn't use our QuestionStorming method per se (see chapter 3), the team's initial process looked very similar and centered on asking questions to better understand what to look for as they shifted to the data-gathering phase of observing and networking. As the team members asked questions, they wrote them on small sticky notes to easily rearrange and prioritize them. Matt Adams, a project leader at IDEO, told us, "By having the right questions, it becomes clearer how you might go about answering those questions." Then IDEO teams gained a much better sense of "what to ask, how to ask it, and what kinds of people to ask" as they moved to the next processes, observing and networking.

Process #2: Observing

This phase involved sending the IDEO design team members out into the field where they observed and documented customer experience firsthand. "Our process is to go in and try to really understand the people that you are designing for," says Kelley. "We try and look for a latent customer need, a need that's not been seen before or expressed in some way."[6] So the Zyliss team spent hours and hours observing various product users, particularly extreme users, in Germany, France, and the United States, trying to intuit what they were thinking and feeling. They took photos and videos of customers using kitchen gadgets to document what they noticed.

Through observations, the team captured many problems with using traditional kitchen gadgets. For example, they saw that traditional cheese graters easily clogged, were hard to clean, and often required considerable dexterity for safe use. They noticed that the mandoline, a slicer well beloved by advanced cooks, presented severe safety hazards due to extremely sharp blades being exposed. They looked for ways to optimize ergonomics (ease of use), cleanability, and functionality. For example, they carefully observed hand and arm movements to make subtle adjustments in handle shape or tool angle for tremendous ergonomic benefit.

Process #3: Networking

As IDEO team members observed, they also talked to as many product users as they could about kitchen gadgets they were using. In particular, they visited with users while they were operating a particular kitchen gadget, because this is when users are most likely to offer ideas or insights about things they like and hate about it. They especially like to talk to "experts" (e.g., full-time professional chefs or highly competent home cooks). They are the most demanding and difficult-to-please users and often have great product improvement suggestions.

Through unscripted conversations, IDEO team members gained critical insights for designing novel kitchen gadgets. They tried to gain deep empathy to the point that they could champion a particular user, such as a chef. They tried to understand what she loves, what her challenges are, and what's really important to her, so they could share that person's story later with other team members. Peter Killman, a project leader at IDEO, says that during the observing and networking phase, IDEO teams "go out to the four corners of the earth and come back with the golden keys of innovation."[7] Those keys, observation and idea networking, help unlock the doors to innovative ideas.

Process #4: Brainstorming Solutions and Associating—the Deep Dive

The next phase involved bringing all the insights acquired through observation and interviews back to a brainstorming session that IDEO calls a "Deep Dive." During the Deep Dive brainstorming session, everyone openly shared all the acquired knowledge during the data-collection phase (called "downloading"). It's basically a storytelling session with lots of details about individual lives, in which team members capture insights, observations, quotes, and details, and share photos, videos, and notes.

The team leader facilitated the discussion, but there are no real titles or hierarchy at IDEO. Status comes from creating the best ideas, and everyone gets an equal opportunity to talk. After they shared ideas, the team members brainstormed design solutions to the problems they've witnessed. To actively support associational thinking during the brainstorming phase, IDEO maintains a Tech Box at every office (full of a fantastic range of odd, unrelated things from model airplanes to Slinkies). They spread the items out in front of the team to stimulate associational thinking as they brainstorm innovative product designs.

Process #5: Prototyping (Experimenting)

The final phase was "rapid prototyping," in which designers built working models of the best kitchen gadget ideas that emerged from the brainstorming session. Kelley describes the value of a prototype as follows: "You know the expression 'a picture is worth a thousand words.' Well, if a picture is worth a thousand words, then a prototype is worth about a million words . . . Prototyping is really a way of getting the iterative nature of this design going through feedback from others. If you build a prototype, other people will help you."[8]

IDEO took its kitchen gadget prototypes to a variety of different product users—from chefs to college students to children—for feedback. For example, the new cheese grater design has a large drum to grate cheese as it rolls and can grate more cheese (or chocolate or nuts) with less cranking. An optimized, clog-resistant tooth pattern provides maximum grating with minimal resistance for older users and people with small hands. The foldable and opposable hand crank makes for efficient drawer storage and for easy use by right- and left-handed users. These innovations are refined with each new prototype because IDEO "builds to think and thinks to build," as Matt Adams put it. Taking the prototype out for a test drive is the fastest way to get great feedback on new product ideas.

Systematically using an iterative process of questioning, observing, networking, and prototyping, IDEO successfully generates one new innovative design after another. IDEO's processes encourage, support, and expect innovation from everyone on the team. It's no surprise then that John Foster, head of talent and organization at IDEO, believes that "leadership is a group outcome," especially innovative leadership.

Our research shows that the DNA of innovative organizations mirrors the DNA of innovative individuals. Just as inventive people systematically engage in questioning, observing, networking, and experimenting behaviors to spark new ideas, innovative organizations and teams systematically develop processes that encourage and develop these same skills in employees. Moreover, as the IDEO example demonstrated, they systematically combine these processes into an overall process for generating novel solutions to problems. By creating organizational processes that mirror their individual discovery behaviors, innovative leaders can build their personal innovator's DNA into their organizations.

10

Putting the Innovator's DNA into Practice

Philosophies

"Innovation is deeply ingrained in all of the nooks and crannies of our culture."

—Jeff Bezos

WHAT FOUNDATIONAL PHILOSOPHIES permeate the world's most innovative companies? To tackle this question, we first explored the inner world of their entrepreneurial founders and senior executive teams. We asked about the philosophies and beliefs that kept their personal innovator's DNA skills in perpetual motion. The most frequent answer was, "I don't know. It's just the way I am." They simply took it for granted that innovation was their job, not someone else's. It was a core part of who they were. They devoted significant time and energy to hunting down new ideas. They pursued a range of innovative results, from incremental to disruptive, and didn't see themselves as taking extreme risks in the process.

Not surprisingly, the same innovators worked equally hard to infuse a parallel set of taken-for-granted philosophies deep into every nook and cranny of their company's culture (just as Bezos did at Amazon). They recognized that a culture is most powerful when widely shared and deeply held. So how did they do this? They knew that their own innovation example was an important first step to building a highly innovative company. They also realized it was impossible to personally lead or participate in every team and that they would have limited direct contact with most employees (especially as their companies grew). As such, they worked hard to instill a deep, companywide commitment to innovation. Not only did their companies pay attention to picking innovative people and putting innovative processes into place, they also lived by a set of key innovation philosophies.

Here's what innovative entrepreneurs and executives told us about their innovation philosophies. We heard that innovation is everyone's job. We learned that disruptive innovation is part of their company's innovation portfolio. We found out that having lots of small project teams, properly organized, is central to the way their companies took innovative ideas to market. Finally, we realized that they *do* take more risks than other companies in the pursuit of innovation, but they take actions that mitigate those risks, thereby turning them into "smart risks." These four philosophies permeate the world's most innovative companies and are not only expressed through words but punctuated powerfully through reinforcing actions.

Philosophy #1: Innovation Is Everyone's Job, Not Just R&D's

Innovation is obviously R&D's job. We've never seen any company question this. However, we have witnessed significant debate in companies around the world about whether innovation is *everyone's* job. In one organization, we watched the chairman and CEO pitted against each other on this issue. The chairman was convinced that everyone should innovate, while the CEO took the opposite stance, believing that only R&D or consumer marketing should spend energy on innovation. *While* this debate raged at the top, the company launched a new initiative to focus everyone on spending some of their workweek discovering new products, services, and processes. It was no surprise that few employees jumped at the chance to innovate until they saw senior-level executives settle their debate.

In rejecting the limiting belief that innovation is R&D's job alone, leaders of highly innovative companies—such as Jobs, Bezos, and Benioff—work hard to instill "innovation is everyone's job" as a guiding organizational philosophy. When Jobs returned to Apple after a twelve-year hiatus, he launched the "Think Different" advertising campaign. The ad paid tribute to a wide range of innovators saying, "Here's to the crazy ones. The misfits. The rebels. The trouble makers . . . the ones who see things differently. They're not fond of rules. And they have no respect for the status quo . . . they change things. They push the human race forward."

The Emmy award–winning Think Different campaign was hailed as one of the most innovative of all time, largely because it inspired people. What most people don't realize, though, is that the campaign targeted Apple employees as much as its customers. "The whole purpose of the 'Think Different' campaign was that people had forgotten what Apple stood for, *including the employees*," said Jobs. "We thought long and hard about how you tell somebody what you stand for, what your values are, and it occurred to us that if you don't know somebody very well, you can ask them, 'Who are your heroes?' You can learn a lot about people by hearing who their heroes are. So we said, 'Okay, we'll tell them who our heroes are.'" To reestablish Apple's innovativeness,

Jobs knew that every employee needed this message: "Our heroes are innovators. We stand for innovation. If you want to work at Apple, we expect you to be an innovator who wants to change the world."[1]

The Think Different campaign is just one of many things Jobs has done to send the message to Apple employees that innovation is their job. He once urged the original Macintosh development team to innovate by saying, "Let's make a dent in the universe. We'll make it so important that it will make a dent in the universe."[2] More recently, he encouraged Disney employees to "dream bigger" (as the largest single shareholder of The Walt Disney Company stock, Jobs has a vested interest in Disney being innovative). These bold statements send a clear message to employees: we expect each of *you* to innovate.

Of course, bold actions must follow bold statements to reinforce the message. P&G's Lafley pursued the "we innovate" philosophy when he remarked, "The P&G of five or six years ago depended on eight thousand scientists and engineers for the vast majority of innovation. The P&G we're trying to unleash today asks all hundred thousand-plus of us to be innovators." To reinforce his commitment to organizationwide innovation, he actively solicited ideas from throughout the company, and if the concept showed promise, he put it into development. For example, Lafley backed a successful hair-care product line for women of color because a few African American employees explained to him that existing products didn't work well and "we can do better." P&G did better, launching a successful new line, Pantene Pro-V Relaxed & Natural. Lafley's actions set the tone for a we-innovate philosophy to take hold. Yet, key leaders' personal actions alone are not enough. We saw that highly innovative companies, compared to typical companies, reinforce this philosophy by giving people more time and resources to innovate.

Creating a Safe Space for Others to Innovate

Establishing an "innovation is everyone's job" philosophy requires creating a safe space for others to take on the status quo. Researchers call this "psychological safety," in which team members willingly express opinions, take risks, run experiments, and acknowledge mistakes without punishment. "If you foster an environment in which people's ideas can be heard," says Azul and JetBlue founder David Neeleman, "things naturally come up."

Many leaders think they encourage others to develop and use their discovery skills, but in reality colleagues often don't see it that way. On average, *team leaders in our research thought they were significantly better at encouraging discovery activities in others than did their managers, peers, or direct reports.* (This sounds a bit like the "better-than-average" effect where over 70 percent of us see ourselves as above average in leadership ability and only 2 percent view ourselves as below average. Clearly, this data shows room for improvement. See figure 10-1.)

How do leaders build a safe space for others to innovate? The most important *first step* to creating a safe space is to encourage questions. At Southwest Airlines, Kelleher creates a safe space by soliciting challenging questions from direct reports, as well as others. "I just watch, I listen," he says. "And I want them to ask me tough questions." Another innovative leader encouraged everybody, even veterans, to ask why on a daily basis, because "they stop using their minds; they've moved into this execution mode and stop asking questions."

(continued)

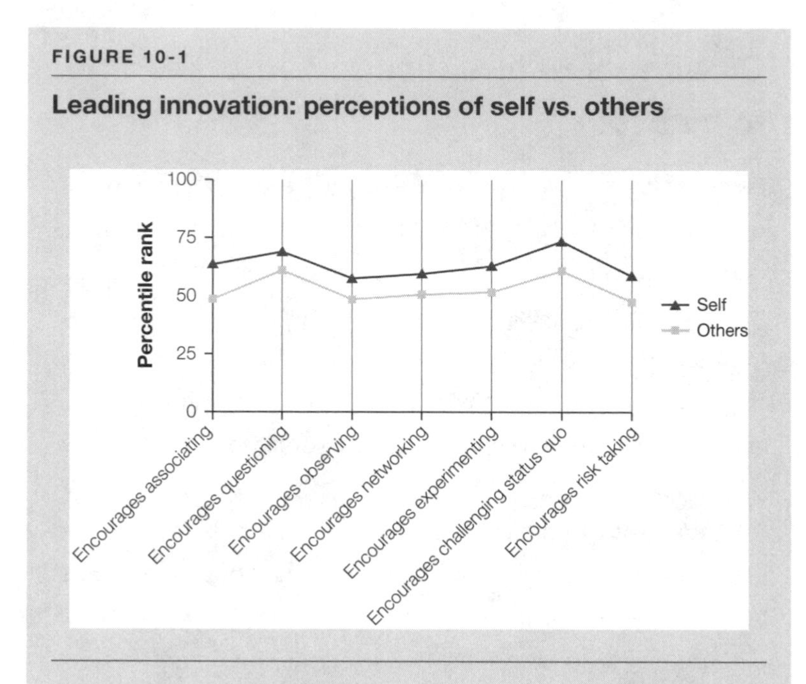

FIGURE 10-1

Leading innovation: perceptions of self vs. others

Another key to encouraging others' innovation efforts is to cheer them on when they use their discovery skills. One senior executive excelled at generating new ideas, but expressed intense frustration with team members failing to do the same. An innovator's DNA 360-degree assessment helped her better grasp what was going on. The data revealed that she had not created a safe space to innovate. Compared to all other assessors, she consistently rated her team members far lower than anyone else (her evaluation put her direct reports at the thirty-fifth percentile on their discovery skills, while her direct reports ranked each other—with confirming evidence from other peers in the company—at around the sixty-fifth percentile).

Why did she do this? Two explanations surfaced during a team-building workshop we conducted. First, she liked her ideas more than others' and often devalued their creative ideas. Second, even though she talked about the importance of creativity, she praised and rewarded delivery skills with her everyday actions. This attention to successful execution, combined with her dismissing others' new ideas, led some team members to change their behavior when around her. They were innovative elsewhere, but flicked the switch off in her presence.

This leader's challenge is not uncommon. Dan Ariely's research in *The Upside of Irrationality* shows a simple cognitive bias that causes all people to do this all the time. Ideas that are "not invented here" are always suspect because people tend to discount or ignore evidence from sources they don't know or trust, which is especially true if the idea contradicts an existing belief or something they already favor. This bias creates a real leadership challenge that innovative leaders conquer by demonstrating an authentic commitment to hearing and supporting others' ideas. Collectively, these actions help establish a widely shared and deeply held belief that innovation is everyone's job.

Give People Time to Innovate

As we mentioned in chapter 1, founder CEOs on our list of most innovative companies spent almost 50 percent more time on discovery behaviors than did CEOs of typical companies. Innovative leaders know innovation doesn't just happen, but requires a significant time commitment. Consequently, they do what other companies do not: budget more human and financial resources to innovation activities. For example, Google reinforces the "innovation is everyone's job" philosophy with its 20 percent project rule, when it encourages engineers to spend up to 20 percent of their time (the equivalent of one day a week) working on pet projects they choose. Even Brin, Page, and Schmidt try to adhere to the 20 percent rule. Management does not specify how to use time, but projects must receive a green light, and employees must account for their time. Moreover, since projects are reported and documented, they wind up on an intracompany idea-sharing forum for companywide input and vetting, which leads to collaboration. Others within Google who learn about the idea may contribute a portion of their 20 percent time to help nurture an idea. Several highly successful projects have come from 20 percent projects—including Gmail, Google News, AdSense (contextual ads that generate advertising revenues), and Orkut (a popular social networking site in Brazil). Roughly half of Google's new product launches in recent years emerged from 20 percent time projects. The 20 percent project rule visibly symbolizes that management believes everyone can and should innovate.

Like Google, 3M has long been known for a similar 15 percent rule, and at P&G, some employees said they were encouraged to devote 75 percent of their time working "in the system" (e.g., executing tasks) and 25 percent working "on the system" (e.g., discovering new and better ways to execute). Other companies, such as Apple and Amazon, give no explicit time allocation, but regularly ask employees to run experiments and work on innovation projects. Alternatively, Atlassian Labs (an innovative Australian-based company that makes software development and collaboration tools) employs a unique variation of the 20 percent innovation time rule. It conducts an annual "FedEx" day when all software developers devote twenty-four hours nonstop to generating new product ideas. Developers work intensely to build a viable "FedEx Shipment Order" that sufficiently details a new idea for others to review. Twenty-four hours later, Atlassian holds a "FedEx Delivery" day when developers rapidly prototype and then demonstrate new software ideas for others in the company. This annual innovation effort has proved highly successful, as developers experience more fun and growth in their work and ultimately help product managers fill in product holes with new options.

Consider where your company stands on this innovation philosophy. One acid test that we've used to see whether an organization has successfully ingrained this innovation philosophy into its culture is to walk in and ask a random group of a hundred employees (selected from the top to the bottom and across every function or geography) these questions:

1. Does your organization expect you to innovate in your job?
2. Is innovation an explicit part of your performance reviews?

In highly innovative organizations, 70 percent or more of the employees respond with a resounding yes. Innovating is an obvious, taken-for-granted component of their everyday work.

Establishing an "Innovation Is Everyone's Job" Philosophy

Our exploration of the world's most innovative companies suggests that the "innovation is everyone's job" philosophy gains greater organizational traction and visibility when:

1. Top leaders actively innovate, and everyone sees or hears about it.
2. All employees receive real time and real resources to come up with innovative ideas.
3. Innovation is an explicit, consistent element of individual performance reviews.
4. Companies allocate at least 25 percent of human and financial resources to platform or breakthrough innovation projects.
5. Companies incorporate innovation, creativity, and curiosity into their core values, in word and deed.

Philosophy #2: Disruptive Innovation Is Part of Our Innovation Portfolio

Beyond encouraging all employees to spend time on innovation tasks, highly innovative companies also allocate a greater percentage of both human and financial resources to innovation projects. They spend more dollars on R&D and initiate more innovation projects compared to similar sized companies in the same industries. Such concrete investments signal an organization's real commitment to innovation.

Of course, most organizations invest in R&D to pursue new products or services. However, we would describe over 90 percent of their innovation projects as "derivative," producing very incremental improvements to existing products (e.g., next-generation products or services) based on established technologies that are well known to the company (and usually its customers).[3] For example, Sony's introduction of the game console PS3—which outperforms the PS2 by providing superior graphics, a Blu-ray player, and Internet connection—is a derivative project. Sony has added features to an existing product to make it more appealing. But it has failed to create a new platform of products, thereby pulling in a whole new segment of customers, or an entirely new market.

In contrast, companies design disruptive innovation projects to establish entirely new markets by offering a unique value proposition through more radical technologies. (Technologies become more radical by incorporating entirely new components—compared to established products—and offering new linkages among components within a new product architecture.) Sony's Walkman was disruptive because it opened up a fundamentally new market by offering a music device that was far more portable than any other music device. The Walkman was based on new miniaturized components and new linkages (interfaces) between those components. Apple took a similar leap forward with iPod and iTunes that, compared to Walkman, were based on very different components and product architecture to open up portable music to a far larger customer group. Over 95 percent of iPod buyers had never used an Apple computer and over 80 percent had never used a portable music device. *That* is opening up an entirely new market. The iPhone is also disruptive, not so much because the technologies employed were so different (though some were), but because it had a very different architecture (one button, touch screen) and because of the "App store," which allowed the device to do so many more jobs than a typical cell phone. Amazon's Kindle e-reader and cloud computing services represent similar disruptive innovations by opening up completely new markets.

Finally, sandwiched between derivative and disruptive innovations are what Steve Wheelwright and Kim Clark refer to as "platform" innovation projects (see figure 10-2; note that Wheelwright

FIGURE 10-2

Aggregate project planning: a framework for prioritizing a company's innovation projects

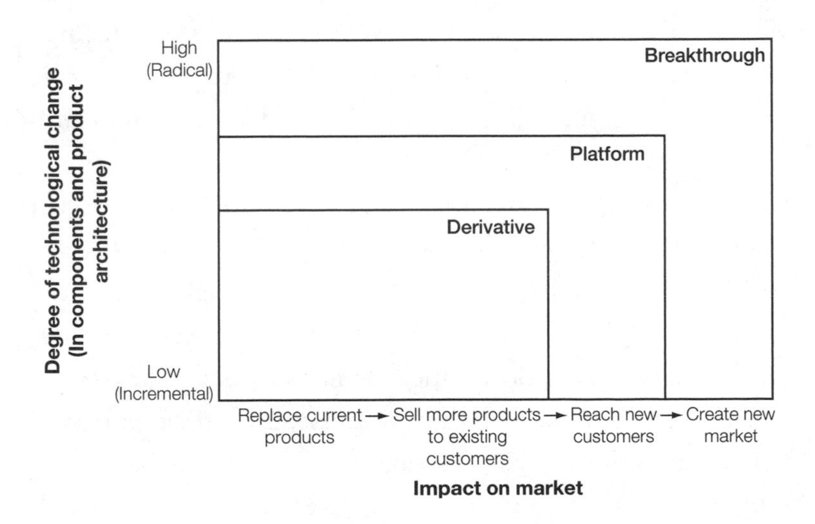

Steven C. Wheelright and Kim B. Clark, "Creating Project Plans to Focus Product Development," *Harvard Business Review,* March–April 1992, 10–82.

and Clark use the term "breakthrough" projects to refer to what we have called "disruptive" projects).[4] We see Apple's MacBook Air laptop as a platform innovation project because it's different enough to be viewed as a new product category but fails to open an entirely new market as the iPod did, since most MacBook Air users are already users of small laptops or other Apple computers. Moreover, the technologies behind MacBook Air are a bit less radical than for breakthrough products like the iPod and iTunes. (Of course, we can always debate the degree to which any given product is based on radical technologies [new components, new linkages among components] or whether it opens up a new market by offering a value proposition markedly different from other products.)

For us, the framework in figure 10-2 illustrates how *innovative companies consciously allocate a significantly greater proportion of people and resources to platform and breakthrough (disruptive) innovation projects*. For example, Google uses a 70-20-10 rule for allocating engineering efforts, including the 20 percent project time granted to technical staff. Google devotes 70 percent of engineering time to expanding and developing derivative products within the core business, that is, Web search and paid listings; 20 percent to projects designed to "extend the core," such as Gmail or Google Docs; and 10 percent to build "fundamentally new businesses," such as the Nexus One phone (its first device), a new collaborative tool called Wave, free Wi-Fi service in San Francisco, or Google Editions (its own e-book store). From our perspective, the 70-20-10 prioritization maps well with Wheelwright and Clark's "derivative," "platform," and "breakthrough" innovation project categories. Google's prioritization demonstrates a willingness to invest in platform and breakthrough innovation projects. "We will not shy away from high-risk, high-reward projects because of short-term earnings pressure," wrote Page in a letter to shareholders at Google's IPO. "For example, we would fund projects that have a 10 percent chance of earning a billion dollars over the long term. Do not be surprised if we place smaller bets in areas that seem very speculative or even strange."[5]

Similarly, Apple and Amazon allocate significant resources to platform and breakthrough innovation projects (though they don't appear to follow any specific resource-allocation guidelines). As far as we can tell, Apple was the only computer manufacturer to allocate real resources to pursue a music business, a phone business, and a digital camera business (the Apple QuickTake, which failed). These businesses were certainly not direct computer derivatives. As an online retailer, Amazon has devoted significant resources to create an e-reader product, the Kindle—which cleared the way for a new product category—and more recently, a cloud computing service. These products unlocked entirely new markets for Amazon, but rarely without deep resistance. Bezos explained, "Every new business we've engaged in has initially been seen as a distraction by people externally, and sometimes internally. They'll say, 'Why are you expanding outside of media products? Why are you entering the marketplace business with third-party sellers?' We're getting these questions right now with our new web infrastructure services: 'Why take on these new web developer services?'"[6] Yet, Bezos and Amazon press forward in their habitual pursuit of breakthrough business ideas.

To summarize, innovative companies invest more absolute time and resources in platform and breakthrough innovation projects. The acid test of whether an organization has adopted a philosophy of pursuing more than just derivative innovation projects is to ask: what percentage of your innovation projects is devoted to platform or breakthrough innovations? If this percentage is small, less than 5 percent, the company is unlikely to be very innovative and certainly wouldn't be seen that way by investors. If this percentage is at least 25 percent, the company shows tangible signs of buying into Jobs's advice to "dream bigger" by actively pursuing more disruptive innovations.

Philosophy #3: Deploy Small, Properly Organized Innovation Project Teams

Every new product or service idea needs a vehicle to take it from inception to the marketplace. A small project team (e.g., breakthrough, platform, or derivative) is the vehicle in most innovative companies. Smart leaders know that the way to empower individuals to innovate is to organize them into very small work units with *big goals* where individual and team performance is visible. Amazon employs a "Two Pizza Team" philosophy, meaning that teams should be small enough (six to ten people) to be adequately fed by two pizzas. By keeping teams small, Amazon can work on a larger number of projects, thereby allowing its teams to go down more blind alleys searching for new products or services.

In similar fashion, Google engineers typically work in teams of only three to six people. Chairman Schmidt explains the intention: "We try to keep it small. You just don't get productivity out of large groups."[7] The result is an empowered, flexible organization with small teams pursuing hundreds of projects, an approach that Schmidt claims "let[s] a thousand flowers bloom."[8] With hundreds of small team projects developing new ideas, it is little wonder that Google can create so many new product offerings.

Providing the right structure and right mix of skills for these project teams is also critical. Many organizations fail with innovation projects, especially breakthrough ones, because they fail to understand a basic organizing principle: *the more radical the innovation, the more autonomy the project team will require from the organization's existing functions and structure.* To illustrate, a company's least radical projects are "derivative," meaning that they typically involve incremental improvements to components or features. For example, Sony designers and engineers who are very familiar with the PS3's components and architecture will likely develop the next generation of its PS3 game console (we'll call it the PS4). Most likely they will modify or improve existing components, for example, improved graphics, more storage, more convenient online gaming. Maybe they'll add a new component, for example, the ability to digitally record TV shows as a DVR/TiVo does. The best type of team for this sort of derivative innovation project is a *functional team* in which engineers who specialize in each type of component work to innovate at the component level. Alternatively, they might use a *lightweight team* that primarily comes from the game console group but includes a light allocation of engineering resources from other functional areas within Sony.

But imagine that Sony wants to develop an iPad-like device that possesses features that leapfrog iPad (let's call it the sPad). If Sony attempts to develop the new sPad device *within* the PS3 engineering group, the new device will likely reflect the knowledge and technology of an existing Sony game console. The same would be true if the Sony computer engineering group or the Sony TV group developed the device. To get something more radical, Sony would be better off pulling folks from each of these areas (and perhaps elsewhere) into a *heavyweight team* or *autonomous business unit*. A heavyweight team enables members to transcend the boundaries of their functional organizations. Heavyweight teams are co-located and led by a manager with significant clout. Members bring functional expertise to the team, but their primary loyalty and innovation mind-set must move beyond the limited interests of their functional group. For that reason, they become part of a real team (and not just a group of people who happen to meet together), possessed by a compelling collective responsibility to figure out a better way—new processes, new knowledge—to meet the project's goals.

In some cases, the innovation project differs so radically from a company's existing offerings that it requires an entirely different business model (e.g., to serve different customers using different technologies). Then it makes sense to create a fully autonomous business unit to pursue the breakthrough innovation opportunity. For example, when Amazon decided to pursue and then launch a cloud computing service business, it created an autonomous business unit because the new opportunity demanded an entirely different business model from its online discount retailing business.

The bottom line? Allocating resources to lots of platform or breakthrough innovation projects will not pay off if project teams don't have the right level of autonomy to do their work. The more radical the innovation project, the more autonomy and the more diversity the project team requires. Remember, disruptive innovation demands a team staffed with folks displaying a broad diversity of knowledge in order to generate more radical ideas.

Philosophy #4: Take "Smart" Risks in Pursuit of Innovation

Most companies push platform and breakthrough innovation projects off the table as strategic priorities because derivative projects leverage existing competencies more effectively. They view the success of derivative projects as more certain and less risky. To counter this dysfunctional resource-allocation dynamic, highly innovative companies exploit a fourth innovation philosophy to soundly back up the first three: "Take smart risks in the pursuit of innovation."

Breakthrough innovations require risk taking to make them happen. Long ago, Edwin Land, inventor of the Polaroid technology and camera, noticed that the most essential part of creativity is "not being afraid to fail." For innovators—and innovative companies alike—mistakes are nothing to be ashamed of. They are an expected cost of doing business. "You do enough new things and you're going to bet wrong," says Bezos. "But if the people running Amazon don't make some significant mistakes, then we won't be

How Smart Is Your Company or Project Team about Risk Taking?

To judge your organization's propensity to take risks and learn from failure, reflect on the following questions:

- Does your organization encourage people to take risks *in order to* learn from them?
- Does your organization reward people for learning from failures? Or is punishment its default response?
- Can you name at least one successful innovation when your company celebrated learning from at least one failure to make the innovation ultimately work?
- Has your company built a higher-than-average discovery quotient in its people to ensure against the inherent risks of disruptive innovation?
- Do your company's top managers understand that they need to take risks and fail frequently in order to innovate?

doing a good job for our shareholders because we won't be swinging for the fences."

IDEO's slogan "fail often to succeed sooner" frames a fundamental philosophy behind its success as the world's leading innovation design firm. It posts the phrase companywide to remind employees that if they aren't failing, they aren't innovating (see chapters 8 and 9 for more about IDEO's people and processes). Virgin's Branson also acknowledges the "ability to fail" as a core value. "It is impossible to run a business without taking risks," he says. "The very idea of entrepreneurship . . . conjures up the frightening prospect of taking risks and failing."[9]

Of course, innovative companies like IDEO and Virgin aren't *trying* to fail. They just know that when a company tries out lots of new ideas, some won't work. That's the very nature of pushing the envelope. But they're smart enough to recognize the difference between good and bad failures. Good failures at Google have two defining characteristics: (1) you know why you failed and have gained knowledge relevant to the next project; and (2) good failures happen fast enough and aren't big enough to compromise your brand. As Google's leaders have acknowledged, "we're going to try things, and some things aren't going to work. That's okay. If it doesn't work, we'll move on."[10]

Apple echoes the same philosophy. "One of the hallmarks of the [Apple] team, I think, is this sense of looking to be wrong," says Jonathan Ive, principal designer of the iMac and senior vice president of industrial design. "It's the inquisitiveness, the sense of exploration. It's about being excited to be wrong because then you have discovered something new."[11] By embracing failure *as a vehicle for learning*, innovative companies embolden their employees to try new things. Companies would do well to embrace, as a company slogan, the innovation philosophy of creativity researcher and author Sir Ken Robinson: "If you're not prepared to be wrong, you'll never come up with anything original."[12]

But we emphasize that the innovative companies we studied were wrong less often. Why? Because they took smarter risks by hiring and developing discovery-driven people and institutionalizing processes that support people's questioning, observing, networking, experimenting, and associating (as we recommended in chapters 8 and 9). Imagine that your company wants to invest in a new disruptive innovation project. What if you could assemble a dream team of innovators to pursue the project, including Jobs (Apple), Bezos (Amazon), Benioff (Salesforce.com), Kelley (IDEO), Lazaridis (RIM), Lafley (P&G), and Gadeish (Bain & Company)? Would you invest in their innovation project? Our guess is yes.

Somehow pursuing disruptive innovations with this type of team feels less risky (than doing it with a more common delivery-driven management team) because these folks boast strong discovery skills and understand the behaviors (and processes) required for generating a successful disruption. No wonder the risk seems more calculated with them. The actual risk *is* low because putting the right people and innovation processes into place increases the probability of success (and decreases the probability of taking disastrous steps).

The *financially successful* innovators in our study demonstrated a higher discovery quotient (stronger discovery skills) than less successful ones. We see the same equation at work in the world's most innovative companies. Innovation failure (in a financial sense) often results because companies fail to consistently engage all discovery skills. They likely don't ask all the right questions, don't do all of the necessary observations, don't talk to enough diverse people, or don't run the right experiments to reduce the inherent risks of innovating. Quite the reverse is true for our dream team filled with innovators who know from experience that fully leveraging their innovator's DNA actually reduces the likelihood of failure. Similarly, making sure that your organization pays careful attention to putting the right *people, processes,* and *philosophies* in place takes out an insurance policy that tones down the risks associated with innovation.

Highly innovative companies live by a set of key innovation philosophies that instill a deep, companywide commitment to innovation. First, these companies make clear that innovation is everyone's job. Second, they make sure that disruptive innovation is an important part of the company's innovation portfolio. Third, they create lots of small project teams and endow them with the right people, structure, and resources to power new ideas to market. Finally, they knowingly take risks in the pursuit of innovation. But they mitigate the inherent risks associated with innovation by deploying the right people and processes in their teams and by providing the right structure so that teams have proper autonomy levels. Ultimately, innovative companies rely on these philosophies to create a culture that not only ignites new ideas, but takes them to market. When this happens, people work in a company culture that helps them answer the following four questions with a hearty yes:

Philosophy #1: In your company, is innovation everyone's job?

Philosophy #2: Is disruption part of your company's innovation portfolio?

Philosophy #3: Are small project teams central to taking innovative ideas to market?

Philosophy #4: Does your company take smart risks in the pursuit of innovation?

Conclusion

Act Different, Think Different, Make a Difference

"Care about something enough to do something about it."

—Richard Branson, founder, Virgin Inc.

BY THE END of our eight-year research project on some of the most innovative people and companies in the world, we came to believe that if individuals, teams, and organizations want to think different, they must act different. Now that you've nearly finished *The Innovator's DNA,* we wonder where you stand. Do you believe that if *you* act different, *you* can think different? That if *your organization* acts different, it can think different as well? We hope so, because the innovator's journey, individually or collectively, can often feel like a road "less traveled."

Yet, the road is worth taking because it just might make "all the difference" in your life and the lives of many others.

Mastering the five discovery skills of disruptive innovators and demonstrating the courage to innovate are what we've tried to share in this book. Doing so requires practice, personally, professionally, and organizationally (for a road map of how to master the five discovery skills, and even how to build them in the next generation, see appendix C). Consistent practice produces mastery, and mastery makes for new habits or, in organizations, new capabilities. By developing heavy-duty discovery skills, we really are different. We act different, think different, and by doing so we can make a concrete difference.

Of course, there are a variety of ways to leverage your discovery skills to make a difference. Ideally, you will uncover a big, disruptive idea, initiating meaningful change in many lives. Certainly, Bezos, Jobs, Benioff, and other innovative entrepreneurs have had an immense impact on the world. Their organizations employ hundreds of thousands of people, and their products influence—and most would say improve—the lives of hundreds of millions. No wonder many of these business innovators moved from disrupting industries to seeking an even greater impact by aiming their attention and resources (including innovator's DNA skills) at some of the toughest world challenges, such as poverty, education, and disease.

Take a look at Salesforce.com, where Benioff built a company to not only disrupt the entire enterprise software industry, but also to make a difference wherever it operates. He did this through a 1-1-1 philosophy where 1 percent of all employees' time, 1 percent of all its products, and 1 percent of all its equity go toward improving communities and promoting compassionate capitalism. As Benioff puts it, he's in the "business of changing the world." His approach relies on hundreds of thousands of employee hours and millions of dollars to tackle problems ranging from sanitation to homelessness. Benioff is not alone in taking on tough issues. Bill and Melinda Gates, Richard Branson, and many others do the same in their own shape and form.

On a smaller scale but a highly similar focus, we have also worked with social innovators around the world who rely on innovator's DNA skills to create profound solutions to some of society's most difficult problems. For example, Andreas Heinecke founded a for-profit social enterprise, Dialogue in the Dark, when working as a newspaper journalist in Germany. Heinecke's boss had brought a blind coworker to his desk and asked him to teach the person how to become a journalist. Heinecke had no idea how to approach the situation, but quickly threw himself into the task of figuring out how to make it work, in part because he had less than perfect hearing. Heinecke not only helped his blind colleague to become a journalist but, in the process, used his innovator's DNA skills to found Dialogue in the Dark, which hires blind experts to take sighted visitors into a world of complete darkness for one to three hours. (Our assessment showed Heinecke as exceptional at idea networking and questioning.) Heineke observed that to better understand and appreciate blind people, you must experience the world as they do.

To date, over 6 million visitors in thirty different countries have experienced the exhibitions where people learn to navigate through parks and across streets, and to eat in completely dark spaces. Dialogue in the Dark also conducts very successful leadership development sessions at companies and conferences, including the World Economic Forum Davos events. (We regularly collaborate with Heinecke to produce "Innovator's DNA in the Dark" experiences that deliver a unique and profound learning context for cultivating the innovator's DNA skills with companies like the leading logistics firm in the Middle East, Aramex, to the world's leading art business, Christie's.) Dialogue in the Dark is now one of the largest worldwide employers of blind people (hiring and training over six thousand so far). All this was triggered because Heinecke decided to focus his persistent questions and conversations on a search for new ways to create jobs for the blind and to overcome barriers in all walks of life.

In the end, most of us will likely make a difference through many minor (derivative) innovations. An idea with impact might be a new process for hiring that helps your company find more talented people (such as Google's Code Jam tournament described in chapter 9). It might be a new approach to marketing your company's products (such as P&G's new use of bloggers and customer-generated content described in chapter 9). Or it might be building a business model based on the premise that for every pair of shoes sold, the company will give away one pair, as Blake Mycoskie did when he founded TOMS Shoes (after traveling to Argentina in 2006 and seeing so many children with foot diseases because they lacked shoes).

Clearly, the process of creative discovery can be difficult, but the rewards far outstrip the challenges. Being a creator is exciting, and to author or coauthor an idea that leads to a new product, service, process, or business energizes. Being an innovator is psychologically and emotionally gratifying in a way that money simply isn't, even though the financial rewards of successful innovation can be significant. Mark Ruiz, co-founder of MicroVentures and finalist for the Entrepreneur of the Year Philippines 2010 award, admitted the same when he told us, "even though I'm an entrepreneur, what drives me is not really the money. What really drives me is a deep sense of mission and purpose. I just see problems that are screaming for new and innovative solutions." Ruiz works nonstop to build new venture after new venture to take on these problems in his home country, the Philippines.

Ruiz and all the other disruptive innovators we encountered while working on this book take seriously the questions, "If not you, who?" "If not now, when?" They do not sit still. They are physically active, always asking questions, observing, networking, and experimenting. Others can actually "see" their discovery skills at work because their innovation work is far from sedentary. Judi Sandrock, CEO of the Branson Centre for Entrepreneurship, told us that she lives by the question, "How do I do this now?" and works tirelessly to help emerging entrepreneurs in South Africa do the same. In his path-breaking research on risk and uncertainty, economist Frank Knight saw innovative entrepreneurs as a class of individuals with the "disposition to act" in spite of the uncertain context in which they operated. We heard this over and over from various innovators, including Virgin's Branson who lives by, "Screw it, Let's do it," and Skype's Zennström, who made the following analogy between action and entrepreneurial success:

> Say that you have one of those reality shows on TV and you drop a bunch of people in the middle of a desert island. The winner is the person who gets to the shore the quickest. Some people try to analyze where they are, which direction to go. Some of them say, "Let's climb up a tree or a rock or hillside and maybe we can see further and figure out what is the best direction to go." They will spend time planning and analyzing how to find the best direction to go. But some other people will just look around, follow their intuition, and start running in a direction.
>
> If there are a lot of people that have been dropped on the island, I can almost guarantee that whoever starts climbing up the tree to start analyzing where he is and which direction to go will not win the competition. Why? Because there are a few other maniacs who will follow their intuition and just start running. They're much more likely to get to shore quicker. The point is: if you have a good gut feeling for which general direction to go, then you should just run as fast as you can.

Zennström's challenge: act and figure it out as you go. That way, you get valuable feedback by acting, and you get even better feedback by fully engaging your innovator's DNA skills along the way. But act now or it may be too late. Windows of opportunity exist for capturing the full value from any innovative business idea. No wonder successful innovators move fast to implement an idea before its window closes.

In the end, innovation is an investment—in yourself, in others, and if you're a senior manager or emerging entrepreneur, in your company. Whether you're working at the top of an organization or as a technical specialist at the bottom, eBay's Whitman advises everyone "to have the courage to plant acorns before you need oak trees." Innovation is all about planting acorns (ideas) with less than complete confidence that each will grow into something meaningful. The alternative, however, is little or no growth when no acorns emerge as trees. By understanding and reinforcing the DNA of individual innovators within innovative teams and organizations, you can find ways to more successfully develop not just growth saplings but the real oak trees of future growth. As you continue your innovation journey, let your life speak[2] the final line from Apple's Think Different campaign: "The people who are crazy enough to think they can change the world are the ones who do." So just do it. Do it now!

Appendix A

Sample of Innovators Interviewed

Interviewees

Name	Company	Innovative aspect of company*
Nate Alder	Klymit	Among the first to offer Klymit Kinetic vests and jackets insulated with noble (argon) gases.
Marc Benioff	Salesforce.com	Among the first to offer online/on-demand CRM/Salesforce Automation Software.
Jeff Bezos	Amazon.com	Among the first online book retailers; developed online fulfillment capabilities.
Mike Collins	Big Idea Group	Intermediary between product inventors and innovative product-buying companies/distribution channels.
Scott Cook	Intuit	Among the first to offer personal finance and tax software Quicken and TurboTax.
Gary Crocker	Research Medical Inc.	Introduced disposable medical products for beating-heart surgeries to reduce excessive blood loss and visualization visibility problems for surgeons.

(continued)

Name	Company	Innovative aspect of company*
Michael Dell and Kevin Rollins	Dell Computer	Developed direct-to-customer sales model in PCs, allowing for mass customization.
Orit Gadeish	Bain & Co.	Bill Bain founded Bain & Company, but Gadeish is known to have initiated innovative ideas in numerous client engagements.
Aaron Garrity and Joe Morton	XANGO	Among the first to offer juice and other nutritional products using mangosteen and a network marketing approach.
Diane Greene	VMWware	Among the first to offer virtualization software technology allowing virtual servers and desktops to host multiple operating systems and multiple applications locally and in remote locations.
Andreas Heinecke	Dialogue in the Dark	A social enterprise that hires blind experts to take "sighted" novices visitors into a world of complete darkness for various training and educational purposes.
Jennifer Hyman and Jenny Jennifer Fleiss	Rent the Runway	Among the first to offer designer dresses for rent over the Internet.
Eliot Jacobsen	Freeport.com; Lumiport	Among the first to launch a free ISP with unique reach to local retailer community; helped launch Lumiport, a topical light for acne treatment.
Josh James and John Pestana	Omniture	Among the first to develop and deploy Web analytics software.
Jeff Jones	NxLight; Campus Pipeline	Among the first to offer a digital offering to campus allowing users to access data remotely.
A. G. Lafley	Former CEO, Procter & Gamble	Initiated major organizational process changes at P&G to focus the company on innovation, including the "Connect and Develop" process that has been a major source of new product introductions.
Mike Michael Lazaridis	Research In Motion	Developed "BlackBerry," a handheld wireless communication device that has frequently been first with new technologies.
Kristen Murdock	Cow Pie Clocks and greeting cards	Invented the "Cow-Pie Clock," a clock embedded in a glazed cow pie with a funny saying attached (e.g., "Happy birthday, you old poop").

Name	Company	Innovative aspect of company*
David Neeleman	Morris Air; JetBlue; Azul	Pioneered ticketless air travel at Morris Air, Live TV at Jet Blue, and free bus travel to the airport at Azul Airlines in Brazil.
Pierre Omidyar; Meg Whitman	eBay	Launched online auction site facilitating person-to-person auctions.
Ratan Tata	Tata Group Chairman	Ratan's father founded Tata, but Ratan initiated the Tata Nano project, which led to the Tata Group's launching of the world's cheapest car.
Peter Thiel	PayPal	Among the first to offer financial services over the Internet. With Max Levchin, developed software that essentially attached money to an e-mail.
Corey Wride	Movie Mouth	Movie Mouth is building an interactive, Web-subscription application that has an embedded media player accessing copyrighted media, such as DVDs and CDs, on the local machine, and remote content from the Web.
Niklas Zennströom	Skype	Used "supernode" technology to place calls via the Internet and deployed a unique viral marketing approach.

*We use the wording "among the first" to launch a product or service offering because we have not verified that the company was indeed the first to offer the product or service. However, the innovators we interviewed claimed that this was their original idea and they were not simply imitating another company's offering.

Appendix B

The Innovator's DNA Research Methods

Our research project consisted of two phases: (1) an inductive study of innovators compared with noninnovators, and (2) a large sample study comparison of roughly eighty innovators and roughly four hundred noninnovator executives (we later expanded this to a larger sample). We conducted exploratory interviews with a sample of roughly thirty innovative entrepreneurs and a similar number of senior executives in larger organizations (see a subsample of innovators we interviewed in appendix A). The goal of our interviews with innovators was to understand when and how they personally came up with creative ideas on which they built new innovative businesses. We asked questions such as:

1. What was the most valuable strategic insight or novel business idea that you generated during your business career? Please describe the details of the idea. (For example, how was the idea novel and how did you come up with it?)

2. In your opinion, do you have any particular skills that are important to helping you generate novel business ideas?

> How did those skills influence your ability to generate strategic insights or novel business ideas?

To get an outside perspective, whenever possible we also interviewed senior executives who were well acquainted with the innovative entrepreneur. For example, we interviewed Dell CEO Kevin Rollins about Michael Dell and former eBay CEO Meg Whitman about eBay founder Pierre Omidyar, Skype founder Niklas Zennström, and PayPal founder Peter Thiel.

Through the interviews, we identified four behavioral patterns—questioning, observing, networking, and experimenting—that were more pronounced in innovators and which seemed to trigger associational thinking. These four behavioral skills and one cognitive skill comprise the five discovery skills that we discuss in the book.

We then developed a set of survey items to measure the frequency and intensity with which a person engaged in questioning (six survey items), observing (four survey items), experimenting (five survey items), and idea networking (four survey items). Response options ranged from 1 or *strongly disagree* to 7 or *strongly agree*. We also conducted an exploratory and confirmatory factor analysis (EFA) to uncover the underlying factor structure of the nineteen items measuring the behaviors.

We then conducted a negative binomial regression to test the relationship between the four discovery behaviors and starting innovative ventures. The results showed that observing, networking, and experimenting were significantly correlated with starting an innovative new business (and questioning was significant when combined with one of the other three behaviors). The four behavioral patterns were also significantly correlated with each other—with correlations typically greater than 0.50—suggesting that an individual who engages in one of the behaviors is more likely to engage in some level of the other behaviors. Results were stronger when each of the behaviors was used in combination with another behavior. Full details of the initial study can be found in: Jeffrey H. Dyer, Hal B. Gregersen, and Clayton M. Christensen, "Entrepreneur Behaviors, Opportunity Recognition, and the Origins of Innovative Ventures," *Strategic Entrepreneurship Journal* 2 (2008): 317–338.

Appendix C

Developing Discovery Skills

Years ago, Arnold Glasow, an entrepreneur and humorist, concluded that "improvement begins with I." We couldn't agree more. The focus of this appendix is to suggest how you might personally improve your discovery skills—associating, questioning, observing, networking, and experimenting.

Developing *Your* Discovery Skills

To develop your skills, we provided a number of practical tips in chapters 2 through 6. To decide which tips make the most sense to follow, we suggest that you take five steps: (1) review priorities to see where you spend your time, (2) assess your discovery skills systematically, (3) identify a compelling innovation challenge that matters, (4) practice your discovery skills ruthlessly, and (5) get a coach to support your ongoing development efforts. When combined, these steps can help you—and your team—build the relevant innovation skills required to make a bigger, better impact at work and beyond. (If you also want to build your team's discovery skills, take the steps outlined , but focus your development work on your team.)

Step 1: Review priorities

Consider how you typically spend your time at work. We suggest dividing your core tasks into three broad categories: discovery, delivery, and development. *Discovery* focuses on innovation and includes actively engaging the five discovery skills in search of new products, services, processes, and/or business models. *Delivery* is all about producing results, analyzing, planning, executing, and implementing strategies. Finally, *development* centers on building your capabilities and those of others (primarily direct reports, if you are a manager). This task includes selecting the right people for your team and training them well in the innovator's DNA skills.

Now, look at your calendar for a typical workweek. What percent of your time do you personally spend on each task—discovery, delivery, and development? You may want to answer this question by filling out the chart in table C-1, using the following simple process. First, make your best guess about how you currently spend your time (the "today" column). Second, record your best judgment about where you think you *should* be spending your time ("tomorrow"), given your team's purpose and your company's strategy. Third, calculate the difference or "gap" between today and tomorrow for each category.

Next, focus primarily on the gap. Is it large? Negative? Positive? Or neutral? If the gap is zero, you're spending the time and energy that you think you should on discovery. However, a negative gap reflects a need to devote more time to discovery activities to improve your ability as a discovery-driven leader.

Innovative CEOs and founder entrepreneurs spend roughly 50 percent more of their typical week on discovery activities than

TABLE C-1

Tracking your time spent

Leadership task	Today	Tomorrow	Gap
Discovery			
Delivery			
Development			
Total	100%	100%	

noninnovative CEOs and entrepreneurs do. So if you aren't devoting at least 30 percent of your time to discovery, you probably aren't leading the innovation charge. Creative problem solving takes time, so increase the amount you spend on discovery to have a bigger impact on innovation.

Step 2: Assess your discovery skills

After reflecting on your time spent (discovery versus delivery), get a more refined, specific sense of your discovery and delivery skill strengths and weaknesses. You can gain an idea of your performance on these skills through the brief self-assessment in chapter 1. You can also visit http://www.InnovatorsDNA.com to take a more comprehensive online self-assessment or a 360-degree online assessment (which provides feedback from your manager, peers, and direct reports) to capture a better sense of your strengths and weaknesses.[1] These assessments can prove valuable in helping you answer: "What is my everyday discovery versus delivery orientation? In which discovery skills am I strongest? Which ones do I want to develop? In which delivery skills am I strongest? Which delivery skills do I need to develop?"

Step 3: Identify a compelling innovation challenge

After assessing your strengths and weaknesses in discovery and delivery, the next step is to find a specific, current innovation challenge or opportunity so that you can practice your discovery skills. This challenge might range from creating a new product or service, reducing employee turnover, or coming up with new processes that reduce costs by 5 percent in your business unit. With your innovation challenge clearly in mind, develop a plan to practice some of the discovery skills as you search for creative solutions.

Step 4: Practice your discovery skills

We propose that you work on your questioning skills first, since innovation often starts with a compelling question and innovative teams have a culture that supports questioning. Write down at least twenty-five questions about your innovation challenge and conduct a QuestionStorming activity (or other questioning tips) with your team, as outlined at the end of chapter 3. A personal habit of asking questions helps create a safe space for other team members to also ask questions.

After strengthening your capacity to question, identify your *strongest* skill among observing, networking, and experimenting and seek to practice it as you tackle your innovation challenge (unless it's so strong that more practice provides diminishing returns; in that case, working on a weaker discovery skill may be a better development option). Again, refer to each of the chapters about these skills (chapters 4 through 6) for suggestions about improving them. Involve your team as much as possible in whatever discovery skill you are working on (observing, networking, or experimenting) as you search for a solution to your challenge. Finally, engage in frequent brainstorming sessions (alone and with your team) to practice associating (see chapter 2 for tips on associating).

Step 5: Get a coach

Innovation is habit forming or, rather, innovation requires forming new habits regarding the five discovery skills. Our friend Stephen Covey, author of *The 7 Habits of Highly Effective People,* might call this book *The Innovator's DNA: The Five Habits of Highly Creative People.* How can you increase the probability that if you try out the new skills suggested, you will turn them into new habits? One place to start is asking someone to serve as your creative mentor or coach—someone who can motivate and coach you while you work on developing new behavioral patterns. Personal change is difficult, and asking someone you respect to help with the change effort is an important step (getting one person engaged in the change process will bump up your success rate 15 percent to 20 percent). The coach can be a boss, peer, professor, classmate, or even someone you live with (you might practice these skills with other family members as you attempt to creatively solve problems at home). But whomever you pick, make sure he or she is someone you can trust to give you honest feedback and suggestions. A creative mentor and coach can make a big difference in helping improve your creativity skills.

Master the Five Skills of Disruptive Innovators

Mastery of any skill comes by practicing specific elements of that skill. For example, world-class athletes, musicians, or managers break down a skill into very specific parts of their "game." Then they practice these minute elements relentlessly. For a golfer, it might mean short putts on the green, over and over for days until she masters one small element of the swing. Concert pianists do the same with a small part of a musical piece. Practice over the course of weeks, months, and years ultimately provides mastery of not only one skill, but a set of skills.

The disruptive innovators in our research did precisely this, either consciously or unconsciously. They practiced skills relentlessly, on almost anyone or anything they interacted with. The mystery of innovation is far less mysterious when people practice the innovator's DNA skills regularly so the skills become new habits. This takes time and self-discipline. So start with realistic expectations and actively allocate time to improving your discovery skills. Most of all, remember that your personal development efforts send a serious signal to your team and organization about how high innovation ranks in your priorities and how important it might become to theirs.

Developing Discovery Skills in the Next Generation

The most important innovation work any of us might do is within the four walls of our home, the boundaries of our neighborhood, or the classrooms of our local schools. Why? Almost all the disruptive innovators we interviewed mentioned at least one adult in their lives who paid personal attention to their innovation skills and helped nurture them as they grew into adulthood. That's why we think it's so important for adults to honor and amplify young people's discovery skills worldwide.

Consider Steve Jobs's life. Early on, his father set aside part of his workbench for Jobs to experiment on mechanical things. Later, Jobs's neighbor, Larry Lang, taught him (and other interested neighborhood kids) a lot about electronics by building Heathkits together (products like transistor radios that were purchased in do-it-yourself kits). In retrospect, Jobs realized that building Heathkits with a neighbor and exploring things on his father's workbench ultimately gave him an understanding of what lurked inside a finished product. More importantly, Jobs acquired the sense that "things were not mysteries" and, as a result, he also gained "a tremendous level of self-confidence" about mechanical and electronic things.

Jobs was not the only fortunate one when it came to developing the next generation of disruptive innovators. Jeff Bezos's grandparents played an equally powerful role in fostering his experimentation skills during the summers on their Texas farm. Richard Branson's mother supported his curiosity to carry on a family legacy of discovering new terrain. Orit Gadiesh's parents and schoolteachers not only tolerated her questions, but valued them. In short, disruptive innovators had one or more adults play a key role in keeping their *natural* innovator's DNA alive beyond childhood. You can play that same important role with a future generation of innovators.

Developing Discovery Skills in Homes and Neighborhoods

What better place to start building the five skills of disruptive innovators than in our homes and neighborhoods? If you take on this challenge to "send the elevator down," as entrepreneur (and founder of Ariadne Capital) Julie Meyer put it, and bring up a new generation of disruptive innovators, here are a few concrete, helpful tips.

Associating Skills

1. One game you can play, particularly when traveling in the car, is called, "What's the connection?" Two people each think of a random word. A third person is the player. Once they decide on random words, each of the first two people announces his or her word. The third person must then create a logical connection between the two words, but try to be creative in doing so. For example, the words *pickle* and *stitches* might be connected with: "We make sour faces when getting stitches at the hospital and when we bite into a sour pickle." Similarly, the board game TriBond (distributed by Mattel) gives you three word clues and asks you to

figure out what they have in common. (You can also try out the game at http://www.TriBond.com, where there's a new combination of three words to connect every day.)

2. Search for books that foster associational thinking. One of our favorites is *Not a Box*. The main character, a rabbit, tries to convince readers that boxes are not boxes. Instead, boxes might be anything, if we let our imaginations run wild (ranging from a race car to a spaceship). After one of us read *Not a Box* to a three-year-old grandchild, he discovered him sitting in a box later that day. It was not a box, but a pirate ship! If you enjoy reading creative books with children, a few others are: *Harold and the Purple Crayon* (by Crockett Johnson,), *Ish* (by Peter Reynolds), *The Anti-Coloring Book* (by Susan Striker and Edward Kimmel).

Questioning Skills

1. When most children come home from school, parents often ask: "How was your day?" or "Did you learn anything interesting today?" The second question is better than the first (in terms of insights gained), but what if you regularly asked your child (or neighbor's child): "What questions did you ask today?" "What questions did other children ask today? "What questions didn't you have time to ask today?" Then listen; really, really listen. You may be surprised by what you discover. (You may also want to take a moment to watch *What Is That?*, a short video by MovieTeller films about how a father's and son's questions powerfully affect each of them).

2. Whenever you face a family, school, or community problem or challenge that needs a solution, try using a modified

version of our QuestionStorming approach with young people. Kids don't have the patience to brainstorm fifty questions, but they usually have the patience to brainstorm ten questions. For example, suppose you have a problem with your child not doing chores or homework. Asking just ten questions together about the "problem" can often yield interesting insights. For example, you might ask, "Why isn't science interesting to you?" "What can I do to be helpful?" Your child might ask, "Why do I need to know science?" "Why is science so important to you?" This process of asking questions about a problem can often trigger ideas or insights that will lead to novel solutions.

Observing Skills

1. Give children a chance to see you at work. You never know what surprises they might have by joining you for a day. Pay attention to what they notice as they enter your world; become a fly on the wall and watch the world through their eyes as they try on the likely new, adult world of work. For Jon Huntsman Jr., going to his father's workplace when he was eleven years old altered the course of his life. He was visiting his father, who worked as a special adviser to President Nixon, at the White House. While there, he met Henry Kissinger, who was on his way to a secret meeting in China. When young Jon asked Kissinger where he was going, Kissinger replied, "China." Until then in Jon's life, China had not been a real place with real people. But hearing that one word from someone who was actually going to China sparked a lifelong interest. Huntsman later studied Asian history and Asian languages in school. In total, he spent fifteen years learning Mandarin and spoke it fluently as the U.S. Ambassador to China.

2. Take frequent walks in old places and new ones. Take a child on a walk and look at the experience through her eyes. What does she see? Hear? Taste? Touch? Smell? You may be surprised at what you've never noticed before. Watch carefully for what surprises her; it just might surprise you as well. When traveling or living in new places, do the same, especially in moments of transition (just arriving or just leaving) when we sometimes see things that otherwise remain invisible. Keep a journal together that captures your observations. *How to Be an Explorer of the World* (by Keri Smith) is a great guide for adults and children who are interested in making better observations of the world.

Networking Skills

1. You can start building networking skills with young people by occasionally bringing a work (or even family) problem to them and asking for their opinion. Explain that problems are best solved when you get a variety of people looking at them from multiple perspectives. If they express interest in the problem, you might even invite them to join you as you bring the same problem to someone else with a different background. This becomes a powerful example of the importance of networking for ideas and demonstrates a process for doing it.

2. Occasionally, whenever you face a family, school, or community problem or challenge, think about inviting a focus group of three or four people with different backgrounds to give their perspectives on how to best solve the problem. This could involve a dinner invitation or drinks and refreshments to accompany the discussion.

3. If you have young people in your home, do some idea networking together by socializing with a diversity of people. For example, pick a person from a different country, different ethnic group, different religion, different age, or unusual occupation and invite him or her to a meal with your family. Explore together how other people live and see the world.

Experimenting Skills

1. Conduct experiments at home or in your neighborhood and discuss them with children. For example, Bill Dyer (a sociologist and father of Jeff Dyer) placed an ironed white shirt on the floor of the central walkway in his home. He watched for two days as his children carefully stepped around it, as no one bothered to pick it up. He then discussed with his children why they didn't think to pick up the shirt and, more broadly, what they viewed as their responsibilities around the house. On another occasion, he swapped a teenage son for a neighbor family's teenage son for a week. After the week, the two families got together to discuss what each boy, and each family, learned from the experience.
2. Take a young person to a junkyard or flea market to find something to take apart. Pick something for yourself at the same time. Take the items home and dismantle them together to see what new insights emerge about how and why things work. One father and son did this with an old airplane engine. The experience sparked a future aviation career, as the young boy grew up to become a pilot.
3. Engage young people in prototyping efforts. Select a product you'd like to improve (or imagine a new one) and

design and construct a crude prototype together. Children love the chance to create something new, particularly if Play-Doh is involved; you never know what new feature of the prototype they might discover.

4. Take your child on a trip to a foreign country (or even a "foreign" part of your hometown) with the explicit goal of experimenting with everything new. Try out new foods, customs, and local products and services. If possible, live in a home to experience life as a local. Try out as many new interactive experiences as possible.

Final Call for Action

What is our final call for action? *Adopt a young innovator!* Find at least one child (your own, a relative's, or a neighbor's) and help that young person appreciate and strengthen his innovation skills. Every child deserves at least one adult who values her innovation skills, at least one adult who listens to her honest questions. As Dr. Seuss knew so well, "Unless someone like you cares a whole awful lot, nothing is going to get better. It's not." If we don't collectively nurture the next generation of disruptive innovators, who will? There are far too many children in need for any adult to slack off when it comes to nurturing the next generation. If we collectively do this task well, many young people will grow up acting different, thinking different, and, in the end, making a difference in a world bursting with complex, challenging problems. Naively perhaps, we believe in the power of one, that one adult honoring one child's innovation skills can make all the difference in building a new generation of disruptive innovators. That is our hope.

Notes

Introduction

1. IBM, "Capitalizing on Complexity: Insights from the Global Chief Executive Officer Study," May 18, 2010.

2. Jeffrey H. Dyer, Hal B. Gregersen, and Clayton Christensen, "Entrepreneur Behaviors, Opportunity Recognition, and the Origins of Innovative Ventures," *Strategic Entrepreneurship Journal* 2 (2008): 317–338.

3. Todd Kashdan, *Curious?: Discover the Missing Ingredient to a Fulfilling Life* (New York: Harper Collins, 2009).

Chapter 1

1. M. T. Hansen, H. Ibarra, and U. Peyer, "The Best Performing CEOs in the World," *Harvard Business Review,* January–February 2010.

2. J. Young and W. Simon, *iCon: Steve Jobs, The Second Greatest Act in the History of Business* (Hoboken, NJ: John Wiley & Sons, 2005), 37.

3. Ibid., 38.

4. Ann Brashares, *Steve Jobs: Thinks Different* (New York: Twenty-first Century Books, 2001).

5. Steve Jobs, commencement address, Stanford University, 2005.

6. Marvin Reznikoff, George Domino, Carolyn Bridges, and Merton Honeyman, "Creative Abilities in Identical and Fraternal Twins," *Behavior Genetics* 3, no. 4(1973): 365–377. For example, the researchers gave them the Remote Associations Test (RAT), where they would present twins with three words and ask them to find a fourth word linking the three; they also gave them the Alternative Uses Test, where they would ask the subjects to brainstorm as many alternative uses for a common object—like a brick—and code how many total and divergent responses the subjects provide.

7. See K. McCartney and M. Harris, "Growing Up and Growing Apart: A Developmental Meta-Analysis of Twin Studies," *Psychological Bulletin* 107, no. 2 (1990): 226–237.

8. Other studies that have found that nurture trumps nature as far as creativity goes include: F. Barron, *Artists in the Making* (New York: Seminar Press, 1972); S. G. Vandenberg, ed., *Progress in Human Behavior Genetics* (Baltimore: Johns Hopkins Press, 1968); R. C. Nichols, "Twin Studies of Ability, Personality and Interest," *Homo* 29 (1978), 158–173; N. G. Waller, T. J. Bouchard, D. T. Lykken, A. Tellegen, and D. Blacker, "Creativity, Heritability, and Familiality: Which Word Does Not Belong?" *Psychological Inquiry* 4 (1993): 235–237; N. G. Waller, T. J. Bouchard Jr., D. T. Lykken, A. Tellegen, and D. Blacker, "Why Creativity Does Not Run in Families: A Study of Twins Reared Apart," unpublished manuscript, 1992. For a summary of research in this area, see R. K. Sawyer, *Explaining Creativity: The Science of Human Innovation,* 2nd ed. (New York: Oxford University Press, forthcoming).

9. A. G. Lafley and Ram Charan, *The Game Changer* (New York: Crown Business, 2008).

10. Indeed, the goal of "gene therapy" is to insert new genes into an individual's cells to replace a genetic defect with a properly functioning gene.

11. L. W. Busenitz and J. B. Barney, "Differences between Entrepreneurs and Managers in Large Organizations: Biases and Heuristics in Strategic Decision-Making," *Journal of Business Venturing* 12 (1997): 9–30.

12. R. C. Anderson and D. M. Reeb, "Founding Family Ownership and Firm Performance: Evidence from the S&P 500," *The Journal of Finance,* 58, no. 3 (June 2003): 1301–1327. This study found that companies led by the CEO founder were *29 percent more profitable* (net income to assets) and had *21 percent higher market valuations.* These results cannot be attributed to the fact that founder-led companies are smaller and more likely to grow (they controlled for size and age) or are in more attractive industries (they controlled for industry). The authors conclude that "founders bring unique, value-adding skills to the firm that result in superior accounting performance and market valuations" (p. 1317).

Chapter 2

1. Walt Disney Company, 1965 Annual Report.

2. Gary Wolf, "Steve Jobs: The Next Insanely Great Thing," *Wired,* wired.com/wired/archive/4.02jobs_pr.html (accessed November 10, 2009).

3. We prefer the term *associational thinking* to *pattern recognition* because the latter term seems to suggest that there is an identifiable *pattern* innovative entrepreneurs recognize. As innovators described how they discovered or recognized ideas for innovative new ventures, it seemed to us that while they connected disparate ideas together, they often did not necessarily recognize a pattern, or even recognize that it would be a viable business opportunity. They often discovered that things fit together through trial and error and adaptation.

4. While Frans Johansson coined the term "The Medici Effect" for his bestselling book, we prefer a less time and place bound version of the term. Hence, we use the "Innovation Effect" when referring to places past, present, and future where a powerful convergence of different ideas generate substantial innovative results. Historically these were geographic spaces that promoted intersections between people with different backgrounds and knowledge. Today these can be geographic places or virtual market spaces that are designed to foster connections between people with different knowledge.

5. In short, the Medici effect was not limited to the Medici family or the renaissance period in Florence, Italy. Instead, the Medici effect was simply a specific example of the common experience within science and elsewhere that innovations often result at the intersection of disciplines.

6. Mihaly Csikszentmihalyi, *Creativity* (New York: Harper Perennial 1996).

7. "Leslie Berlin, "We'll Fill This Space, but First a Nap," *New York Times*, September 28, 2008.

8. If you want books chock-full of ideas about how to connect ideas more creatively, pick up either of Michael Michalko's books, *Cracking Creativity* or *Thinkertoys.* They're exceptional.

9. Bill Taylor, "Trading Places: A Smart Way to Change Your Mind," *Harvard Business Review* Blog, March 1, 2010.

Chapter 3

1. Quinn Spitzer and Ron Evans, *Heads You Win: How the Best Companies Think* (New York: Simon and Schuster, 1997), 41.

2. Peter Drucker, *The Practice of Management* (New York: Wiley, 1954), 352–353.

3. Mihaly Csikszentmihalyi, *Creativity* (New York: Harper Perennial 1996).

4. Karen Dillon, "Peter Drucker and A.G. Lafley want you to be curious," October 8, 2010, http://blogs.hbr.org/hbr/hbreditors/2010/10/what_will_you_be_curious_about.html.

5. Land not only created the Polaroid camera, but held 532 other patents for a variety of scientific and commercial purposes (a patent output second only to Thomas Edison).

6. Marissa Ann Mayer, "Turning Limitations into Innovations," *BusinessWeek*, Feburary 1, 2006, http://www.businessweek.com/innovate/content/jan2006/id20060131_531820.htm.

7. Rekha Balu, "Strategic Innovation: Hindustan Lever Ltd.," *FAST Company*, May 31, 2001, http://www.fastcompany.com/magazine/47/hindustan.html.

8. Alan Deutschman, "The once and future Steve Jobs," October 11, 2000, http://www.salon.com/technology/books/2000/10/11/jobs_excerpt.

9. Brooks Barnes, "Disney's Retail Plan Is a Theme Park in Its Stores," *New York Times*, October 13, 2009.

10. Since our serendipitous discovery of QuestionStorming, we have since learned that others also stumbled across similar practices (e.g., Jon Roland, *Questorming* (http://www.pynthan.com/vri/questorm.htm); or Marilee Goldberg, *The Art of the Question* (New York: Wiley, 1997).

Chapter 4

1. Bob Sutton, a professor at Stanford, has used this expression, but Tom Kelley of IDEO says he's also heard that it originated with the comic George Carlin.

2. Tom Kelley, *The Art of Innovation* (New York: Doubleday, 2005), 16.

3. http://www.wired.com/magazine/tag/trimpin/, November 12, 2009.

4. Howard Shultz and Dori Jones Yang, *Pour Your Heart Into It: How Starbucks Built a Company One Cup at a Time* (New York: Hyperion, 1997), 51–52

5. Ethan Waters, "Cars, Minus the Fins," *Fortune*, July 9, 2007, B-1.

6. See http://www.nytimes.com/1991/01/27/books/notes-from-a-more-real-world.html?src=pm.

Chapter 5

1. Ron Burt, "Structural Holes and Good Ideas," *American Journal of Sociology* 110, no. 2 (September 2004): 349–399.

2. See http://www.ted.com/pages/view/id/47.

Chapter 6

1. Steve Jobs, Stanford Commencement Speech, June 12, 2005.

2. M. Carpenter, G. Sanders, and H. Gregersen, "Bundling Human Capital: The Impact of International Assignment Experience on CEO Pay and Multinational Firm Performance," *Academy of Management Journal* 44, no. 3 (2001): 493–512.

3. Walter Isaacson, *Einstein* (New York: Simon and Schuster, 2007), 2.

Chapter 7

1. How the innovation premium is calculated:

Step 1: In assessing a company's current valuation, HOLT determines the next two years of cash generation from existing businesses for each firm based on the consensus estimate of earnings and revenues by analysts. The consensus estimate of earnings and revenues is based on the median of the combined estimates of carefully screened analysts covering a public company as selected by Institutional Brokers Estimate System [I/B/E/S]). Benchmarks for historical periods (as are used in the innovation premium) use actual reported profitability and reinvestment rates as the starting point for the cash flow forecasts.

Step 2: HOLT then projects future free cash flows over the next 38 years from existing businesses based on *fade* algorithms developed from an analysis of historical cash flows from over 45,000 firms and more than 500,000 data points. The concept of fade embodies the commonsense notion that competition is the one enduring constant in free markets (à la Schumpeter's "creative destruction") and that technological change and changing market dynamics all militate against the persistence of excessively high returns (this is consistent with prior research that consistently shows a "regression to the mean" effect with regard to firm profitability).

The fade algorithm for a given company is based on the following:

a. *The forward two-year consensus estimate of ROI level.* Firms with higher levels of profitability and ROI maintain higher returns into the future. However, the historical experience of most firms shows a "regression to the mean" effect, meaning that high ROIs will gradually fade toward the average ROI of firms in the economy. The higher the current level of profit, the faster the expected decline. (Firms will tend to maintain their rank order; however, the spread between the top and bottom performers tends to narrow.)

b. *Historical ROI volatility* (over the previous five years). The greater the volatility of ROI historically, the faster the firm's ROI tends to fade toward the average of all firms going forward. Firms with consistent and stable ROI are more likely to maintain a consistent ROI into the future.

c. *A company's reinvestment rate.* The faster a company's recent growth and the greater the amount of cash it has reinvested, the faster the firm's ROI will fade toward the mean profitability of firms in the economy. It's hard enough for a management team to maintain high levels of financial performance; doing this while also growing rapidly is even more difficult.

Step 3: The difference between the company's total enterprise value (market value of equity plus total debt) and this *value of existing business* constitutes the innovation premium, expressed as a percentage of the enterprise value.

While HOLT's fade algorithm is based specifically on the historical and future projected performance of the given firm, it may appear to reflect sector identification or industry position. To the extent that firms in an industry or sector share the characteristics of ROI level, variability, and reinvestment, the pattern of fade will also be similar. There is also an apparent correlation between a company's fade expectations and its position in the industry, since most industry leaders have higher and more stable rates of ROI and, having been through their growth phase in achieving their leadership position, no longer need to grow at above-average rates.

We require at least 10 years of financial data for a given firm in order to be considered on our list of most innovative companies. We also use a "research and development" screen requiring that companies make some investment in R&D. Also, to control for size differences, we include only those with a market value greater than $10 billion. In very rare cases when a company derived more than 80 percent of their revenues from a single high economic growth market (e.g., India, China), we assumed a small portion of the company's innovation premium [5 percent of the difference in growth] was derived from domestic market growth rather than entering new products, services, or markets. Accordingly, we made a slight downward adjusted to the firm's innovation premium, but this only made a minor change in a firm's ranking and did not move any companies on, or off, the list. The innovation premium shown in the tables in this chapter reflect a weight average innovation premium over five years with the weighting as follows: most recent year (30%), years 2–4 (20%), year 5 (10%).

2. Our ranking must exclude private companies like Virgin (#16 on the *BusinessWeek* list) and Tata (#25) because they do not have publicly traded stock and report financial results.

3. A. G. Lafley and R. Charan, *Game Changer* (New York: Random House, 2008), 21.

Chapter 8

1. As quoted in Carmine Gallo, *The Innovation Secrets of Steve Jobs* (New York: McGraw-Hill, 2011).

Chapter 9

1. Carmine Gallo, *The Innovation Secrets of Steve Jobs* (New York: McGraw-Hill, 2011), 31.

2. http://www.shmula.com/987/jeff-bezos-5-why-exercise-root-cause-analysis-cause-and-effect-ishikawa-lean-thinking-six-sigma.

3. Gallo, *The Innovation Secrets of Steve Jobs*, 96.

4. Google's Culture of Innovation, Innoblog, November 14, 2005, http://www.innosight.com/blog/index.php?/archives/36-Googles-Culture-of-Innovation.html.

5. *Nightline*, "Deep Dive" video, February 9, 1999.

6. David Kelley interview at Stanford University's business and design school, August 21, 2006, http://sites.google.com/site/wyndowe/iinnovateepisode3:davidkelley,founderofideo.

7. *Nightline*, "Deep Dive" video.

8. David Kelley interview, August 21, 2006.

Chapter 10

1. Steven Levy, *The Perfect Thing: How the iPod Shuffles Commerce, Culture, and Coolness* (New York: Simon & Schuster, 2006), 118.

2. Jeffrey S. Young, *Steve Jobs: The Journey Is the Reward* (Glenview: IL: Scott Foresman and Company, 1988), 176.

3. The categorization of innovation projects as "derivative," "platform," or "breakthrough" comes from the Aggregate Project Planning framework introduced by Steven C. Wheelwright and Kim B. Clark. See: "Using Aggregate Planning to Link Strategy, Innovation, and the Resource Allocation Process," HBS N9-301-431 (Boston: Harvard Business School Publishing, 2000).

4. The concept of aggregate project planning was first introduced in Steven C. Wheelwright and Kim B. Clark, "Creating Project Plans to Focus Product Development," *Harvard Business Review,* March–April 1992, 10-82.

5. Larry Page and Sergey Brin, "Letter from the Founders: 'An Owner's Manual' for Google Shareholders," Google Inc., Form S-1 Registration, April 29, 2004, 1, via Thomson Research/Investext, http://research.thomsonib.com.

6. "The Institutional Yes. An interview with Jeff Bezos," *Harvard Business Review,* October 2007.

7. David Vise and Mark Malseed, *The Google Story* (New York: Delacorte Press, 2005), 256.

8. John Battelle, *The Search: How Google and Its Rivals Rewrote the Rules of Business and Transformed Our Culture* (New York: Penguin Group, 2005), 141.

9. See http://www.virgin.com/aboutvirgin/allaboutvirgin/richard replies/default.asp.

10. Keith Hammonds, "How Google Grows . . . and Grows . . . and Grows," FastCompany.com, http://www.fastcompany.com/online/69/google.html, March 2003.

11. Jonathan Ive, "Lessons On Designing Innovation," interview, Radical Craft Conference, Art Center College of Design, Pasadena, CA, March 25, 2006.

12. Ken Robinson with Lou Aronica, *The Element* (New York: Penguin, 2009), 15.

Appendix C

1. These online assessments also provide a development guide with your customized assessment report to help you understand your strengths and potential areas of improvement with regard to your discovery skills and delivery (execution) skills. The development guide also helps you build a skill development plan to leverage your strengths and improve on any major weaknesses that could derail your career.

Index

Acknowledgments

Almost a decade ago the innovator's DNA research project started to take shape and evolved through the contributions of hundreds, even thousands, of people from around the world. Each of us feels deep gratitude for the colleagues who played critical roles in advancing our ideas much further than they might otherwise have gone. We thank many of them individually below, but many others played a pivotal role in moving this project forward and ultimately bringing it to a conclusion.

No doubt this book would not have been possible without the gracious gift of time given to us by so many disruptive innovators who shared insights into the personal characteristics that helped them innovate. While we interviewed close to a hundred such innovators, we give special thanks to the following: Nate Alder (Klymit), Marc Benioff (Salesforce.com), Jay Bean (ah-ha.com; OrangeSoda, Inc.), Jeff Bezos (Amazon.com), Mike Collins (Big Idea Group), Scott Cook (Intuit), Gary Crocker (Research Medical, Inc.), Michael Dell and Kevin Rollins (Dell Computer), Orit Gadeish (Bain & Co.), Aaron Garrity and Joe Morton (XanGo), Diane Greene (VMware), Andreas Heinecke (Dialogue in the Dark), Jennifer Hyman and Jenny Fleiss (Rent the Runway), Eliot Jacobsen (Freeport, Inc.; Lumiport), Josh James and John Pestana (Omniture), Jeff Jones (NxLight; Campus Pipeline), A.G. Lafley (Procter & Gamble), Mike Lazaridis (Research in Motion), Kristin Murdock (Cow-Pie Clocks and Greeting Cards), David Neeleman (JetBlue; Azul), Pierre Omidyar and Meg Whitman (eBay), Mark

Ruiz (Hapinoy), Ratan Tata (Tata Group), Peter Thiel (PayPal), Corey Wride (Movie Mouth), and Niklas Zennström (Skype).

Lisa Stone, assistant to Clayton Christensen, worked hard to coordinate many aspects of the project, but most of all she excelled at setting up interviews with high-profile innovators. While this might sound straightforward, it was at times a Herculean task to coordinate the schedules of four busy people across three continents. Thanks, Lisa, for making miracles happen.

We would also like to extend special thanks to Michael McConnell of HOLT (a section of Credit Suisse), who conducted the research we used to calculate the innovation premium for the companies we analyze in the book. Michael's thoughtful guidance and careful analysis made our ranking of the world's most innovative companies possible. We cannot thank him (and HOLT) enough for his expertise and insights.

When the writing finally came to a close, we reached out to several innovators and best-selling authors who gave their valuable time to carefully read the manuscript and provide us with feedback. For those efforts we'd like to thank Marc Benioff, A.G. Lafley, Stephen Covey, and Scott Cook.

At Harvard Business Review Press many people extended themselves throughout the life of the project to make this a better book. Melinda Merino, our editor, listened intently to our original pitch and took it forward with vision and commitment. We appreciate her thoughtful guidance on the book's structure and content, as well as her unwavering support and encouragement. More than once her optimism came through with a cheery voice and a warm smile that kept the creative ideas flowing and the manuscript moving along. At *Harvard Business Review*, Sarah Cliffe gave us valuable feedback and guidance on our original HBR article, "The Innovator's DNA." Bronwyn Fryer, our HBR editor and later a freelance editor who worked with us on the book, was indispensable in making our writing more coherent. She constantly pushed us to make the ideas within each chapter more interesting, compelling, and accessible—and she did it with exceptional speed and professionalism. As the book moved into production and marketing, many others played key roles in sustaining the energy behind our ideas and keeping us focused on key deadlines. In particular, Jen Waring, Courtney Cashman, Julie Devoll, and Alex Merceron fully leveraged their professional skills in handling every aspect of the manuscript.

Beyond Harvard Business Review Press, two organizations and their people were especially helpful in making this book a reality. At Innosight, Scott Anthony, Mark Johnson, and Matt Eyring worked tirelessly with us to shape our ideas for practical use by leaders around the world. Their efforts helped keep the ideas solidly on the ground where the greatest good can be done. Similarly, at Stern+Associates, Danny Stern and his team were exceptional at helping us frame the ideas for an even broader audience—and, we hope, maximum impact.

From Jeff Dyer

When we started this project almost ten years ago, I had no idea of the joyful, but challenging, journey before me. The innovator's DNA research has opened my eyes to the fact that all of us can make creative contributions towards a better world. I would first like to acknowledge my sage and insightful coauthors, Hal Gregersen and Clayton Christensen, who have taught me much and have made this book possible. In particular, Hal excels at asking great questions and stepping back to look at the big picture; Clay is a master at theorizing and knowing how to use "the case" to make theory interesting and practical. Moreover, they are both great friends and wonderful human beings.

The data collection effort for this book has been immense, and I have many research assistants to thank who have worked untold hours to make this manuscript possible. I would especially like to thank Nathan Furr, Mihaela Stan, Melissa Humes, Ryan Quinlan, Jeff Wehrung, Nick Prince, Brandon Ausman, Jon Lewis, Stephen Jones, Andrew Checketts, and James Core. In addition, I would like to thank Spencer Cook for developing the tools to capture individual assessment data on our website, as research without data is not possible. Thanks also to Greg Adams for his expert analysis of the data that was used to test hypotheses in our *Strategic Entrepreneurship Journal* article, "Opportunity Recognition, Entrepreneur Behaviors, and Origins of Innovative Ventures." I would also like to recognize and thank the scores of MBA students at Brigham Young University who took my Creative Strategic Thinking course and interviewed innovative entrepreneurs as part of their class projects. Their work—and the interview transcripts they provided—was invaluable in helping us to understand the processes by which innovators discover new business ideas. Corey Wride, one of those MBA students, was particularly helpful in reading the manuscript and offering very useful suggestions. The transcriptions of all of the innovator interviews, including the ones conducted by Hal, Clay, and me, were done by Nina Whitehead and her staff, who always managed to meet my ASAP deadlines. Indeed, all of the staff members that support me at Brigham Young University are terrific and deserve my thanks, especially my assistants Holly Jenkins, Stephanie Graham, and Stephen Powell. I also must extend my heartfelt thanks to Dean Gary Cornia and the other deans at the Marriott School at Brigham Young University for the research funding that has supported this project over the last ten years.

I must also acknowledge the contribution of my parents, Bill and Bonnie Dyer. My mother has been a constant source of love and support throughout my life. My father was an amazing example to me in every aspect of life; but for this book, in particular, I thank him for teaching me that it's okay to ask questions.

Finally, I owe a deep debt of gratitude to my wife Ronalee and my children, Aaron, Matthew, and McKenzie, who have always supported me on this project despite the fact that it has taken a great deal of my time and attention. Ronalee, especially, deserves recognition for always taking such great care of our children and me—we are all greatly blessed because of her love. So thanks, Ronnie—the book is finally done.

From Hal Gregersen

For me the innovator's DNA speaks deeply about the genesis of ideas with impact. Now at the project's end, it's rewarding to reflect on the ideas and actions of others that have shaped my innovation journey. Let's start with parents.

My father was a master at many things, ranging from the repair and maintenance of anything mechanical to playing the clarinet, saxophone, and bass with such intensity and mastery that his feet often tapped out the beat in his sleep. My mother was equally adept at making music with the flute and piano, but more important, she always paid attention to what wasn't being said when others spoke. Her inquisitive ears and eyes reflected a heart in search of, and then in service of, hidden needs. Thank you, Mom and Dad, for constantly questioning the world (albeit from different angles) and passing that legacy on to your children.

Shifting from home to school, one teacher stands out above all in terms of unbridled curiosity—J. Bonner Ritchie. I worked with him intensely during my master's program, where he single-handedly rewrote the maps in my mind by constantly confronting my worldviews. Put simply, Bonner personified the innovator's DNA long before we ever put these ideas onto paper. His unsettling questions, uncanny observations, and unusual dexterity with metaphor lifted my own sense of inquiry to an entirely different level. For that gift, Professor Bonner, thank you.

After finishing my PhD, I started a twenty-year search to understand what makes great global leaders great. That search, however, was certainly not a solo effort. Many colleagues in the academic world and executives in the business world played an important role in the hunt. In particular, Stewart Black, as well as Mark Mendenhall, Allen Morrison, and Gary Oddou, demonstrated unbridled inquisitiveness in our work (and friendships)—just as we had discovered global leaders doing in theirs. To each I give heartfelt thanks, professionally and personally.

During the 1990s and early 2000s, I experienced a perfect incubator at BYU for uncovering some of the early innovator's DNA ideas—especially around questioning and curiosity. These inklings took shape and took hold in discussions with colleagues across the campus, especially Gary Cornia, Matt Holland, Curtis LeBaron, Lee Perry, Jerry Sanders, Michael Thompson, Greg Stewart, Mark Widmer, Dave Whetten, and Alan Wilkins, along with a cadre of exceptional research assistants including Cyndi Barrus, Chris Bingham, Bruce Cardon, Jared Christensen, Ben Foulk, Melissa Humes Campbell, Spencer Harrison, Mark Hamberlin, Julie Hite, Marcie Holloman, Rob Jensen, Jayne Pauga, Alex Romney, Laura Stanworth, and Spencer Wheelwright. On the administrative side, Holly Jenkins always excelled at supporting this work and was a joyous breath of fresh air when things seemed deceptively heavy.

Crossing the Atlantic to teach at the London Business School and then INSEAD shifted my role in the innovator's DNA project onto a truly global trajectory. INSEAD's tagline, "The Business School for the World," is much more than marketing hype. Colleagues, administrative support, and executive education participants come from every corner of the earth. Numerous innovation and entrepreneurship-focused colleagues from each campus (Fontainebleau, Singapore, and Abu Dhabi), including Phil Anderson, Henrik Bresman, Steve Chick, Yves Doz, Soumitra Dutta, Charlie Galunic, Morten Hansen, Mark Hunter, Quy Huy, Roger Lehman, Will Maddux, Steve Mezias, Jürgen Mihm, Mike Pich, Subi Rangan, Gordon Redding, Loïc Sadoulet, Filipe Santos,

Manuel Sosa, James Teboul, Ludo Van der Heyden, Hans Wahl, and Luk Van Wassenhove have been exceptional at nurturing insight-laden conversations. Administrators in the dean's office—Frank Brown, Anil Gaba, Dipak Jain, and Peter Zemsky—and in the organizational behavior area—Paul Evans, Martin Gargiulo, and Herminia Ibarra—have been equally generous in their support of the innovator's DNA research. In addition, several INSEAD research grants have been pivotal in moving the research along at critical stages, and coaches from the INSEAD Global Leadership Center have debriefed numerous Innovator's DNA 360 Assessments with consistent professionalism. Other INSEAD support staff have been truly helpful to the project, while personal assistants Jocelyn Bull, Melanie Camenzind, and Sumy Manoj have played a key role in keeping my work (and often my life) on track over the years. Finally, many thanks to at least a couple thousand INSEAD executive education participants (executives, entrepreneurs, and social entrepreneurs) who contributed key insights about the innovator's DNA over the years and provided reams of critical research data.

In the business, government, and social enterprise world, many executives were particularly generous with their time and talents related to nurturing my evolving insights on innovation. Stefan Bauer at Eli Lilly has been a dedicated collaborator and constant source of wisdom and insight when it comes to understanding what innovation is and how to make it happen. His ideas and his life have helped transform my own. Similarly, Schon Beechler, an academic, consultant, and executive coach, has done the same while working with me on numerous innovation-centered projects, ranging from recent professional development workshops on questioning at the Academy of Management to ongoing research with Teach for America about its teachers' innovation skills. Others include David Breashears (filmmaker, photographer, adventurer); Larry Kacher at ADIA; Fadi Ghandour at Aramex; Edward

Dolman, Steven Murphy, Lisa King, Karen Deakin, Gillian Holden, and Naomi Graham at Christie's International; Ahmet Bozer and Stevens J. Sainte-Rose at Coca-Cola; Andreas Heinecke, Orna Cohen, and Meena Vaidyanathan at Dialogue in the Dark; Mark Ruiz at Hapinoy; Pat Stocker at Marriott; David Daines and Denice Jones at Nu Skin; and Dave Ulrich, Wayne Brockbank, and Norm Smallwood at RBL (Results-Based Leadership).

Now I give deep thanks to my incredible coauthors, Jeff and Clay, for their contributions to this book and to my life. When Jeff joined BYU, he brought along his father's "institution builder" mentality. Jeff not only worked tirelessly to support colleagues' creative efforts in the strategy group; he reached beyond the strategy world to collaborate with me on an experimental MBA class, Creative Strategic Thinking. We hoped to merge a strategic perspective on how companies innovate with a psychological perspective on how individuals innovate. This merger created a perspective-changing classroom experience that continues on, with Jeff at the helm. The unexpected side benefit of that course was an increasing level of collaboration around where innovative ideas come from and how they successfully move forward. Our collaboration has been powerful, both professionally and personally. Jeff's capacity to craft clear ideas and to exert discipline onto a project when it might otherwise drift is exceptional. These gifts proved invaluable during a decade that rocked the Gregersen family in many unexpected and difficult ways. Through it all, Jeff not only kept the project on track, but even more important, he provided steady personal support in the midst of difficult life challenges. I will always be grateful to him for his professional excellence *and* his personal friendship.

Almost ten years ago I first met Clay Christensen. I still remember the conversation as though it were yesterday. We talked in depth about the transforming power of questions in our lives, at home and at work. It was a dialogue steeped with insight and a bit of a precursor to the disruptive questions—in a good way—that Clay would come to pose throughout the project. However, little did any of us know that Clay (and his family) would tackle a series of serious health challenges in the coming years: his heart attack, then cancer, and then a stroke. Each took a heavy toll on Clay's health, and with each he faithfully clawed his way back to well-being. Through it all, I stand amazed at his capacity to continue taking on work and to do so with his characteristic kindness. When I discussed innovator's DNA ideas with Clay—whether he was in good health or fighting to recover—he more often than not would reset a theoretical framework for the book or a chapter that almost always made it better. His passion for theory and his capacity for *building* good theory left indelible marks on the innovator's DNA. No wonder he's the author of disruptive innovation. Most of all, I express gratitude to Clay that during his own physical challenges he still found the time to supply energy-giving support and insight into my own family's ups and downs.

Finally, my gratitude comes full circle back to home. Our grandchildren Elizabeth, Madysen, Kash, Brookelynn, and Stella endlessly surprise me with innocent nuggets of insight about the subtle and often unseen nuances of life. Our children Kancie, Matt (and Emily), Emilee (and Wes), Ryan, Kourtnie, Amber, Jordon, and Brooke continue to roam the world (literally and symbolically) in pursuit of ideals and actions that make a difference. Collectively and individually, their resilience through difficult times inspires and encourages my own hope in a brighter future—and with good reason. Almost ten years ago my wife, Ann, bravely took on the frightening challenges of breast cancer. Unfortunately, two years later, physicians acting on automatic pilot completely misdiagnosed the rapid return of her cancer and, as a result, she passed away suddenly and perhaps unnecessarily (raising profound questions for which there will likely not be clear answers in this life). Out of that tragedy, though, another miracle walked into my life: Suzi, who grabbed my hand and heart to start a global journey that neither of us expected. We married and later left the United States to experience more cultures and people than I ever thought the world could dish up. Living and traveling with Suzi always includes unplanned excursions that create wonder, awe, and, at the core, a restoration of the heart. On those journeys it's inspiring to watch her completely engaged with sketching and painting her keen observations of the world. Her counterintuitive take on life and her deeply intuitive sense of direction are solid anchors in my sometimes topsy-turvy world. Indeed, "forever and always" have taken on even deeper meaning as we face the joys and sorrows of earthly experience (including Suzi's own experience with breast cancer). What a gift it is to be married to your best friend. Nothing better—especially when so much time and energy went into writing this book. So thank you, Suzi, for joining me on the journey and infusing it with such joy. I have never seen blue like that before.

From Clayton M. Christensen

I feel the same sense of gratitude to the many individuals Jeff and Hal have already mentioned. I add to these my wife Christine, who takes over most things when writing a book takes over my life.

In addition I wish to thank the hundreds and hundreds of managers—some senior executives, but most in the middle ranks, who also taught us profound lessons about how to be innovators—because they have repeatedly failed at it. Few of these managers will find their names in this book despite the fact that they shaped our thinking profoundly. But I hope that they hear their voices within its pages—not attributed, unfortunately, because there literally are too many to mention. Great theories only emerge from work in which researchers repeatedly try to find anomalies that the theory can't explain—which is why I am so thankful for those who were willing to explain to us why things don't always work as expected.

I am grateful for the opportunity Jeff and Hal gave me to work on their team. Hal taught me the value of asking the right questions. Jeff taught me how to get the right answers. My role on our team was to stand in the coach's box by third base. I would wave Hal and Jeff on to home plate, chapter after chapter. I hope that we can play again.

About the Authors

Jeff Dyer is the Horace Beesley Professor of Strategy at the Marriott School, Brigham Young University, and adjunct professor of strategy at the University of Pennsylvania's Wharton School. Dyer holds a PhD in Management from UCLA. He is the only strategy scholar in the world to have published five times in both *Strategic Management Journal* and *Harvard Business Review*. The impact of his work is evidenced by the fact that he was recognized by *Essential Science Indicators* as the fourth most cited management scholar and seventeenth most cited overall scholar (1996–2006) in the combined fields of management, finance, marketing, operations, and economics. His Oxford book, *Collaborative Advantage*, was awarded the Shingo Research and Professional Publication Award.

Dyer, a former Bain & Company manager, regularly gives speeches, consults, and conducts training programs in the areas of innovation and strategy. His past clients include Baxter International, Boeing, Ford, Kraft, General Electric, Johnson & Johnson, and Medtronic.

Hal Gregersen is a Professor of Leadership at INSEAD, where he pursues his vocation of executive teaching, coaching, and consulting by researching how leaders discover new ideas, develop the capacity to realize those ideas, and deliver high-impact results. He holds a PhD from the University of California, Irvine. Before joining INSEAD, he taught at the London Business School, Dartmouth's Tuck School of Business, and Brigham Young University.

He also served as a Fulbright Fellow at the Turku School of Economics in Finland.

Gregersen has coauthored many books, including *It Starts with One: Changing Individuals Changes Organizations,* and has published over fifty scholarly articles. Putting this research into practice, he consults with senior teams, conducts workshops, and delivers keynote speeches with global clients, including Adidas, Aramex, Cemex, Christie's, Coca-Cola, Daimler, IBM, Intel, LG, Lilly, Marriott, Nokia, Sanofi-Aventis, Twinings, and the World Economic Forum. He also works with social enterprises such as Teach for America, Dialogue in the Dark, and Room 13 to help build the next generation of leaders. Traveling the world, he pursues a lifelong avocation—photography—as part of a global community of social entrepreneurs committed to creating positive change through the arts.

Clayton M. Christensen is the Robert and Jane Cizik Professor of Business Administration at Harvard Business School. He is regarded as one of the world's foremost experts on the management of innovation and technological change. Christensen holds a BA in economics from Brigham Young University; an MPhil in economics from Oxford University, where he studied as a Rhodes Scholar; and MBA and DBA degrees from Harvard Business School, where he graduated with highest honors as a George F. Baker Scholar. His publications on the management of technological innovation have received numerous academic awards, including the McKinsey Award and the Global Business Book Award. One of his most recent articles, "How to Measure Your Life," published in the *Harvard Business Review,* won the 2010 McKinsey Award. In addition to his academic pursuits, Christensen is the founder of three successful companies: CPS Technologies, Innosight LLC, and Rose Park Advisors. During the administration of President Ronald Reagan, he served as a White House Fellow.